ANNEX

THE AUSTRALIAN
WOOL MARKET
1840-1900

The wool floor, Goldsbrough, Mort & Co. Ltd, Melbourne,
in the nineties

THE
AUSTRALIAN
WOOL MARKET
1840-1900

by

ALAN BARNARD

Research Fellow, Department of Economics
The Australian National University

MELBOURNE UNIVERSITY PRESS
ON BEHALF OF
THE AUSTRALIAN NATIONAL UNIVERSITY

First published in 1958

Printed and bound in Australia by
Melbourne University Press, Carlton, N.3, Victoria

Registered in Australia for transmission
by post as a book

London and New York: Cambridge University Press

ACKNOWLEDGMENTS

ECONOMIC history, perhaps more than other branches of history, is dependent on unpublished records of our past. In particular, economic historians already owe a considerable debt to the records of business enterprises; they are also realizing that this material could be the source for studies wider than the narrowly conceived business history. I have been fortunate, in working on the history of the wool market, to have secured the enthusiastic co-operation of a number of firms in the wool trade without which, and without the records they put at my disposal, no satisfactory conclusion could have been reached.

Permission to use business and other records retained by them was readily given by Goldsbrough, Mort & Co. Ltd, the Australia and New Zealand Bank Ltd, T. S. Beaumont & Sons Pty Ltd and the Victorian and South Australian Wool-buyers' Association, all of Melbourne, and by the Australian Pastoral Co. Ltd (through the managing agent Gibbs, Bright & Co. Ltd of Melbourne). The Librarians of the Mitchell Library, Sydney, and the Public Library of Victoria made available for my use manuscript collections, noted in the bibliography, which are in their care. Many people in these concerns, and in these and other libraries, have willingly shared their knowledge with me and patiently endeavoured to correct my misconceptions. I must particularly record the assistance I have received from Messrs G. A. Manning, R. B. Bebarfald, T. Young, R. S. Southey, D. Gibbs, D. H. Merry, C. Greenwood and G. Dewez.

In England I received equally liberal help. Robert Jowitt & Sons Ltd of Bradford, and Browne, Eagle & Co., Hughes, Willans, Irwell & Co. and Kreglinger & Fernau Ltd of London kindly consented to my use of their records. Manuscript collections from the Brotherton Library in the University of Leeds were made available to me and the help of the staff in the British Museum, the Goldsmiths' Library and the libraries of the Royal Empire Society and the Royal Statistical Society was invaluable. Sir Geoffrey Gibbs and Messrs R. Mackenzie and G. Renouf shepherded me through the City of London.

A financial grant from the Commonwealth Bank of Australia made it possible for me to use these libraries and records in

England. It also made possible a fruitful contact with workers in the Dean Research Project and the Department of Economics at the University of Leeds and in the London School of Economics.

To all those mentioned here, and to the many whose assistance has been acknowledged in the text, I am deeply grateful.

The substance of this book was originally prepared during the tenure of a Research Scholarship at the Australian National University and was presented as a doctoral dissertation. Its present publication owes much to the encouragement and aid I have received from Goldsbrough, Mort & Co. Ltd. Professors H. W. Arndt and H. Burton, Dr A. R. Hall and Miss P. Croft undertook the arduous task of reading the manuscript and their suggestions have served to clarify the argument and make the work more presentable to the reader. The Mapping Section of the Geography Department in the Australian National University produced the graphs and charts. The frontispiece is reproduced by courtesy of Goldsbrough, Mort & Co. Ltd, the other plates by courtesy of the Commonwealth National Library, Canberra. To Mr N. G. Butlin, ever a source of stimulation and encouragement, and to my wife, for her patience and understanding, I owe a particular debt.

A.B.

CONTENTS

APPENDIX

ILLUSTRATIONS

PLATES

FIGURES

ABBREVIATIONS

A.A. Co.: Australian Agricultural Company.

A.I.B.R.: The Australasian Insurance and Banking Record and Statistical Register.

A.M.L. & F.: Australian Mortgage Land and Finance Co. Ltd (from 1910, Australian Mercantile Land and Finance Co. Ltd).

J.R.A.H.S.: Royal Australian Historical Society. Journal and Proceedings.

N.S.W. V. & P.: Votes and Proceedings of the Legislative Assembly of New South Wales.

N.Z.L. & M.A.: New Zealand Loan and Mercantile Agency Co. Ltd.

Proc. Vic. Leg. Ass.: Proceedings of the Legislative Assembly of Victoria.

S.A.P.P.: South Australian Parliamentary Papers.

The Sales of Australian Wools in London. . ..: The Joint Sub-committees of Enquiry appointed by meetings in New South Wales, Victoria and South Australia, *Report on the Sales of Australian Wools in London. . . .* (London, 1870).

Y.B.E.S.R.: Yorkshire Bulletin of Economic and Social Research.

W. & P.: T. A. Coghlan, *The Wealth and Progress of New South Wales*, Sydney, annually 1887-1905.

1 Advanced sheep-washing methods in the seventies

2 Shearing, 1874

INTRODUCTION

THE growth of the pastoral industry is usually accepted as a major feature in Australian history. Socially and politically the importance of the industry is, perhaps, clear enough: wool was probably the main influence which, in the eighteen-twenties and thirties, led to the break-down of the penal system and the triumph of free Australian enterprise; wool was an important source of political influence throughout the nineteenth century and the focus for a large part of government legislation and administrative action; wool was the chief means of the successful spread of colonial settlement, and the pattern of that settlement, based on a highly profitable pastoral industry, had a basic influence on the character of Australian urban development, communication systems and service occupations.

Yet, the contribution of the pastoral industry to Australian economic development can too easily be misunderstood. Wool did not produce an overwhelming part of Australia's national income and provided, probably, an even smaller part of Australian employment. Directly, it produced a substantial demand for investible funds and was an important avenue for private capital formation. Its outstanding place in the Australian economy of the nineteenth century arose from its dominating position as an export commodity. The growth of a large, highly profitable export industry encouraged a related growth of services, not only in the form of transport and personal services but also of highly specialized banking and marketing agencies.

The fact that, by the extensive utilization of cheap land resources in a new country, it met some of the growing raw material requirements of the European wool textile industries forms a large part of the explanation both of its profitability and its magnitude in the colonies in the nineteenth century. And it was on these two characteristics that its importance in the economy largely turned. Yet we know virtually nothing of Australian wool in an international context, of the export market and how it worked. The growth of the industry coincided with a general relocation of wool production from the northern to the southern hemisphere. The second half of the nineteenth century also witnessed the expansion of wool textile production in continental European countries which sought their raw materials from South America, South Africa, New Zealand and Australia. We know that within this changing world structure Australia first became the leading supplier of wool to the British industry and later the world's leading producer of fine merino wool. Among other things, we are ignorant of such basic matters as the relations between the growing outputs of these other new countries and that of Australia; between the development of these new textile industries and the colonial wool producer; and even of the identity of the consumers of Australian wool.

As a step in the investigation of these problems this study is essentially concerned with the institutions of this export market—with the way in which the Australian producer was linked with the European consumer.

How the connection was effected depended mainly on the point at which the grower disposed of his interest in the produce. Throughout the greater part of the nineteenth century this point was London, where the wool was sold by public auction to textile consumers and distributive dealers. Consequently there arose a set of agents whose task was to arrange the transport and sale of the wool on the growers' behalf. From this large and heterogeneous group emerged a relatively small number of specialized agencies, with whom were specifically associated some of the services whose performance constitutes the market. These specialist agents also assumed other functions—particularly that of financing the production as well as the export of wool—and behaved in certain ways which tended to introduce rigidities into the marketing structure.

In the last third of the century, however, the location of the market was changed from London to centres in the colonies. This, it will be argued, was part of a world-wide movement in wool trading which was intimately associated with changes in the structure of the producing and consuming industries. It was also dependent on the prior development of a set of institutions in the colonies which to a certain extent ran parallel, and competed, with those that served the London sales system. Their original function was to provide a means of permitting growers to transfer to middlemen the responsibility of exporting their produce; it became one of bringing the producers and the consuming and distributive trades together in the colonies. This change altered the whole technique of wool exporting, but it could not become wholly effective until the rigidities of the marketing agencies centred on London were either overcome or transformed into similar rigidities centred on the colonial markets.

A consideration of these matters forms the substance of Part II of this book. It is evident that the whole problem might be approached from two points of view: first as a study of the institutions of the market, conceived, primarily, as the story of the men and concerns who exploited their command of the necessary lines of communication between the producers and consumers to exact tribute from the lucrative Australian wool industry. This would concentrate attention on the rigidities of the market structure and on the elements of 'finance capitalism' which it might be said to contain. Alternatively, the problem might be studied, as it is here, in terms of the men, the institutions and the relations which serviced the producing and consuming industries and which contributed to the smoothness and the rapidity of the growth of each. In this story market rigidities obviously have their place, but the basic interest lies in the connection that was effected rather than in the narrow relations between producers or consumers and marketing functionaries.

It is partly for this reason that Part I, in which the market to be examined is defined by identifying the product, the producers and the consumers, is also designed to provide a background sketch of the producing and consuming industries. It outlines the expansion of Australian output, the conditions under which it was produced, and the uses to which it was put. In addition, attention is drawn to certain features in the structure of the wool-growing industry, in the nature of the consumers and in the organization of the wool textile industries of Britain and Europe which were important in creating or encouraging the establishment of behaviour trends in the market participants, and of the channels and methods of wool marketing.

Finally, in Part III, the outcome of the operation of the market is considered briefly. Since the function of the market was, in each year, to dispose of the current clip, the main interest attaches to the prices reached to clear this stock. The main features of the prices realized are discussed, both as total movements and as patterns of relative prices. The market also realized another quantitative variable, marketing costs. These, in conjunction with realized prices, were important factors in determining the growers' net returns. Although some guide to these costs has been attempted, any effective analysis must await the completion of a great deal more statistical work.

PART I

THE EXTENT OF
THE MARKET

1

THE PRODUCTION OF AUSTRALIAN WOOL

I THE PRODUCT

Wool is not a homogeneous commodity. The fibre varies in diameter, in softness, crimp and elasticity, and in the length and soundness of the staple; and the variations of these qualities, in different combinations, suit wool to quite different manufacturing purposes and processes. The differences between various types of wool, created in this way, are most marked in sheep of different breeds—between, for example, an Australian merino and an English Leicester. But even within one broad breed of sheep they are still appreciable.

'Australian wool', then, is simply a shorthand way of referring to a large number of types of wool, the composition of which changed during the nineteenth century. Different sheep were bred in different regions; different strains were introduced from other countries; and the wool was marketed in different forms—washed, scoured or greasy—which, from the point of view of the market, created a further series of wool types.

Australian production is based on the merino sheep, but the nature of this breed has changed very widely. The original Spanish merino blood introduced and changed by Macarthur, Marsden, Cox and other pioneers was modified by the addition of British merino strains from Thomas Henty's West Tarring flock. Further modifications resulted from the Saxon merinos imported into Van Diemen's Land and Port Phillip where they formed the basis of famous flocks such as those at 'Ercildoune' and 'Belle Vue'. Later, after the fifties, merinos from the Rambouillet stud in France were imported in considerable numbers and, mainly through the influence of the Peppin studs at Wanganella and Boonoke, had a far-reaching effect on the future characteristics of the Australian merino. In the eighties American Vermont merinos were imported and for a short while provided the main emphasis in breeding.

All these breeds were originally Spanish stock which had been imported into Saxony, England, France and America in the last half of the eighteenth century. The differences in climate, pastures

3

and handling had created differences in the wool they bore. Thus the infusion of Saxon stock into the Australian flocks increased the fineness, density and elasticity of the wool, that of the Rambouillet the length, and the Vermont the quantity of wool carried.

Broadly, the introduction of these strains meant that the Australian merino could produce wool for either of the two main wool textile processes. The short, fine wool of the Spanish, Saxon and British breeds was eminently suited for carding by the woollen industry, while the longer fibres of the Rambouillet-influenced Wanganella sheep, which were well adapted for the Riverina district, could be utilized for combing by the worsted branch.[1] Indeed, the introduction of the Rambouillet coincided with, and was stimulated by, an acute shortage of long wool suitable for combing by the English industry during the sixties, and later it suited the increased demand for soft combing wool.[2] In New South Wales, nearly three-quarters of the merino flocks towards the end of the century were of strains that produced wool for the worsted industry, while the remainder was more suited for the woollen industry.[3]

This division of sheep into different breeds and types, however, is not sufficient to allow accurate determination of the proportions of wool produced for different manufacturing purposes, for the fleece of any one sheep contains different types of wool. Figure 1 illustrates the types of wool shorn from select groups of sheep run on Warrah Station on the Liverpool Plains of New South Wales by the Australian Agricultural Company. It will be seen that, although the flock was cultivated primarily for combing wool, the average proportion of explicitly clothing wool from one sheep could rise as high as almost 30 per cent while if the 'pieces', generally used in the woollen industry, are included it rose as high as 79 per cent. Apparently the proportion of each type was at least partly determined by breeding, levels of nutrition and care, sex, age and perhaps even the state in which the sheep were shorn. The clip from the rams and stud ewes yielded over 60 per cent of combing wool, while that from the purchased sheep only 21 per cent; greasy breeding ewes produced 46 per cent of combing wool while washed breeding ewes yielded only 27 per cent; from the three-year-old wethers the yield of combing wool was 52 per cent, while that from

1 Wool used in worsted processes is called 'combing' wool; that used in woollen processes, 'clothing' or 'carding' wool. The crudest distinction is that the former are long and the latter short. See p. 19, n. 2, for an account of the main differences between worsted and woollen production.
2 See p. 24.
3 See Appendix, Table I.

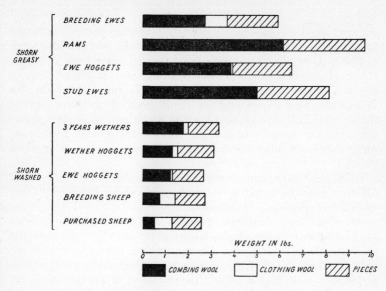

FIG. 1.   Classing of part of Warrah Station clip, 1881
(See Appendix, Table II)

the wether hoggets was 43 per cent. The influence of breeding can also be readily discerned in the comparative yield of combing wool from the highly selective stud stock—the rams and stud ewes—and from the purchased stock. Moreover, the proportion of each variety of wool shorn from a sheep varied with the season. The portion of the fibre which grew while stock were underfed during drought was appreciably more tender than the rest, and formed a fault at which point it broke during combing. This meant that tender wool otherwise suited to combing could only be used in woollen processes requiring, on the whole, shorter fibres.

In addition to the different types of wool that could be produced by breeding and by seasonal accidents, regional differences in climate and soil produced their own particular types of wool. The salt pastures and limestone soil of the Liverpool Plains, for example, were not suited to the growing of long silky combing wool;[4] the Riverina, partly because it suited that breed of sheep, and partly

[4] Australian Agricultural Co. 'Despatches from London', no. 194, 26 Aug. 1864. The records of this company, which are invaluable to the Australian historian, are held in the Business Records Collection at the Australian National University.

because of the soil and climate there, grew combing wool of excellent quality—long, bloomy, deeply grown and compact in the staple. The wools from the Western District of Victoria and the south-east of South Australia gained wide fame for their excellence and their colour. By contrast, the Lower Darling area produced fine to medium quality wools which were generally soft and which, like those from other regions, carried the distinctively coloured dust of the district. This dust content itself played a part in product differentiation, for the dust from some regions was difficult to remove, while that from other regions hid wool that was very white when scoured.

There were, then, many varieties of Australian wool which suited different manufacturing needs and which were therefore subject to differing conditions of demand.

One of the more significant trends in wool growing in the colonies in the last forty years of the last century was the shift from the production of clothing wool for the woollen industry to combing wool for the worsted. It is not possible to measure this change in so far as it was effected by selective breeding of merino sheep. By the eighties, when appropriate statistics first became available, the change had already been made. Three-quarters of the New South Wales merino flocks in 1886 grew combing wool and the proportion remained substantially the same in 1900 (Appendix, Table I). On the other hand the number of long-woolled sheep and crossbreds increased by $\frac{3}{4}$ and $1\frac{1}{2}$ million, a trebling and doubling, respectively. Their combined proportion of the New South Wales flocks rose from 2.7 per cent to 8.2 per cent. The wool from these sheep was suited to worsted production, and the growing popularity of these breeds was another indication of the changing composition of Australian wool growing. This change had been much greater, and apparent for much longer, in Victoria and Tasmania than in New South Wales. That colony, in fact, remained a predominantly merino-raising area, while by 1908 only a third of the Victorian flocks were still pure merino. Unfortunately there are no adequate stock statistics indicating the breeds of sheep raised in colonies other than New South Wales. One indication of the growing production is found, however, in the United Kingdom imports of crossbred wools from Australasia. In the decade 1871 to 1881 those imports rose from 25,000 to 176,000 bales. Although a considerable proportion of this was attributable to New Zealand, where crossbred production was more popular, the order of magnitude of the expansion of Australian crossbred production is evident.

The reasons for the change were complex, but three major ones stand out. The change occurred mainly in the southern colonies, where the wetter, colder climate suited crossbreds better than in New South Wales. In those colonies it came to be associated with mixed farming. The expansion of agriculture, therefore, provided a particular stimulus to the production of crossbred wools. As the newer breeds, especially the crossbreeds, were coarser and larger than merinos, they not only produced longer, coarser wool (suited to combing) but their carcasses were better adapted for meat production. Consequently the rising demand for meat for home consumption and, with the development of refrigerated transport, for export also increased their popularity. The main reason for the change, however, was the rising industrial demand for crossbred type wools, the growing importance of which was reflected in the United Kingdom imports. Between 1889 and 1899 the proportion of crossbred to merino wool imported from the colonies and South America rose from 17 per cent to 45 per cent.[5]

In the predominantly merino-producing areas of Australia this demand resulted in the evolution of another breed, known as the comeback—a refined cross between the merino and long-woolled breeds—which throve in conditions which also suited merinos but not the normal crossbred.

All these varieties of wool were further subdivided according to the state in which they were marketed. Wool buyers differentiated between wools on the basis of their cleanliness and of the methods used to clean them. As between wools of the same quality the different scales of values established for washed, scoured, and greasy (unwashed) types ideally reflected only the varying quantities of foreign substances such as grease, dirt, grass-seeds, etc. which they contained, and the relations between them were theoretically determined by the technical efficiency of the cleaning processes. In fact, quite independent factors caused those relations to vary during the second half of the century. It is this that gives significance to the product differentiation which cleaning implied.

From the sixties an increasing proportion of Australian wool was sold in the grease. Greasy wool had been exported since the thirties and forties, and there had been periods when special factors caused sharp but short-lived increases in the proportion of greasy to scoured and washed wool.[6] From 1873, the first year in which a separation

---

[5] Bradford *Observer*, 31 Dec. 1900.
[6] Examples are provided by the early fifties, when the shortage of labour led to increased shearing in the grease as a labour-saving device, and by other

between them was made in the statistics of New South Wales exports, to 1900 the proportion of the clip exported in the grease rose from 18 per cent to 71 per cent.[7] This phenomenon was general, and appears in the statistics of the other colonies from the time the separation was first made.[8] There are no reliable estimates of the relative quantities before those dates, but the high proportion— 49 per cent—of the Australasian clip brought to market in the grease in 1875[9] indicates that the change had been begun some time earlier. The reasons for this trend may be sought in three developments: the reduction of inland carriage rates as a result of rail and river transport—which meant that growers could more easily afford to freight the heavier product; the growing practice of selling in the colonies rather than in England—which meant that the incentive to scour in order to reduce the ocean freight charges was progressively reduced; and the narrowing differential, in money terms, between scoured and greasy wool prices—which was not matched by a comparable fall in scouring costs.[10]

This, then, is the commodity the market for which is the subject of this study. It was in fact a group of products that changed over time. In the forties it consisted primarily of clothing merino wool which was washed or scoured. This was supplemented and later overshadowed by merino combing wool, obtained by introducing foreign merino strains into the Australian flocks. Towards the end of the century long-woolled sheep, crossbreds and comebacks began to increase their relative numbers and to add increasing quantities of their distinctive wool to the Australian output. There was, finally, a general change from scoured and washed to greasy wool.

2 THE GROWTH AND LOCATION OF PRODUCTION

Although we are dealing primarily with marketing institutions, it will be convenient as a background to the main theme to discuss briefly the movements in output and to consider some of the conditions under which production was carried on. The remainder of this

---

years in which the drying up of creeks and dams on pastoral properties during droughts prevented graziers washing in the customary fashion.

[7] *New South Wales Statistical Register*, 1900, pp. 384-5.

[8] This occurred in Queensland in 1868, in Victoria in 1873, in South Australia in 1876, and in Tasmania in 1903.

[9] A. Sauerbeck, *The Production and Consumption of Wool*, p. 8. See Appendix, Table IV, n., for a discussion of the problem before the seventies.

[10] The prices of scoured and greasy wools fell by similar proportions despite the divergent output movements. This was due to a growing consumer preference for greasy. On this preference, see J. Leach, *Australia v. London as the World's Wool Depot, passim*.

chapter is devoted to some of the salient features of the progress of wool growing in Australia, to the difficulties facing individual producers, to the obstacles to the expansion of the industry as a whole and to the ways in which they were overcome. Attention will be concentrated on the measure of production, the location of sheep raising, the technology which it employed, and on the structure of the industry.[11]

During the nineteenth century Australia became the world's largest exporter of merino wool and a dominant force in the world wool markets. Expressed in national terms, Australian production rose continuously, though not evenly, in each of the quinquennial periods from 1840 to 1894, growing from c. 12 m.lb. to 596 m.lb. More detailed figures are given in the Appendix (see Table IV). The expansion, which had gathered pace during the 'squatting' rush of the thirties, was slowed down but not halted during the depression of the forties. From those depression years emerged measures which eased two of the industry's basic difficulties—the Liens on Wool and Mortgages on Stock Act of 1843 which made sheep and the growing wool legal security for loans, and the Order in Council of 1847 which confirmed the squatters in their occupation of lands beyond the authorized limits of settlement and gave them some right to their improvements.[12] The economy was hardly out of the depression when the discovery of gold led to a dislocation of pastoral production. The gold discoveries drew labour from the industry and meant an increase in the costs of provisions, while to a certain extent the demand for meat reduced wool output. For a time the relative attractiveness of wool growing as a field of investment declined. Nevertheless the industry continued to expand. In the early sixties there was a boom in the formation of new pastoral enterprises. It was encouraged by the renewed availability of labour and capital and by the fact that the export price of wool maintained its level, while import prices and the domestic price level fell. Despite a fall in wool prices in the second half of the decade, which reacted unfavourably on the establishment of new stations, output bounded upwards as those formed during the boom became fully

[11] See also the treatment of these subjects in B. Fitzpatrick, *The British Empire in Australia: an economic history, 1834-1939*; E. Shann, *An Economic History of Australia*; and T. A. Coghlan, *Labour and Industry in Australia*.

[12] The Liens on Wool and Mortgages on Stock Act was originally accepted by the imperial government as an emergency measure; it was renewed with difficulty in succeeding years until 1850, when its permanence was accepted. The 1847 Order replaced squatting licences by pastoral leases which carried pre-emptive rights and which, in the 'unsettled' areas, were for an initial period of fourteen years.

productive and as the capital improvements executed then became fully effective. The severe fall in prices at the end of the sixties was reflected by a much slower expansion of production in the early seventies, but the rate of growth once again became high during the second half of the decade. Throughout the eighties the expansion continued steadily, although at a reduced rate. The rise in the rate of expansion in the first half of the nineties was, however, followed by an actual reduction in output in the second half. This was the product of drought, and of a readjustment of the industry to the changed relations between wool and other prices and to the introduction of a real alternative to wool production in the form of frozen meat for export.

These aggregate figures tend to conceal very different rates of growth in the different colonies. Victorian and South Australian production was declining through the eighties just as Queensland's expansion gathered speed; and the increase in Tasmanian production was slow and much more unstable than that of the other colonies. The high rate of growth in the late seventies and early eighties was almost entirely a product of the expansion of the industry in New South Wales, and the magnitude of the rise in output in 1890-4 is a result of developments in that colony and Queensland. These differences are even more obvious when one studies, instead of statistics of wool output, the growth of the sheep flocks.[13] They form a necessary supplement to the production statistics as an indication of the growth of the industry, even when quinquennial averages are used, because they are free from the distorting effects of minor climatic variations (which often cause a difference in the yield of wool per sheep) and, though subject to their own errors of collection, are free of the complications arising from wool washing. To demonstrate these divergent rates of development between the different colonies, however, serves merely to underline the importance of the changing geographical distribution of wool production and to direct attention to divergent rates of growth of much smaller areas within colonial boundaries.

Initially, the expansion of the industry was accomplished by pushing out the geographical frontiers of grazing. Pastoral occupation followed the discovery of new pastures by official explorers, overlanders and the pastoral pioneers themselves. This method of increasing production was obviously limited by, and at the same time aggravated, the two main problems of the pastoral industry: transport and drought. How these limitations were overcome to

[13] See Appendix, Table V.

allow progressive extensions into previously sub-marginal regions will be considered more fully below (section 3). It is sufficient here merely to indicate some of the consequences.

Pastoral occupation went well ahead of organized transport and communication. The pioneers blazed the trails and established their stations; carriers, wagon tracks, roads and eventually railways followed them. But even in 1870 the railways of New South Wales terminated at Lithgow in the west, Goulburn in the south and Murrurundi in the north. By that time occupation of substantial areas west of the Bogan and Lachlan Rivers was complete, and a broad band of settlement existed along the Darling River. Settlement on this basis was possible, of course, only because wool was a commodity whose value was high compared with its weight. Yet carrying costs were high, and as settlement proceeded even farther beyond the railheads the carriage of wool to the ports and of supplies and rations back to the stations became an increasingly important element of pastoral costs. There was obviously a limit beyond which they became prohibitive. The occupation of some regions was, therefore, impossible until some provisions were made for transport. The clearing of the Murray, Murrumbidgee and Darling River systems for navigation in the fifties and sixties opened up large areas of New South Wales in this way.

The spread of pastoral occupation is well known. In New South Wales it moved from the Nineteen Counties west and north to the Bathurst and Liverpool Plains, south to the Monaro and Riverina, then west towards the Lachlan in the south and the Upper Darling in the north, and finally filled out the Western District. In Victoria squatters first occupied the central and western coastal plains, then followed the northern rivers to the Murray, filled in the north-eastern corner, and later spread north-west into the fringe of the Mallee country. In South Australia and Queensland it followed a similar pattern, exploiting first the coastal and river areas and then moving to the drier north and west respectively. After 1860 this pattern of extension came increasingly to mean an expansion into areas of low rainfall and few natural permanent waters.

The sparse pastures and the scarcity of drinking water for stock natural to such areas seemed, at the time, to have been satisfactorily overcome by technological innovations. Nevertheless, even in those inland regions where pastoral occupation was firmly established, the incidence and severity of droughts was much higher than in areas closer to the coast and the mountains. Further, the large-scale operations necessary for sheep raising in low rainfall areas, together with the ready growth of annual herbage plants immediately after rain, induced graziers to stock the land more heavily than the relatively sparser growth of drought-resistant shrub herbage warranted; stocking tended to be determined by the maximum, not the minimum, capacity of the land. This overstocking meant not merely temporary embarrassment in drought periods but also permanent deterioration of the vegetation as well as erosion of the surface soil. It was such considerations as these, at least equally with the depredations of rabbits and other wild animals, that made untenable the graziers' positions on stations north of Goyder's Line in South Australia in the late sixties and west of the Darling in the nineties.[14]

In other words, as the pastoral industry moved outwards to the semi-arid regions, transport became an increasingly heavy burden and the vulnerability of those regions to droughts and deterioration made production and income more unstable.[15] It was from these very regions, however, that a large part of increase in Australian production came before the end of the eighties.

In this early occupation of the more favoured areas and the later dependence on semi-arid zones for subsequent expansion may be found part of the explanation of the differential rates of growth between the colonies noted above. The topography of Tasmania placed a natural limit to this expansion, which was reached in the fifties. In Victoria, though grazing was later extended to the Mallee district,[16] the process had been substantially completed by the sixties. By the mid-sixties occupation had spread as far as Lake Eyre in South Australia. Disastrous droughts at the end of that decade forced it to retreat, and though the re-occupation of the area was complete by the nineties, the process was so cautious and gradual that it cannot be considered an example of the dynamic extension of productive frontiers. In New South Wales, on the other hand, the late seventies and eighties saw the expansion of produc-

---

[14] In both these cases, of course, there was an aggravating interaction between changes in wool prices and the effects of overstocking. *Either* lower prices *or* diminished carrying capacity could have been borne, for a time at least; in combination they spelt disaster.

[15] The report of an overseer to his absentee employer sums up the devastation which drought could imply: 'We eat, drink and sleep well, and play quoits, sheep being all dead. We have nothing else to do, and would rather not meet you in Sydney, till the rain comes . . .' quoted in the *Australasian Insurance and Banking Record and Statistical Register* (Melbourne, monthly), vol. 8, p. 179 (henceforth referred to as *A.I.B.R.*).

[16] This story is admirably told in A. S. Kenyon, 'The Story of the Mallee', *Victorian Historical Magazine*, vol. iv, nos. 1, 3 and 4.

tion into the back country on both sides of the Darling, while in Queensland the occupation of reasonably watered country was completed and then sheep raising moved westward beyond the Warrego and beyond Longreach toward the South Australian border.

3 THE TECHNOLOGY OF PRODUCTION

Before the industry could be profitably and permanently extended to these semi-arid areas, measures were necessary to secure the survival of the stock. Drinking water was the main problem despite the relative abundance of some types of water-retaining vegetation. In country where the soil was largely sandy—where rivers petered out to a muddy end in the middle of a plain and then re-appeared some hundreds of miles away—and where the evaporation rate was high, artesian bores provided the only answer. After 1870 thousands were sunk by colonial governments and individual stockowners throughout the areas served by the Great Artesian and River Murray Artesian Basins. But the sparse growth of pastures made it necessary for graziers to develop new techniques of husbandry appropriate to light stocking. At the same time protection against rabbits and wild animals, which threatened both the stock and their feed, was needed. Fencing in huge paddocks reduced the depredations of the animals and made light stocking possible on an economic scale. The construction of vermin-proof fences, undertaken on a tremendous scale by graziers and colonial governments,[17] together with appropriate legislation, represented the greatest though still unsuccessful attempt to eliminate rabbits, dingoes and kangaroos.

With the exception of artesian water supplies, these techniques differed only in degree, however, from those that had been adopted previously and were to find even wider application in the future, in the higher rainfall districts. There their importance lay not so much in ensuring survival as in increasing productivity. Fencing had originally been introduced as a labour- and cost-saving device, and it was largely on those grounds that its popularity spread so

[17] At the end of 1900 it was estimated that some 18,000 miles of rabbit-proof fencing had been erected in N.S.W., of which 1,157 miles had been constructed by the state (T. A. Coghlan, *The Wealth and Progress of New South Wales, 1900–01*, p. 612. Appearing annually, this series of publications formed the official year book of N.S.W. from 1806 to 1904. It will henceforth be referred to only as *W. & P.* with the appropriate year). This probably refers only to leasehold properties and should be multiplied two or three times for a full coverage. In Queensland, the state constructed virtually all this type of fencing.

rapidly in Victoria where the process of enclosing grazing lands was virtually completed during the sixties. In addition, however, it greatly increased the percentage of lambing, maintained the sheep and their wool in better condition, and made heavier stocking of the pastures possible.[18] It was partly for those reasons that in the late seventies and eighties most of the grazing land in New South Wales was fenced.[19] Similarly, even the early settlers had dammed creeks to provide permanent water. It was soon found that the country without river frontages—the areas into which secondary waves of occupation were carried—needed excavated dams or artesian wells to increase the carrying capacity of the land to economic levels.

Other technological changes to reduce costs or improve the quality of the product were, of course, most important, especially as production moved into marginal areas.[20] In the early days of the industry, for example, wool was sent from the runs to the coast wrapped as whole fleeces in sheets, in the English fashion. Sheets were soon replaced by bales, into which the fleeces, and later the divided and classed wool, were squeezed with a hand press. From the sixties hand pressure was gradually replaced by hydraulic

[18] Coghlan's classical statement of the advantages to be derived from fencing a sheep property into paddocks is worth repeating: 'the country will carry one-third more sheep, the wool will be longer and sounder, and the fleece as a whole one-third better; the feed will be cleaner and less liable to grass-seed; the sheep will increase in size; they will live longer and continue longer profitable; they will be freer from foot-rot and other diseases; the expenses of working the station will be less than one-quarter of what it would be if the sheep were shepherded; and finally, the owner will be able to devote the principal part of his time to improving his sheep instead of spending it in attempting to manage a number of shepherds and hut-keepers' (*W. & P., 1900–01*, p. 584). One might add that some system of paddocking, and the separation of flocks, was essential to any attempt to improve sheep by selective breeding.

[19] As late as 1867 the policy of the Australian Agricultural Co. (A.A. Co.) was that while 'the subdivision of the whole estate by wire fencing is the result that we have in view . . . the cost of it will be very heavy, and without experience of our own we should not be justified in recommending the shareholders to incur it. Our wish, therefore, is that you should proceed experimentally' (A.A. Co., 'Despatches from London', no. 236, 26 Nov. 1867). The contrast in fence building in N.S.W. between the sixties and seventies is of 50,000 miles to 750,000 miles— N. G. Butlin, *Private Capital Formation in Australia, Estimates 1861–1900*, The Australian National University, Social Science Monograph No. 5 (Canberra, 1955), p. 93.

[20] The actual purpose of developmental investment in pastoral properties is often unclear. It could be argued, for example, either that fencing was designed to reduce the costs of production of a given quantity of wool or that it was effected with the object of increasing the amount which could be produced from a given piece of land (cf. the arguments advanced in the *Sydney Morning Herald*, 23 March 1891 and *A.I.B.R.*, vol. 15, p. 330). Whatever the object, however, one result was to make possible the occupation of otherwise unprofitable areas.

pressure and side-pressing by end-pressing, and by the end of the century many bales were double-dumped. The result was wool packs more regular in size and shape and with progressively more weight compressed into a smaller space,[21] and a substantial saving in inland carriage and handling charges. Again, washing sheep before shearing was a practice common throughout Europe and one imported into the colonies by English migrants at the advice of the English trade. In the early years buyers refused to contemplate wool from which the grease and foreign matter had not been at least partly removed, and their bids rose with the quality of the washing. Accordingly, colonial graziers who had used running streams for washing sheep, soon abandoned these for specially constructed washing pools, and in the fifties and sixties they imported special washing soaps from England and France and installed pumps—all at considerable expense—so that sheep, or later their shorn wool, could be washed under pressure with either hot or cold water to approximate as closely as possible the buyers' ideals. In other cases the wool was scoured, either on the station or in the cities, after it had been shorn. After the seventies, by contrast, there was a growing tendency to market it in its original greasy state. This eliminated all the costs of washing or scouring and met the increasing buyer preference for greasy wool, while improved transport facilities meant that it did not involve greatly increased carriage costs, which might have offset these advantages.

Some improvements increased the carrying capacity of the land; others increased the yield of wool per sheep. In general, over the whole period 1860 to 1890 there was possibly an average annual increase in yield of 1 per cent, though it may have been more significant after 1870 than before.[22] This cannot be attributed to

[21] The Australian Agricultural Co., accustomed to using a screw press at Warrah Station, found, in 1876, that the use of a hydraulic press would reduce the number of bales by one-third. The cost of installation would have been covered in two years by the savings in colonial transport charges. (A.A. Co., 'Despatches from London', no. 381, 18 Feb. 1876, and 'Warrah Papers', Memo of the estimated cost and gain of dumping wool at Warrah, 2 Aug. 1876.)

[22] Quinquennial average yields of sheep and lambs' wool calculated from Tables IV and V show a rise from 2 lb. in 1860–4 to about 5.8 lb. in 1875–9, 5.6 lb. in 1885–9, and 6.7 lb. in 1895–9. In 1910–14 it was 8.3 lb. This grossly exaggerates the actual improvements that took place, for the production statistics make no allowance for the changing proportions of greasy and scoured wool. The change from 1875–9 to 1910–14 more closely approximates the magnitude of the increase due to better breeding, better production methods and better shearing. By contrast, the scoured wool shorn from the sheep and lambs of the Australian Agricultural Co. flocks increased from an annual average of 2.97 lb. in the period 1869–71 to 3·29 lb. in 1876–8; the greasy wool yield rose from 6·02 lb. in 1876–8 to 6.75 lb. in 1896–8 (A.A. Co., 'Annual Returns'). It must be remembered,

capital improvements alone, of course, for the introduction of new breeds of sheep played an important role. But fencing increased the average weight of the fleece, while machine shearing added an average of two ounces to each fleece shorn on one station.[23] (Machine shearing does not seem to have reduced costs appreciably except by preventing waste and ensuring even shearing.)[24]

One of the most important factors not only in increasing the wool yield per sheep but also in improving the carrying capacity of the land was the development of mixed farming associated with the growth of agricultural production. Mixed farming provided, in effect, a continuation of the trend to more intensive grazing in well-watered regions which was considered above. While one tends, perhaps, to think of agriculture expanding at the expense of grazing —the conversion of pasture to arable and the displacement of stock by crops—in fact in Australia the conversion was slow and never wholly complete. Agriculture, and particularly wheat growing, tended to mean mixed sheep and crop husbandry, and frequently in the nineteenth century developed as a diversification of, and side by side with, existing grazing activities. In New South Wales, where it developed late in the century, small selections designed for agricultural occupation were largely used for grazing and perhaps some cropping until a favourable conjunction of markets, transport and technology led to an expansion of the agricultural side— but without any significant reduction in the flocks. In Victoria and South Australia, where agricultural activity had been stimulated from the sixties by a complex of factors, sheep were often grazed on farms both because of their value as sideline production and because they increased the agricultural yield.[25] This tendency to raise sheep

---

however, that this company was one which bred for quality wool rather than quantity alone.

[23] Australian Pastoral Co., 'Manager's Annual Reports', 1901. I am indebted to the company and to Gibbs, Bright & Co., the managing agents in Australia, for permission to view and use material from their archives.

[24] Under the most favourable circumstances, including a low contract price, the Australian Pastoral Co. found that the saving amounted to only ½d. per sheep ('Manager's Annual Reports', 1906). H. Munz, *The Australian Wool Industry*, p. 95, gives an account of the very slight differences in the speed of hand and machine shearing at the end of the century. In 1894 Jacomb & Co., London wool-selling brokers, lamented that 'practical consumers somehow refuse to recognise any material differences between machine and hand shorn fleece' (A. A. Co., 'Letters from the Secretary', enclosure with 22 March 1894).

[25] 'My idea' wrote 'A Northern Farmer', 'is that in farming operations in this colony we can only guard against exhaustion of the land by combining cultivation and pasturing of sheep' (*South Australian Advertiser*, 2 Dec. 1875). Many farmers, in fact, empirically appreciated the beneficial effects of grazing

in conjunction with farming had two important consequences. It meant, firstly, that the number of sheep did not fall significantly as agriculture expanded; it might even be claimed that flocks increased as a by-product of the agricultural expansion. Secondly, because of the nature of the soil and climate, in many regions mixed farming tended to be more highly productive of wool than extensive grazing.

In Victoria and South Australia the effect was a redistribution in the ownership and a change in the size distribution of the flocks. Closer settlement did involve cutting up large grazing estates. But not all that land was withdrawn from grazing. The large station flocks were reduced and their places taken by small farm flocks. In the censal year 1871 the average size of Victorian flocks reached a peak of 8,092; by 1901 it was 2,075.[26]

In New South Wales the same process of running sheep with crops had begun by the eighties. In the Cootamundra and Molong districts mixed wheat and sheep raising was common by 1886;[27] by 1890 it was general between the Murrumbidgee and the Murray and well known as far west as Hillston.[28] It was not until the nineties, however, that agriculture expanded at all rapidly, and its effects may then be seen in the increase in stock numbers despite the rapid decline of the large flocks of the Western Division. The number of flocks of over 50,000 sheep declined from 208 in 1894 to 81 in 1900, while the number of flocks of less than 2,000 sheep increased from 10,415 to 12,798. This was associated with a far greater decline in the number of sheep in the Western Division (from 15.4m. to 6.3m.)

---

sheep over wheat stubble long before it was officially recommended by the scientists in the colonial Departments of Agriculture.

Even the smallest holdings often ran sheep too; see the Royal Commission on Crown Lands, 'Minutes of Evidence', *Proc. Vic. Leg. Ass.*, 1879–80, vol. 3, paper 72, *passim*.

[26] These have been calculated by dividing the census returns of the number of persons entered as pastoral employers in each colony into the number of sheep at those dates. The comparisons are not entirely accurate, as dairymen are included among the pastoralists and no account is taken of pastoralists owning more than one flock, but the changes are so very great that this is not important. The full comparison between the censal years 1861, 1871, 1881, 1891, and 1901 is: 6,986, 8,092, 2,933, 2,756, 2,075. Analogous figures for New South Wales in the same years are: 5,307, 12,491, 11,510, 9,109, 4,872.

[27] W. S. Campbell, *Extracts from Reports on Certain Agricultural Districts* (Sydney, 1888), pp. 28, 42.

[28] Standing Committee on Public Works, 'Report on the Proposed Railways for the Riverina, with Minutes of Evidence', *N.S.W. V. & P.*, 1891–2, vol. 5, evidence of C. Uphill, A. S. Joss, T. Lutham, and P. P. Sandral; also 'Report on the Proposed Temora-Hillston Railway', ibid., *passim*.

than in the Tablelands and Western Slopes which were more suited to wheat growing.[29]

The greater productivity of mixed farming remained a matter of dispute for some years, possibly because the quality of the sheep and the wool from small holdings lacked the breeding of station stock. Nevertheless, it was apparent that sheep grazed over wheat stubble in the autumn were better fed, healthier, and less afflicted by disease than others. The stock-carrying capacity of the land was increased by 25 per cent,[30] and because coarser breeds of sheep were run, the weight of the fleece tended to be greater.

That the increasing importance of small flocks was not merely the product of mixed farming is shown, however, by the gradual decline in the size of flocks in New South Wales after 1861, and particularly after 1881 (see n. 26). The entry of many small-scale producers in the eighties and the various schemes for closer settlement, involving government resumption of large estates and the imposition of progressive land taxation at the turn of the century, helped both to increase the number of small flocks and to diminish the number of large ones.

These changes, both in location and technology, implied changes in the scale on which wool production was conducted. The carrying capacity of semi-arid lands was low, and, as the pastoralists advanced further into them, the net returns per sheep tended to fall. This called for cheap handling and large flocks—for profits derived from small returns on many sheep. But though this meant a high initial investment in stock (or a relatively long period of waiting while flocks multiplied by natural increase) and had important consequences for financing production, the heavy capitalization that came to be associated with the industry did not begin until the seventies.[31] Then the improvements necessary to stock stations to their full capacity and to prepare clips more efficiently—fencing and water conservation, washing pools, scouring plants and more elaborate shearing sheds—were reflected in mounting capital costs. On the other hand, of course, where pastoral production was carried on together with farming, the scale of activity and of capitalization tended to decrease.

[29] *W. & P.*, *1900-01*, pp. 574, 578.
[30] Standing Committee on Public Works, 'Report on the Proposed Railway from Temora to Hillston, with Minutes of Evidence', *N.S.W. V. & P.*, 1891-2, vol. 5, evidence of Robert Cooper.
[31] Australian new capital formation in agriculture and the pastoral industry rose from an average of £893,000 in the period 1863-5 and £862,000 in 1866-70 to £2,953,000 in 1871-5 and £6,679,000 in 1876-80 (N. G. Butlin, *Private Capital Formation*, p. 133).

2

THE CONSUMPTION OF AUSTRALIAN WOOL

THE growth of Australian wool output coincided with a sustained expansion of the European and North American wool textile industries which continued to absorb, year after year, the production not only of Australia but also of South America, South Africa and New Zealand without appreciable difficulty. In broad terms it is indisputable that wool production in these new countries was stimulated, up to the sixties at least, by the extension of demand implicit in the mechanization of these industries[1] and that, in turn, the continued industrial expansion after the sixties was made possible, in part, by the huge inflow of cheap antipodean wools.

Generalizations as wide as these are seldom very informative; when referred to particular cases they are sometimes actually misleading. It is, for example, misleading to imagine an Australian output that was absorbed by a ready-made demand which merely grew year after year and with the fluctuations of which it broadly corresponded. When considering the markets for Australian wool what matters is not the general interdependence between pastoral production and manufacturing activity but the changes in the extent, the nature and the sources of the demand.

One of the most important features of the trade in Australian wool has been, in fact, the striking way in which the expansion of output after the sixties, occurring as it did in the context of a generally declining price trend for wool, was absorbed only by an increasing variety of consumers. The use of colonial wools spread from the woollen to the worsted industry,[2] and from Great Britain

---

[1] The thesis advanced by Fitzpatrick in *The British Empire in Australia*, p. 189, that the *raison d'être* of the growth of the Australian pastoral industry lay in the British industry's need for raw materials to sustain its expansion during the forties is seductive but grossly oversimplified, and it is one which becomes increasingly difficult to maintain in the succeeding decades.

[2] Throughout most of the nineteenth century the distinction between the worsted and woollen industries was easy to draw. The basic differentiating process of worsted manufacture was 'combing'. This meant the separation of the short wool fibres (the 'noils') in the raw wool input from the long ones (the 'tops') in such a way that the long fibres were laid out parallel to one another. The tops provided the raw material for the worsted spinner. In woollen manufacture, on the other hand, short fibres (including noils imported from the worsted industry)

to Continental and North American mills. This changed pattern of consumption, and the changes in the structure of the manufacturing industries with which it was partly associated, affected significantly not only the prices paid for colonial wools but also the organization of the wool market. Further, at the same time as Australian output was expanding, wool production was growing rapidly in other countries in the southern hemisphere. The relationships between the consumption of these competing wools are completely obscured by any general statement. These are the problems to which this chapter is devoted. They can be traced in an examination of factory consumption of raw wool, and there is little need, at this stage, to study final consumers' demand for wool textile products.

I   BRITISH CONSUMERS

During the thirties and forties Australian wool gradually displaced other imported wools in the mills of Great Britain, and by 1850 the imports of the Australasian product exceeded those of all other wools combined—a rise to supremacy that is a familiar story.[3] In addition, colonial wool came to overshadow the use of domestic English wool. In 1850 retained imports of colonial and other wools were only one-half the size of the retained domestic production; by 1870, when Australasian wool amounted to two-thirds instead of a half of total imports, the proportion of imported to domestic wool retained had risen to 122 per cent; by 1890 it had risen to 261 per cent.[4] Yet these global figures, and the apparent capacity of the British industry to accept such a growing volume of imports, conceal a complex pattern of adaptation and a changing utilization. Changes in consumers' clothing fashion, a growing shortage of suitable domestic wools and increasingly severe competition from

---

were laid criss-cross on one another by the process known as 'carding', prior to spinning. Each branch, therefore, used broadly different types of wool, and the different types of yarn which these wools and the different processes produced resulted in different types of fabrics. Towards the end of the century and in the twentieth century the distinction between the types of wool and the types of yarn used, and consequently between the fabrics characterizing each branch, tended to become blurred, and it becomes more difficult to define the boundaries between them.

[3] For details see S. H. Roberts. 'The Australian Wool Trade in the Forties', *Royal Australian Historical Society Journal and Proceedings*, vol. xvii, part vi, p. 337. See also Appendix, Table VI.

[4] Source: A. Sauerbeck, *The Production and Consumption of Wool*, pp. 3, 27; The Tariff Commission, *Report*, vol. 2: *The Textile Trade*. Part 2, 'Evidence on the Woollen Industry', para. 1512. The figures for imports include alpaca, vicuna and llama wool and goats' hair. If those products are excluded, which is possible only after 1875, the relevant proportion for 1875 becomes 125 per cent, for 1880 169 per cent and for 1890 241 per cent.

Continental industries forced the worsted industry to enter the market for colonial wool which, until the late sixties and seventies, had in England been the preserve of the woollen manufacturers.

Consumption data for the two English industries are very unsatisfactory, and they relate only to the fifties. The evidence available, however, indicates very clearly both the widely differing combinations of raw material types used and the dominance of the woollen industry in the market for imported wools. In 1851 the worsted industry used an estimated 15 m. lb. of imported wool and 65 m. lb. of English wool; in 1857 an estimate placed the relative consumption at 15 m. lb. and 80 m. lb. The woollen industry, in 1858, used 76 m. lb. of imported wool and 80 m. lb. of English.[5] In other words, in 1858 the woollen industry utilized 83 per cent of the retained imports of wool from all foreign and colonial sources, and indeed until the end of the sixties it remained the only substantial consumer of Australian wool. The first group to buy colonial wool at the London sales had been, in fact, the Yorkshire woollen manufacturers and dealers, and they had been followed, in the forties, by West of England woollen interests.[6] The reason for this particular pattern of demand is not difficult to discern. The industry had been nurtured on relatively short wool from the Downs, and when it outgrew that source it sought its raw materials from the merino flocks of Spain and Saxony. When a similar type of wool became available from New South Wales at a lower price and in greater quantities than the German product, and when the quality of the German flocks began to deteriorate, the choice was made with little hesitation.

The change was smooth because it presented no major technological problem; it was the source of the raw material, not its nature, that was changed. Although German wool was still imported in small quantities, even in the twentieth century, for speciality work,[7] the colonial wool displayed all the characteristics which manufacturers had demanded of it.

On the other hand the worsted industry had always used long

[5] T. Baines, *Yorkshire, Past and Present*, 2 vols. (Lond, n.d.). Chapters in vol. 1 by E. Baines, 'The Woollen Manufacture of England with special reference to the Leeds Clothing District' (1858), and 'Supplementary Account of the Woollen Trade to 1870'. Estimates of the value of worsted production were made by Forbes in 1851 and James in 1857, quoted on pp. 693 and 694 respectively, and of woollen production by Baines in 1858, given on p. 659. The worsted industry's consumption of 15 m. lb. in 1858 is Baines' estimate (p. 660).

[6] W. H. Chard, *Australasian Wool Markets*, p. 12. See S. Macarthur Onslow, *Some Early Records of the Macarthurs of Camden*, ch. xiii, *passim*, for a more detailed identification of the buyers in the twenties.

[7] J. H. Clapham, *The Woollen and Worsted Industries* (London, 1907), p. 80.

domestic wool. Although the perfection of mechanical combing and its general adoption during and after the forties made it technically possible for short wool to be prepared for worsted spinning,[8] it was many years before this allegiance was changed, the reason being increasing concentration, from the thirties on, on the production of mixed lustre goods, in which worsted yarn was combined with such other fibres as alpaca, cotton and mohair.[9] This style of cloth demanded the use primarily of long hard English wool. Consequently, although some relatively long foreign and colonial wool was utilized, combing machines like those of Holden and Donnisthorpe, which could work on short-stapled wool, were discarded in favour of those of Lister and later of Noble, which were more suited to long wool.[10] The rapid expansion of worsted production which the mechanical innovations in combing and spinning permitted and which the introduction of cheaper fabrics from cheap mixed raw materials induced, and the growing demand for wool which that implied, had therefore very little effect on the demand for specifically colonial wool.

The increase in the English demand for Australian wool up to the end of the sixties arose from the expansion of the woollen industry. Mechanization proceeded slowly. (Though the power loom was being used on a small scale in the West Riding from the early fifties, it did not attain widespread use until the seventies,[11] and in 1858 many elements of the domestic system of production remained.)[12] Yet the industry flourished. The Cobden Treaty with France in 1860 and subsequent agreements with the *Zollverein*, Belgium and Austria opened markets into which the Yorkshire and Scottish manufacturers moved with alacrity.[13] New mills were erected, equipment was extended, and the earnings of operatives rose.[14] To some extent the expansion was uneven. The West of

---

[8] T. Southey, *The Rise, Progress and Present State of Colonial Sheep and Wool*, p. 9, says that Donnisthorpe's improved combing machine patented in 1844 could work on a staple down to $1\frac{1}{4}$ inches in length. Normal combing wool was 3 inches or more.

[9] Cf. T. Illingworth, *Our Textile Industries: what is the cause of their so-called depression?* (Bradford and Manchester, 1883), pp. 15-16; also E. M. Sigsworth, 'A History of Messrs. John Foster & Son, Ltd., 1819-1891' (unpublished Ph.D. thesis, University of Leeds, 1954), pp. 78-96.

[10] Lister controlled all the patent rights by 1853 and produced only his own machine for sale in England. After the expiration of the patents in 1860 Noble's machine was widely adopted in Bradford (Sigsworth, op. cit., pp. 71-2).

[11] E. P. Dobson and J. B. Ives, *A Century of Achievement: the history of James Ives & Company Limited, 1848-1948* (London, 1948), pp. 38-9.

[12] Baines, *Yorkshire, Past and Present*, p. 631.

[13] Ibid., p. 668.   [14] Tariff Commission, op. cit., para. 1642.

England manufacturers retained their supremacy in the production of superfine cloths, but the demand for plain cloths, the staple production of the West and of Leeds, was declining. Growth occurred mainly in the increasingly popular fancy cloths and cheap medium and low quality woollens, made mainly in the West Riding.[15] As in the worsted industry, a mixture of raw materials made it possible to exploit an ever-widening market for cheap goods; warps of cotton or worsted yarn were in common use by 1870, silk was woven with a woollen warp, and a vast increase took place in the amount of shoddy and mungo incorporated in woollen cloths.[16]

Meanwhile the worsted industry was expanding even more rapidly and spectacularly. Cost-reducing innovations in combing and spinning[17] and the introduction of new fabrics from cheaper mixed raw materials continued to widen the market for worsted goods. Further stimulus was derived from the treaties with Continental countries and from the expiration of patent rights on combing machinery which permitted a ready expansion of that branch of the industry. There is, once again, no satisfactory measure of the industry's output, but some indication may be derived from the figures of machine capacity and the volume of exports. Between 1850 and 1871 the number of worsted spinning spindles rather more than doubled.[18] In the period 1857 to 1869 the exports of worsted yarn rose from less than 23,930,000 lb. to 35,572,000 and of fabrics from 129,632,000 yards to 250,062,000.[19] Allowing at least an equivalent expansion of the home trade—whose share of output was variously estimated between a half and four-fifths—the export figures suggest an expansion of up to double the 1857 output.

This growth, however, overreached itself: the supply of suitable wool did not expand commensurately with the industry. Accordingly manufacturers turned to consider colonial wool; but it was still long wool they were interested in, not the short merino. The efforts of the Wool Supply Association, established through the Bradford Chamber of Commerce in 1859,[20] were therefore devoted to popularizing the long-woolled breeds of sheep in Australia and New Zealand.[21]

[15] Baines, op. cit., pp. 642, 666.   [16] Ibid., p. 669.
[17] Sigsworth, op. cit., pp. 53 ff.   [18] See Appendix, Table VIII.
[19] See Appendix, Table VII.
[20] Its activities embraced the distribution of information, assistance to emigrants and submissions to the governments.
[21] Commenting on a sample of wool sent to Bradford the chairman said that 'what they wanted at present was a large supply of deep combing wool. As a committee they were doing all in their power to urge on the people in Australia in that direction' (*Argus*, 8 April 1872). As another example of their publicity see

Towards the end of the sixties the worsted industry was faced with a further set of changed conditions which entirely transformed the market for colonial wool. The lustre goods on which the industry had concentrated for so long began to lose their popularity, and consumers tended to transfer their preference to soft all-wool worsteds.[22] For these new wares shorter wool was essential. English domestic wool production had, by this time, switched almost entirely to the long wool which had formerly been in such great demand and which had not been in such close competition with the colonial produce.[23] Consequently the industry had to seek its raw material from Australia. Adaptation to the changed fashion was slow and difficult. In particular, spinning machinery, which had been geared to working long English and colonial wools, had to be adjusted to the novel conditions.[24] Moreover, French superiority in producing these cloths placed the English manufacturer under a severe competitive handicap, despite the breathing space afforded by the Franco-Prussian War.

From the early seventies the worsted industry became the dynamic element in the British demand for colonial wool. In the first place, the use of short merino wool was becoming increasingly necessary and the means of treating it increasingly efficient; at the same time, while the expansion of worsted production continued, the growth of the woollen industry slowed down. Further, the reimposition of foreign protective duties and the growing competition in export markets from foreign manufacturers pressed more heavily on woollen manufacturers.[25] Thus, while the number of worsted spinning spindles increased by 22 per cent between 1871 and 1885, and by 32 per cent between 1871 and 1890, woollen spinning spindles increased by only 11 per cent and 17 per cent during the same periods,[26] and the contrast is even more marked when doubling spindles are considered. The expansion of the worsted industry between 1840 and 1870 had not affected the demand for colonial wool, since long wool was its principal raw material. Now, the coincidence of worsted demand for short wool with a relative decline in woollen demand gave the worsted industry a doubly important

'Omega', *The Sheep, Long Woolled as well as Short Woolled, for Victoria, Tasmania and New Zealand* (Melbourne, 1865).

22 Illingworth, *Our Textile Industries*, p. 16; Sigsworth, 'A History of Messrs. John Foster & Son Ltd.', pp. 127, 187.

23 Baines, *Yorkshire, Past and Present*, p. 662.

24 Sigsworth, op. cit., pp. 150-4.

25 Tariff Commission, op. cit., paras. 1390-2.

26 See Appendix, Table VIII.

role. Secondly, the traditional worsted processes also commenced using colonial wool in increased quantities from the seventies. The relatively fixed nature of the domestic wool supply meant that any expansion of this section of the worsted industry had to rely more and more on the growing colonial production of crossbred long wool and, later, of fine, long, comeback wool. An increasingly large, though unrecorded, share of colonial wool imports were therefore taken by the worsted industry after about 1870.

It would be a mistake, however, to imagine that these developments in the English wool textile industries were the sole, or even the main, set of circumstances affecting the consumption of colonial wool. Though the expansion of the woollen industry and the entry of the worsted industry into the market together meant a great extension in demand, it did not nearly match the growth of colonial output. Great Britain did not for long, in fact, retain the monopoly of Australian wool which she had enjoyed in 1840. After 1860 the re-exports of foreign and colonial wool (mainly colonial)[27] grew rapidly both in absolute terms and as a proportion of total imports. The comparison of retained imports and re-exports in Fig. 2 indicates that by 1880 only half the imports were consumed in

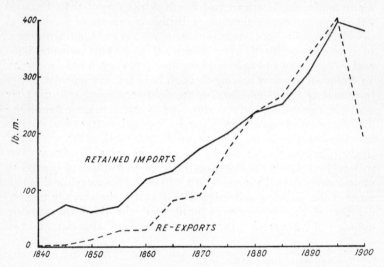

Fig. 2. United Kingdom re-exports and retained imports of wool
(See Appendix, Table IX)

[27] See Appendix, Tables VI and IX.

England. The re-exports went mainly to Continental countries.
France, in particular, became a major force in the market after the
removal of the import duties on raw wool in 1860. Re-exports to
Belgium became significant in the late sixties, to Germany in the
early seventies and to the United States in the late seventies.[28] By
the end of the seventies London's importance was rapidly becoming
that of an entrepôt market for the Continental industries. The growing importance of the re-export trade means that, despite the fact
that British industry remained the largest single consumer, explana-
tions of movements in the market for colonial wool must be sought,
to an increasing extent after 1860, in the implications of Continental
demand.

2   CONTINENTAL CONSUMERS

From 1860 the Continental textile industries grew rapidly. Not
only did the size of the French and German industries, in particular,
rival in size that of the United Kingdom, but their expansion was
more rapid.[29] Their expansion, however, was not based nearly as
much on colonial wool as the English expansion was, for in addition
to large domestic supplies,[30] the Continental industries made use of
far more South American and South African wool than England
did. The apparent destination of British re-exports of foreign and
colonial produce gives one approximate measure of Continental consumption of specifically colonial wool (Fig. 3). This measure, however, suffers from two defects: first, the destination is only apparent,
an unknown quantity passing through Belgium, in particular, either
in transit or for re-shipment to the final consuming country after
preliminary washing and scouring; and secondly, to these figures the
direct exports of wool from Australia, especially after 1880, need to
be added to give a complete picture.[31] Nevertheless three features,
implicit in the figures as they stand, are most significant. The
pattern into which the dates marking the expansion of exports to
various countries falls is one which strikingly illustrates the development of the different industries. The second is the absolute prepon-
derance of French purchases until 1881; the third the growing
diffusion of exports after the mid-seventies. Until that date, that is,

---

[28] See Appendix, Table XI.   [29] See Appendix, Table X.
[30] See Appendix, Table XIII.
[31] In the 1896-7 selling season 362,989 bales were forwarded from the Australian colonies direct to the Continent—Goldsbrough, Mort & Co. Ltd, *Australian
Wool: its position and prospects in 1896* (Melbourne, 1897), p. 14. In round
figures this would be equivalent to about 100 m. lb., or almost one-third of the
amount of foreign and colonial wool re-exported from London.

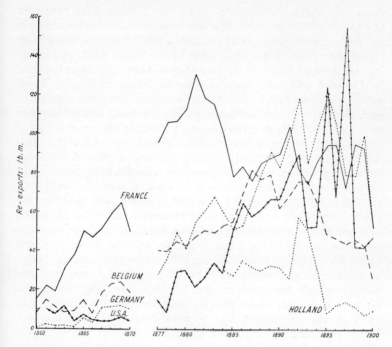

FIG. 3. Destination of United Kingdom re-exports of wool
(See Appendix, Table XI)

the London market virtually served only the textile industries of the United Kingdom and France, and the demand for colonial wool was primarily responsive to conditions affecting them. After that date the effect of the demand from any one country except perhaps England, which still retained nearly half her imports, played a much less prominent role in the formation of prices at London.

In order to explain this diffusion of consumption, and to place it in a setting appropriate to later discussions, it is necessary to consider, in outline, the main features of the history of wool textile manufacture in these countries.

Throughout this period France was the United Kingdom's main textile competitor. Her consumption was higher than England's by 10 per cent by the second half of the seventies,[32] and even by 1860 French manufacturers were in a strong enough position to face the

[32] See Appendix, Table X.

threat of British competition under the Cobden Treaty without undue immediate alarm.[33] The course of technical development in the worsted industry broadly paralleled that of Britain, though the initial moves occurred a little later. In the forties most wool combing was done by hand. At the end of that decade machines invented by Heilman and Schlumberger were beginning to displace handwork, and in the first half of the fifties the industry was revolutionized by their wide-scale adoption. The Heilman machine, which met with the widest approval, made possible the production of greatly increased quantities of better quality tops at less than half the former cost.[34] Machine combing, because it ensured the large, steady flow of tops that was necessary, also made economical the introduction of machine spinning, which had been rare before the mid-forties.[35] Supplementing machine combing and spinning, the power loom began to be used more extensively after the forties. By 1870 combing was entirely mechanized, nearly all spinning was done on mules, mostly of the self-acting type, and the power loom was widely used (though hand weaving still occupied an important place in specialities and novelties).[36] By that time, also, combing had become highly localized in the Roubaix-Tourcoing, Croix and Reims areas, and while weaving was more decentralized, one-third of the 48 million kg. of wool combed in the Roubaix-Tourcoing-Croix area was spun locally.[37]

Unlike the British industry, French worsted production had been specialized on the manufacture of all-wool merino cloths and

[33] A. L. Dunham, *The Anglo-French Treaty of Commerce of 1860 and the Progress of the Industrial Revolution in France* (University of Michigan Publications, History and Political Science vol. ix, Ann Arbor, 1930), p. 222.

[34] The reduction is put at 60 per cent by M. Alcan, *Rapport tendant à accorder à M. Josué Heilman, inventeur de la Peigneuse Mécanique, le prix fondé par M. le Marquis d'Argenteuil* (Société d'encouragement pour l' industrie nationale, Paris, 1857), pp. 5-6.
In a letter to George Marshland (29 Oct. 1838) Isaac Holden described a plan whereby he hoped to capture the combing of fine wool for the French merino cloth trade by cutting the cost from between 1s. and 1s. 6d. per lb. to between 2d. and 4d. Allowing for the exaggeration natural to the circumstances (he was asking for financial backing), the envisaged saving was very great. (This letter is from the manuscript collection, 'The Holden-Illingworth Correspondence', held in the Brotherton Library, University of Leeds. I am indebted to the Librarian for permission to quote from it.)

[35] This relationship, of course, was not one which was confined to France. On spinning machinery see Dunham, op. cit., p. 225.

[36] Clapham, *The Woollen and Worsted Industries*, p. 249; Ministère du Commerce, de l'Industrie et du Travail: A. Picard, *Le Bilan d'un Siècle* (Paris, 1906), p. 352; Dunham, *The Anglo-French Treaty*, p. 225.

[37] W. O. Henderson, *Britain and Industrial Europe, 1750–1870* (Liverpool, 1954). p. 101.

superior worsteds since the end of the eighteenth century.[38] The main raw materials used in these lines were the domestic merino wools, and the combing and spinning techniques developed were those appropriate for treating short wool. There was, therefore, no obstacle, either technical or in the nature of the raw material, to French use of colonial wool in the worsted industry as there was to English. Yet large-scale imports were made only after 1860. Heavy tariffs on raw wool were the hindrance. Imposed between 1816 and 1826, they amounted to 30 per cent of the value. A reduction of one-third was effected in 1836, and in 1856 the *ad valorem* basis of the duties was changed to one of weight. In 1860 wool was admitted free of duty when imported in French vessels.[39]

Basically, it was the development of the French machine combing industry and the tariff liberalizations which that development and the expansion of the worsted industry made necessary that account for the increases in British re-exports in 1850, 1855-60 and 1865 (Table IX).

Although the British industry did in fact present a serious competitive threat after 1860, particularly to Roubaix-Tourcoing in the years immediately following the conclusion of the treaty,[40] worsted production boomed in the second half of the decade. In the fifties the construction of roads and railways had created a national market which was quickly exploited. In the sixties export channels were established and France began to compete with England for markets in Germany; exports of combed goods rose from 0.65 m. francs in 1861 to 7 m. francs in 1867, most of them sent to Germany and most of them produced in Roubaix and Reims.[41] Moreover, the British competition hastened the introduction of power machinery. The number of power looms in Roubaix increased from 1,000 in 1855-6 to 10,000 in 1867, and in the sixties the Reims combing industry doubled its capacity and output.[42]

By the nature of the fabrics produced, this expansion was based largely on the use of South American and colonial wools, which found far wider use in the French than in the English worsted industry. This was made possible by the type of equipment used. French combing with Heilman, Schlumberger and Holden

---

[38] Illingworth, *Our Textile Industries*, p. 16; Dunham, op. cit., p. 216.
[39] Dunham, op. cit., p. 131.
[40] Ibid., pp. 230-2. This was felt mainly in the production of mixed worsteds. Isaac Crowthers writing to Isaac Holden from Croix (5 May 1866) recalled that in Roubaix the trade 'gave themselves up for lost' in 1860, 1861, and 1862 ('Holden-Illingworth Correspondence').
[41] Picard, op. cit., p. 349.   [42] Dunham, op. cit., pp. 230, 233.

machines, as we have already seen, was specifically adapted to short wools.[43] Spinning was done almost entirely on mules which, again, were designed to work short wool and the use of which, in England, was restricted to the woollen industry. In particular, the technique by which the wool was drawn out before and during spinning was not only peculiarly adapted to short wool but enabled manufacturers to produce a yarn of greatly superior quality.[44] One of the main disadvantages which English worsted and woollen manufacturers found in colonial and particularly in South American wools—the presence of burrs and grass seeds—was readily overcome in France, where mechanical and chemical methods were developed to remove them.[45]

As in England, the development of the woollen industry was overshadowed by that of the worsted. The mid-fifties marked the turning-point in its fortunes. The business of the Elbeuf district, one of the main woollen manufacturing regions, reached a peak in 1858 and then declined during the sixties under the combined impact of British and Belgian competition and the handicap of dear fuel;[46] and Elbeuf was typical, in general outline, of the other regions. Mechanical development was slow. Though machine spinning had been known for many years, it was still far from universal in 1860, and there were only a few power looms.[47] The goad of British competition did lead to improvements in carding and preparing machinery, to improved techniques in manufacturing,[48] and to a more extensive use of power looms in the succeeding years. On the other hand, the difficulties of power weaving, the role played by speciality manufactures and the conservatism of the producers, tended to retard the introduction of power looms, especially in Elbeuf where even in the late seventies the transition was most incomplete.[49] The other step taken to meet the competition resulted in a shift of the emphasis of woollen production. Vienne, in the south-east, successfully turned to the production of low-priced goods of cotton and wool and displaced the imports from Huddersfield.[50] The general trend towards the imitation of low-quality English goods, started in the forties, was accelerated during

[43] Holden's was one of the main machines used, mainly because of the importance of Holden's own combing works at Croix, Reims and St Denis.
[44] W. S. B. McLaren, *Spinning Woollen and Worsted* (London, 1884), pp. 148-9.
[45] Ibid., pp. 47-8; Picard, op. cit., p. 343.   [46] Picard, op. cit., pp. 342, 345.
[47] Dunham, op. cit., pp. 225, 227.   [48] Ibid.
[49] Ibid., pp. 323-4; J. Wrigley and C. E. Bousfield, *Report on the Woollen Cloth Manufacture of France* (Leeds, 1878), pp. 7, 9.
[50] Wrigley and Bousfield, op. cit., p. 18.

the sixties and seventies.[51] None of these responses, however, was entirely adequate, and in 1875 and 1881 the industry successfully applied for the re-imposition of protective duties.[52]

The raw wool materials for the French woollen industry differed from those of the English mainly in the use of greater quantities of South American wool and a readiness to use some burry colonial wool. It also utilized a far greater quantity of noils, the short residue removed from long wool by the combing process, which tended to impart a greater softness to the French products.[53] The greater variety of raw materials, however, meant that the industry's demand for specifically colonial wool was relatively small, and a considerable proportion of it was exercised indirectly in the demand for combing wool. This concentration of French demand for colonial wool into the worsted industry, fostered by the suitability of the colonial product for combing and the primacy of worsted production, was intensified during the last twenty years of the century as the distinction between worsted and woollen manufacture became less easy to draw. Fashion changes favoured the soft, all-wool worsteds against woollen products, and there was a growing tendency to mix an increasing proportion of worsted with woollen yarns in products formerly composed entirely of woollen yarns or of mixtures of wool and shoddy, mungo and cotton.[54]

The wool textile industries of other European countries followed a similar, though later, development. Their evolution can be traced in the statistics of British and French wool textile exports and in the changes in the protective tariffs. Protection was first afforded to fabric manufacturers whose raw materials in the form of yarn, and to a slighter degree of tops and raw wool, were admitted free. Then protection was extended to spinners, and only tops and raw wool were freely admitted. Finally, duties were placed on tops, to encourage local combing. Up to 1857 exports of yarn from the United Kingdom expanded more rapidly than raw wool exports, which reflects the expansion of French production before its spinning component was fully equipped to serve it.[55] Similarly, after the early eighties yarn exports expanded more rapidly than manufactured exports,[56] as a result of the initial expansion of manufacturing

---

[51] Picard, *Le Bilan d'un Siècle*, p. 345.   [52] Dunham, op. cit., pp. 323-4.
[53] Picard, op. cit., p. 343.   [54] Ibid., p. 353.
[55] British exports of woollen and worsted yarn, mainly to France, rose from 1.1 m. lb. in 1830 to 3.7 m. lb. in 1840, 13.7 m. lb. in 1850 and 24.6 m. lb. in 1857. Overall, these exports increased over 23 times between 1830 and 1857; raw wool exports increased only 5 times (Baines, *Yorkshire, Past and Present*, p. 640).
[56] See Appendix, Table VII.

in Germany, Austria and Italy. The acceleration of German production is similarly reflected in its growing imports of French tops after the late eighties.

By 1867 Belgian worsted products were presenting a threat to both Bradford and Roubaix,[57] while the woollen spinners were already gaining a wide reputation for the quality of their yarn.[58] By the eighties they were acknowledged masters in producing certain types of yarn which were extensively used by Glasgow woollen manufacturers.[59] To some extent this superiority was founded in natural advantages and the techniques for washing wool which were developed in Verviers. Economies in transport enabled it to capitalize on those advantages, for it was situated on one of the major cross-roads of European commerce. Buyers who obtained their supplies at London or Antwerp were able to have them sent there, before being forwarded to their producing area, at virtually no extra cost. At the same time the machinery and techniques used in spinning woollen yarn were considered better adapted to the type of wool used and the nature of the finished product than any others.[60]

Swiss worsted spinning establishments were founded in the late sixties and seventies. Prussia and Austria began to imitate English woollen wares from the end of the sixties. The main expansion in those countries came, however, towards the end of the seventies. The unification of the German states by Bismarck and the tariff of 1879 provided the opportunity for a vast expansion of worsted production and a considerable one in the woollen industry there. By 1900 Germany had become Britain's 'worst competitor'.[61] The rapid extension of worsted spinning in Germany, Austria and Italy during the eighties may be traced in the history of a firm of Swiss wool merchants, Simonius Vischer & Co.[62] In the first half of the century it supplied raw wool to small woollen manufacturers in Alsace and the southern German states; by the middle of the century the partners were shareholders in a newly formed Alsatian worsted spinning mill; by the seventies and eighties the nature of its trade had changed completely and it was now almost entirely

57 Picard, op. cit., p. 352.
58 Ibid., p. 214; Belgian yarn exports to England rose steadily from 846,500 lb. in 1867 to 3,963,100 lb. in 1871—A. and J. A. Redgrave, Labour, Wages and Production in the Cotton, Woollen and Flax Factories in France and Belgium (London, 1873), p. 28.   59 McLaren, op. cit., pp. 38, 228.   60 Ibid., p. 228.
61 Tariff Commission, op. cit., para. 1383.
62 Simonius Vischer & Co., The Chronicle of a Basle Wool Trading House, 1719–1939 (Basle, 1939). The following discussion in the text is based on this work without further references.

devoted to supplying worsted spinners in Switzerland, Germany and Italy; at the same time the source from which they obtained their stocks of raw wool had changed from the flock-owners of Hungary, Italy and south Germany to the public auctions at London and Antwerp; and finally, the trade with woollen manufacturers was reopened, but entirely as a subsidiary to the worsted trade, for it was based on the sale of the noils not required by the worsted spinners.

From the middle of the century the growth of these Continental industries most probably implied an increase in the world demand for raw wool. Certainly it meant a shift from a demand for imported finished and semi-finished products to one for imported raw wool. These Continental countries exerted, therefore, a growing force in the international raw wool markets. For example, the purchases of colonial wool in London by Continental and North American countries combined rose from thirty million to four hundred million pounds from the beginning of the sixties to the middle of the nineties, while the British share increased only slightly over three times (Tables IX and XI). Despite the importance of these countries in the London market, however, the role of colonial wool in their consumption should not be overestimated. South American and domestic European wools provided the bulk of the European raw wool requirements,[63] and colonial wool did not bear the same relation to Continental textile activity as it did to English.

3 CHANGES IN THE STRUCTURE OF INDUSTRIAL DEMAND

In 1906 Clapham reported that the woollen and worsted industries of England were organized on quite different principles: the woollen industry was composed of unspecialized, relatively small-scale producers; the worsted industry, on the other hand, was marked by large-scale concerns specializing in one process of manufacture.[64] The same division was broadly true of the Continental industries. In this context the essential point of the differentiation is its development, in that particular form, during the preceding fifty years. The specialization of worsted concerns had proceeded from relatively small-scale, integrated mills; in the woollen industry the process was one of concentrating activities formerly performed by specialists into one larger-scale mill.

Apart altogether from their effects on productive capacity and

[63] See pp. 39, 42-3, 171 n. 90.
[64] J. H. Clapham, 'Industrial Organisation in the Woollen and Worsted Industries of Yorkshire', *Economic Journal*, vol. xvi (1906), p. 515.

therefore on the total demand for wool, these changes had most important implications for the expression of demand in, and consequently the organization of, the wool market. Demand became concentrated at fewer and more powerful points. An increasing proportion of the demand for wool for worsted purposes was expressed through large spinners, merchant-combers and a few raw wool merchants, instead of directly by the large number of integrated mills and wool dealers that were characteristic of the first half of the century. In the woollen industry the reduction in the number and the increase in the size of the units of production meant that supplies could more easily be obtained without the intervention of a wool merchant. These structural changes were essential pre-conditions of the relocation of the market for colonial wool from London to Australian centres in the last quarter of the century.

In the worsted industry specialization grew in two fields: combing became an occupation separate from the rest of the worsted processes; and then spinning was separated from weaving.

The specialization of combing was fully apparent in England by the middle of the century. It was fostered initially by the patent protection afforded to newly invented machinery; by 1853 Lister had bought out all the English patentees and was allowing only his own machines, leased at high rentals and returning heavy royalties, to be used.[65] Mills established by Lister and his licensees, as well as by other, less monopolistic, patentees like Holden in France, were necessarily on a large scale and specialized. Other factors independently confirmed this trend to specialized operation of combing mills. In the early years, in particular, machine combing presented a complex task, and modifications were constantly being made to adapt the machinery to different types of wool and to the production of different types of tops.[66] Managerial efficiency could not easily be retained when these activities were undertaken in conjunction with those demanded by the operation of a spinning mill. Moreover, once combing costs had been reduced by mechanization, the value of operating combing machinery lay in the economies of scale; the modifications to machinery and the experience necessary for efficient production were much too costly to be squandered on the few bales a spinner might require combed each day. Uncertainty about the type of yarn, and therefore of tops, that would be required

---

[65] See p. 22, n. 10. Lister charged £1,200 for a set of three machines (Southey, *The Rise, Progress and Present State of Colonial Sheep and Wool*, p. 10).

[66] Clapham, 'Industrial Organisation in the Woollen and Worsted Industries of Yorkshire', p. 519.

in the future was another inducement for spinners to have their wool combed on commission when and as they required it or to buy the tops from a comber. This uncertainty grew as the exports of yarn to France and later to other Continental countries and to the English woollen districts increased.[67] Consequently, even after the expiration of the patent protection in 1860 the tendency towards specialization continued.

Developments in another field altogether also hastened the specialization of topmaking. The English wool stapler had occupied an important place in the worsted trade, buying, sorting, and re-selling domestic wool to the spinners. The growing scarcity of English wool in the fifties induced, and the long credit allowed them by the staplers enabled, the spinners to compete with the staplers and go direct to the sources of supply. The decline in the staplers' importance thus initiated was accelerated by the steadily growing consumption of colonial wool during the late sixties. In general terms, the stapler was forced to become a merchant of colonial wool. This new role, however, was undermined in two ways. The growth of the scale on which the worsted spinners were organized made it easy for them to obtain their own supplies direct from the London sales. At the same time spinners tended more and more to buy tops than to have their own raw wool combed on commission.[68] The stapler-merchant then added combing to his other activities and sold tops as well as raw wool. At first he had it combed on commission but later he did it in his own plant. This combina-tion of merchant-topmaking served two purposes. It enabled the merchant to retain his trade and, as the wool in the tops was indistinguishably blended, he was in a position to profit perhaps more highly than if clearly identifiable raw wool was sold.[69]

The second element of specialization lay in the separation of spinning from weaving. The decline in the importance of the factory that combined spinning and weaving became apparent by the mid-seventies.[70] Some of the factors which produced it, however, were operative from the fifties. The growing use of cotton and other raw

1145108

[67] Ibid., p. 518.
[68] Although it is not readily apparent, it is possible that this practice first found extensive favour during the seventies when raw wool prices were falling, for by not buying raw wool at all spinners transferred the risk of inventory losses to the merchant-topmakers.
[69] This paragraph is based generally on Clapham, 'Industrial Organisation in the Woollen and Worsted Industries of Yorkshire'. The full story of the decline of the stapler and the rise of the merchant-topmaker requires a far more compli-cated treatment than is necessary for our purposes. [70] See Appendix, Table XII.

materials meant that the manufacturer was, in any case, forced to go outside the industry for his supplies and that, therefore, the utility of vertically integrated production had begun to wane. The vast variety of fabrics into which these materials could be manufactured not only tended to narrow the range of products on which any one producer was willing to concentrate[71] but, paradoxically, rendered him more susceptible to the vagaries of fashion, readier to manufacture to order and therefore readier to change, within limits, the style of his product. This implied that the type of yarn he required was likely to vary quite widely over a fairly short period. It was cheaper to buy yarn from specialized spinners than to install machinery which could cope with that variation. In the seventies and eighties, however, these considerations were submerged in the far greater influence of the growth of yarn exports overseas and to the woollen districts—an increase in spinning, that is, unmatched by any worsted weaving.

The same tendencies were apparent in the French worsted industry. Before 1860 topmaking and spinning were separate specialized processes. The Holden works at Reims was combing wool on commission for spinners in the fifties;[72] merchants were then already adding topmaking to their activities (although Holden also did combing for them on commission);[73] and the topmakers were doing some merchanting.[74] The scale of their operations was also extending: in 1866 at Reims and Croix the Holden works alone produced about 4.5 million kg. of combed wool; the combined capacity of Reims and Roubaix, the two largest centres, was only about 22 million kg. in the following year.[75]

In France, however, there was a persistent tendency for the processes to be reintegrated during the following forty years. Concrete evidence supporting this assertion is fragmentary at the best. British competition during the sixties led spinners to try to add combing to their establishments;[76] in 1869 a pamphleteer remarked some factories which took in raw wool and sent out woven products and

[71] Cf. Sigsworth, op. cit., pp. 97 ff.
[72] 'Holden-Illingworth Correspondence': Jonathan Holden to Isaac Holden, 7 June 1859.
[73] Ibid., Edward Holden to Isaac Holden, 7 Nov. 1860.
[74] Ibid., Isaac Crowthers to Isaac Holden, 7 April 1866.
[75] Picard, *Le Bilan d'un Siècle*, p. 349.
[76] Dunham (*The Anglo-French Treaty of Commerce*, p. 154) details the case of a comber who sought a government loan to add spinning to his establishment in order to meet competition. Isaac Crowthers noted the same tendency, in Roubaix after 1864 ('Holden-Illingworth Correspondence': Crowthers to Isaac Holden, 5 May 1866).

commented on the rapidly disappearing specialization in sorting, washing, carding, combing and spinning;[77] and between 1867 and 1878 specialized combing was reduced by 25 per cent.[78] It is unfortunate that more exact statistics are not available to measure this movement and to separate mere surmise and extended generalization from actual fact, for the effect of these changes on the scale of production is uncertain. The alternative implications differ significantly: either the capitalization of the firms concerned was roughly unchanged after the transition was made, spinning capacity being reduced to allow the substitution of combing or weaving capacity, or the spinning plant was maintained intact and the firm's size and capital were greatly increased by the addition of other plant.

By comparison with the worsted industry the scale of woollen enterprises in England was small in 1906. It was, however, considerably greater than it had been in 1850. The trend in this industry was to concentrate, under one factory roof, the processes that had formerly been carried out by scattered out-workers. This was undoubtedly the result of the gradually extended use of power machinery for spinning and weaving. The Somersetshire serge industry is said to have been fully industrialized by the end of the fifties;[79] in the Yeadon-Guiseley district in Yorkshire the process of concentration was not complete until the eighties.[80] What prevented the specialization of the various branches after they were mechanized was mainly the complexity of the blend of raw materials which the woollen manufacturer used—a complexity that demanded unremitting personal attention in spinning.[81]

The very process of concentration tended to increase the economies that could be derived from larger-scale production, and the size of woollen mills continued to grow during the second half of the century. Inconclusive but suggestive evidence of this may be seen in the nature of the trade between Robert Jowitt & Sons, then wool merchants of Leeds, and their woollen manufacturing customers drawn from all the woollen producing districts. A sample from the firm's ledgers reveals that the average size of purchases made by those customers increased by up to one-third between the

[77] P. Pierrard, *Etude sur l'Industrie Lainière en France, et les Moyens de Ramener sa Prospérité* (London, 1869), p. 35.

[78] Picard, op. cit., p. 352.

[79] D. M. Hunter, *The West of England Woollen Industry under Protection and under Free Trade* (London, 1910), p. 24.

[80] Dobson and Ives, *A Century of Achievement*, pp. 43-4.

[81] Cf. Clapham, 'Industrial Organisation of the Woollen and Worsted Industries of Yorkshire', p. 521.

mid-sixties and the early seventies.[82] This tendency was accelerated during the late seventies and early eighties by the effects of the competition from the worsted industry. Changing consumer fashion leading to a substitution of worsted for woollen fabrics and the use of an increasing proportion of worsted yarn in woollen products, together with the effect of foreign tariffs, decimated the ranks of the woollen manufacturers. (The survivors rationalized their enterprises and sought in the economies of large-scale production the answer to their problems.) By the early years of the twentieth century concentration had progressed so far under the dual influences of industrial mortality and the economies of large scale that, to take an extreme example, one firm produced four-fifths of the Somersetshire woollen output.[83]

In 1904 the President of the Elbeuf Chamber of Commerce said 'Twenty-five years ago we were two hundred and fifty manufacturers . . . We have been forced either to start large establishments or vanish . . . Today there are but thirty-five concerns'.[84] Both this end-product and the intermediate stages in the process of concentration and growth of scale in France paralleled those in England. The rate of mechanization was slower and in 1878 French mills were reported to be smaller than those in England.[85] In 1870 the Reims woollen industry was still only partly centralized and some spinning and weaving was done as out-work in the surrounding villages;[86] in 1878 the use of hand mules and looms was still common.[87] The acceleration of the trend to concentration came partly from the effect of worsted competition and partly from a more direct incursion of worsted manufacturers into woollen production. The distinction between regional specialities became a difficult one to draw. In the late eighties Tourcoing, one of the worsted districts, began producing woollens.[88] The same broad development was also observ-

---

[82] Thirty-eight firms, selected on a systematic basis, in 1865 bought an average of 35.9 bales from Jowitt; twenty-five selected in 1872 bought an average of 43.9 bales. Ten other firms in 1865 took an average of 38.6 bales, and in 1872 they took an average of 52.2 bales. There are obvious dangers in generalizing from these samples, for the statistical population is very small, and they may represent simply the nature of the specific business of Jowitt & Sons—the clients, that is, do not necessarily form a representative selection from the industry. (This information is taken from the ledgers in the 'Jowitt Records', an immensely valuable collection in the Brotherton Library, University of Leeds. I am indebted to the firm, now in Bradford, and the Librarian for permission to use them.)

[83] Hunter, op. cit., p. 49.   [84] Quoted, ibid., p. 60.

[85] Wrigley and Bousfield, *Report on the Woollen Cloth Manufacture of France*, p. 7.   [86] Dunham, op. cit., p. 225.   [87] Wrigley and Bousfield, op. cit., p. 13.

[88] J. H. Clapham, *The Economic Development of France and Germany, 1815–1914* (Cambridge, 4th ed., 1936), p. 250.

able in Belgium. In 1846 the number of woollen and worsted factories was estimated at 544, the average employment being 30.4 workers; in 1896 there were only 244 factories, but they employed an average of 73.3 hands.[89]

4 AUSTRALIAN WOOL AND COMPETING FIBRES

The discussion has proceeded so far as if Australian wool were the main one which entered into the consumption of the European wool textile industries. We must now take into account the fact that these countries produced their own wool and that the other new countries of the southern hemisphere were also exporting vast quantities of wool to Europe. That the developments outlined above in section 3 also influenced the marketing organization relating to South American and South African wool does not diminish their importance as far as Australian wool was concerned. The relevance of other sources of wool supply lies, of course, in the fields of comparative consumption and price determination.

It is proposed here simply to identify the main sources of competing wool supplies, to examine the degree to which those wools were substitutable with Australian wool, and to inspect the effect of competing fibres such as cotton, silk and mohair which were used in wool textile activity.

In the first place it must be noted that the consuming countries themselves produced a large proportion of their raw wool requirements. It amounted to 78 per cent in 1860, nearly 57 per cent in 1875 and 48 per cent in 1885.[90] The decline in home production and the increasing reliance on imported wools, even in the United States, is a charactertistic feature of this period. English domestic production declined from 162 m. lb. in 1875 to 141 m. lb. in 1900, while her consumption rose from 340 m. lb. to 474 m. lb.; German production dropped from 83 to 28 m. lb. over the same period and her consumption rose from 150 to 316 m. lb.; in the United States, domestic wool provided almost 85 per cent of the material consumed in 1875, but only 66 per cent in 1900.[91] Despite the fact that the proportion of requirements met from domestic sources was declining,[92] it nevertheless posed a weighty competitive problem

[89] J. St. Lewinsky, *L'Evolution Industrielle de la Belgique* (Paris, 1911), p. 320.
[90] Calculated from estimates of production and imports in Helmuth Schwartze & Co., *The Production and Consumption of Wool* (London, 1887).
[91] See Appendix, Table XIII.
[92] The actual decline is exaggerated because the wool has been measured in the greasy state. On a greasy basis the consuming countries provided 55 per cent of their requirements in 1877; but on a clean basis it was 61 per cent (A. Sauer-

for the producing countries, particularly in the early years when manufacturing techniques were still primarily geared to treating the domestic wools. What caused European production to fall was, of course, the growing bulk and relative cheapness of supplies from the new countries, and the diversion of European pastoral lands to other purposes—including meat production. In England, production tended first to be diverted into long wool suitable for combing (a temporary product of the shortage of those wools during the fifties and sixties) and then to decline entirely as it was supplanted by colonial wool for both woollen and worsted production. In France and other Continental countries events followed a similar course. As early as 1816 the French merino producers had successfully sought protective tariffs against more cheaply produced foreign wool.[93] By the middle of the century antipodean competition was already making serious inroads on the markets of the domestic wool grower, and demands for a reimposition of tariff protection became increasingly frequent—in 1870 and 1890 for example.[94] The difficulties of the industry seem to have arisen primarily from the competition of the imported wools, from the increasing shift to meat production, and from the growing French demand for wool suited to relatively coarser cloths.[95]

The Australian wool grower was in more direct competition with the producers of the new countries. The expansion of Australian output in the context of the world market was large and rapid. Between 1850 and 1886, Australasia's contribution to the total supply of raw wool available for consumption in Europe and North America rose from 4.9 per cent to 22.4 per cent (on a clean wool basis, from 4.4 per cent to 20.1 per cent).[96] But in the same years the Australasian contribution to European and North American imports of raw (greasy) wool rose only from 39 per cent to 43 per

---

beck, *The Production and Consumption of Wool*, p. 17). The difference arises from the greater quantities of dirt and foreign matter in wools from the southern hemisphere.

[93] Dunham, *The Anglo-French Treaty of Commerce*, p. 216.

[94] Dunham, op. cit., p. 224; France, Conseil Supérieur du commerce et de l'Industrie, Enquête sur le Régime Douanier, tome 3, p. 79 contains a request for duties on wool which was made by La Société d'Agriculture de la Nièvre.

[95] The term 'coarser' is, of course, a relative one and refers here mainly to the abandonment of the almost exclusive devotion of the French industry to fine luxury goods which existed before the forties and fifties.

[96] From Helmuth Schwartze & Co., *Production and Consumption of Wool*, the following estimates may be made for the years 1850, 1860, 1870, 1880, 1886: raw wool basis (per cent), 4.9, 6.2, 13.4, 18.8, 22.4; clean wool basis (per cent), 4.4, 5.7, 13.3, 16.8, 20.1.

cent.[97] In a world context, that is, her expansion was neither spectacular nor unique. The production of the Argentine, New Zealand and, to a slighter extent, of South Africa rose at rates comparable to that of Australia. The output of these countries is compared in Fig. 4.

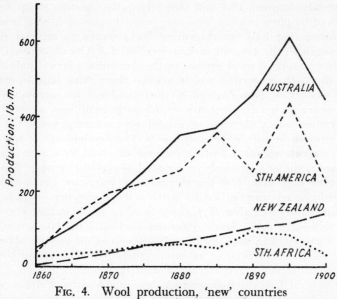

FIG. 4.   Wool production, 'new' countries
(See Appendix, Table XIV)

Argentine production only began to expand from the mid-fifties, when the sheep population was sixteen million, and until the late seventies and early eighties the merino-type breed predominated. Between 1877 and 1884 very wet weather caused heavy losses among merino stock while creating conditions in which the Lincoln and other long-woolled sheep thrived.[98] At the same time the crossbred wools were rising in price in the European markets,[99] and the

[97] Helmuth Schwartze & Co., op. cit., give estimates suggesting that the ratio of Australasian wool to all wool imported into the European and North American markets in the years 1850, 1860, 1870, 1880, and 1886 was: for raw wool, 39, 29, 36, 40, and 43 per cent respectively; and on a clean wool basis, 41, 30, 42, 42, and 46 per cent.

[98] H. Gibson, *The History and Present State of the Sheepbreeding Industry in the Argentine Republic* (Buenos Aires, 1893), p. 37.

[99] See Fig. 6 (p. 194) for the movements in the prices of one type of Australian crossbred wool. The prices of other crossbred varieties, including the South American, exhibit the same general features.

European demand for meat was being appreciated in the pastoral countries. In 1883 the first extensive plants for treating frozen meat for the English market were completed,[1] and in the following year the fall in merino wool prices became steeper. Under the impact of these two forces the composition of the Argentine flocks changed drastically. Between 1888 and 1893 fifty million merino sheep were replaced by pure- or cross-bred long-woolled animals; in 1893 it was estimated that half the Argentine flocks owned to at least one crossing with the Lincoln or Leicester breeds.[2] (One by-product of the importance of meat exports to the Argentine pastoral industry was the high proportion which woolled sheep-skins bore to total wool exports.) In New Zealand, on the other hand, the merino sheep had never been raised extensively. Climatic conditions, as well as the contemporary shortage of English-type combing wools, led to the introduction of the English breeds. The development of frozen meat exports meant a further increase in crossbreeds with large carcasses and long relatively coarse wool. Sheep run by white South Africans were mainly of the merino type, but some coarse (non-English) breeds were raised by natives; the production of mohair became substantial after 1877, rising from 1.4 m. lb. in that year to 17.5 million in 1907.[3] South American wool until the late seventies and South African wool until nearly the end of the century appear generally to have been of relatively inferior quality within their breeds—carelessly raised and indifferently presented.

In general terms the competition between Australian wools and these different wool types was limited. Until the early seventies the use of imported wool by the English worsted industry was restricted to some very long Australian wool; the English woollen industry used short Australian merino; and the French worsted industry used merino which was slightly longer, together with relatively small quantities of very short staple. This meant that, though the borders between the three types of wool were not sharply defined, the three industries did not generally compete for the same types of Australian wool. However, the English worsted processes used very large quantities of English wool, which was in fact preferred; the woollen industry used domestic carding wool as long as it was available; and French combers also used French, South American and South African merino. With these wools and within the specific

---

[1] Gibson, op. cit., p. 160. By 1893 there were five freezing works having a total annual capacity for three million carcasses.
[2] Ibid., p. 41.
[3] F. B. de Beck, *Le Commerce International de la Laine.* p. 110

industries where they were used, the relevant types of Australian wool were more or less satisfactorily interchangeable.

After about 1870 the range of practical substitution was extended. The English worsted industry began to use shorter Australian merino, and it utilized the Australian and New Zealand crossbred wools; the French also took to colonial crossbred; the German worsted manufacturers began to supplement their domestic wool and their imports of South American wool with Australian combing merino. In the woollen industries, some South American merino was added (in increasing proportions after the eighties) to Australian in England, and certain types of superior fine short Australian wool were added to the French consumption of domestic and South American merino and to the German use of domestic and Cape wools.

Despite this tendency, the areas of specialized use remained large. Belgian scouring, combing and carding was predominantly confined to South American wool; her manufacturers did not as readily attain success with Australian varieties. Though considerable quantities of colonial wool were imported there, it was generally processed to the specific requirements of other European industries. German and even French woollen manufacturers, while they did use Australian wool, relied more heavily on South African and South American wool respectively. Moreover, within the various national wool textile industries regional and individual requirements were greatly specialized. At the end of the century, for example, the West of England woollen industry used Australian wool almost exclusively, while the North Country made extensive use of South American supplies. Some regions, and many individuals, concentrated on the production of one type of fabric—blankets, tweeds or superfine cloths—or on production for one particular market.

Australian wool also competed with other fibres. The use of shoddy (wool reclaimed from old woollen cloths) in the woollen industry increased rapidly after 1850. It provided an ever-ready means whereby manufacturers, by varying the content of shoddy and therefore the quality of their product, could offset high prices for Australian clothing merino. Australian wool utilized in the worsted industries came into direct competition with cotton, mohair, alpaca and silk. Though the use of these materials was frequently complementary to the use of wool—one of them being used in either the warp or the weft, the wool completing the weave—changes in relative prices or in fashions could, at times, lead to the production of different fabrics employing, for example, a silk warp and cotton weft. In a wider context, of course, all wool textiles were substitutable with cotton and linen wares, but a detailed consideration of these aspects of the position of Australian wool in the textile world is beyond the scope of this study.

In general, Australian wool appears to have enjoyed a fairly comfortable position in its competition with other wool fibres until the early seventies. Marginal substitutions of different wool types within and between the English and more particularly the Continental industries before that date tended to impose a broad uniformity on the price movements of wool from different countries. But within that limitation divergent movements were common and often long lived. Specializations in raw material utilization and in the finished products tended to make movements in the prices of national wool varieties less dependent on fluctuations in total world wool production and consumption. They became more closely associated with sectional variations in the supply of wool from particular regions, in the demand for particular types of wool textile products, and in the industrial conditions in certain manufacturing regions.[4] At the same time the broad effect of the use of non-wool fibres was complementary rather than competitive. The coincidence, from the seventies, of a significant extension of the substitutability of other wools for Australian—a more general competition between wools from most producing countries, in fact—with the apparent satisfaction of world demand for raw wool may have played a considerable part in the relatively greater decline in merino than in crossbred prices during the last quarter of the century.

    [4] This specialization, and its results, can easily be overstated, but used cautiously the broad generalization is valuable. One of the main facts which might be thought to invalidate it—that during a drought in any one country or one area the price of wool from that region does not often rise—is explicable on entirely different grounds. The drought, besides reducing the output of that area, also produces an inferior product—tender, and dirtier than usual—which naturally commands a lower price than the normal quality.

PART II

THE INSTITUTIONS OF THE MARKET

3 Shearing shed at Yanko Station, New South Wales, 1868

4 Bullock transport, New South Wales, in the seventies

3

THE MARKETING PATTERN

THE Australian wool trade is, above all, one in which the rationale of a highly developed chain of middlemen finds almost classical expression—long distances separating large numbers of small-scale, geographically scattered producers from a numerous body of small-scale consumers. During the nineteenth century the patterns linking the production and consumption of colonial wool were changed basically as the structure of the pastoral and wool textile industries altered, as improvements were effected in transport and communications, and as the financial institutions serving the trade were developed. The nature of these changes forms one of the fundamental features of the history of the wool market during that period.

In the 1840s perhaps 50 per cent of the clip was disposed of at the central auction sales in England on behalf of colonial general merchants who purchased it from the growers; 30-40 per cent was consigned to England through general colonial agents for sale there on the growers' behalf; and the remainder was shipped directly by the growers themselves. By the 1860s some 80 per cent was consigned for sale in England at the growers' risk largely through specialized wool consignment agencies. In both these periods distribution to the consumer was effected in two ways. Manufacturers either purchased their wool, personally or through their agents, at the central sales or they were provisioned by wool dealers who also secured their supplies at the sales. By contrast, in 1900 one-half of the Australian production was sold by auction in the colonies, through specialized selling agencies, to foreign consumers and dealers, and only 30-40 per cent consigned to England through the specialized consignment agencies.

The changes, in other words, embrace three separate though related aspects of the marketing network. The methods by which the growers disposed of their clip changed; the point of disposal was altered (this process is considered more fully in ch. 7); and the structure of the middleman organizations was reshaped. Growers sold first to general colonial merchants and later consigned their wool to England; London gave place to the main Australian cities as the location of the major primary market; general colonial merchants acting incidentally as middlemen in the wool trade were succeeded by large-scale specialized concerns.

It is proposed, in this chapter, by identifying the groups of middlemen through whose hands the wool passed, their nature and their place in the trade, to outline the marketing system and to define the points at which change occurred. As one of the central problems of the market was that of linking widely separated consumers and producers, the incidence of marketing risks at the point at which the wool left the colonies is crucial. It is therefore convenient to consider separately the course which the wool followed before and after its shipment.

I MARKETING WITHIN THE COLONIES

By 1840 the marketing system was already changing rapidly. During the twenties and thirties its organization in the colonies had been, by later standards at least, a haphazard, disordered affair. Most growers sold their wool to general colonial traders who shipped it to business acquaintances in England for sale on their own account. This *method* of disposal was clearly enough defined. Yet the insignificance of the colonial contribution to total raw wool supplies available in England and the consequently small interest taken in it by English wool dealers and consumers, and the extent to which it depended on a colonial mercantile community which was small, inexperienced and cramped by the lack of facilities, together meant that the disposal itself was insufficient and undependable.

In this context, it will be argued below (ch. 6) that the pastoral expansion of the thirties and forties had two main implications. It meant, firstly, a growth in colonial production for the purchase of which mercantile resources proved quite inadequate. The expansion itself was largely based on the activities of a new class of pastoral occupiers, recently migrated from England and having, in many cases, substantial capital backing. The first of these attributes implied that they had relatives or friends in England who might act on their behalf; the second freed them from an entire dependence on a quick local sale to provide them with funds. Thus many growers were in a position to consign their clips to England in the same way as the merchants did.

These two broad alternatives—sale in the colonies or consignment to England—remained open to them throughout the century. Our task is to trace how each of them, and the relations between them, changed. Though they are related, and in many respects similar, the two courses are by no means parallel. Consignment replaced the local disposal of wool in the middle of the century, but by the nineties local sales were once again the predominant form of marketing.

(a) *Local Selling, 1840–55*

As early as 1819 a certain Raines advertised his willingness to pay 10d. per lb. for wool delivered at his Sydney store, washed before shearing and duly tied in separate fleeces.[1] During the twenties and thirties other merchants, such as Robert Campbell & Co., Aspinal, Brown & Co., J. B. Montefiore & Co. and C. W. Roemer, offered similar facilities.[2]

By the forties the number of firms prepared to buy wool in the colonies had grown impressively. Many of them were general import-export merchants, whose interests covered the whole range of the colonies' imported requirements.[3] In Sydney, such firms as Griffith, Gore & Co. (later Griffith, Fanning & Co.), Lamb & Parbury and Cooper & Hunt stood to the fore among the wool buyers. Similarly, in Melbourne, Griffith Borrodaile & Co. (later Dalgety Borrodaile & Co.),[4] and in Van Diemen's Land James Henty & Co.[5] acted both as wool buyers and general import merchants. Other extensive purchases were made in Van Diemen's Land by H. Hopkins whose activities extended, through the grocery firm of Annand & Smith, to Port Phillip.[6] Other buyers, such as S. A. Bryant in Sydney, were shipping agents, an occupation frequently shared by the merchants already mentioned.[7]

This wide combination of activities is no less than one might

[1] Quoted in J. Bonwick, *Romance of the Wool Trade*, p. 199.

[2] Newspaper advertisements provide a rich source of information on the participants in the trade. See for example the *Sydney Herald*, 1 Jan. 1835, from which these illustrations are taken.

[3] A random examination of the advertisement columns of the *Sydney Herald* during 1842 reveals the following sample illustrations of the diverse trading activities of merchants who also bought wool: A. B. Smith & Co., ship's agents, importers of sherry and other goods; Lamb & Parbury, importers and sellers of spirits and tobacco, coffee, sugar and tea, shoes, paper and oil, cloves, iron and starch; Campbell & Co., importers of Sourabaya sugar and other goods; G. L. Robinson, gin, Van Diemen's Land potatoes, etc.

[4] John Cotton of Port Phillip had extensive dealings with the firm. See his letter to his brother William, December 1843. As 'The John Cotton Letters' this, with others, was reprinted from the originals in the possession of the Hon. W. C. Russell Clarke in R. V. Billis and A. S. Kenyon, *Pastures New*.

[5] M. Bassett, *The Hentys: A colonial tapestry, passim*.

[6] A. Joyce, *A Homestead History, being the reminiscences and letters of Alfred Joyce of Plaistow and Norwood, Port Phillip, 1843 to 1864*, p. 76.

[7] During January 1842 the following shipping agents advertised as wool buyers in the *Sydney Herald*: S. A. Bryant & Co., Gilchrist & Alexander, A. B. Smith, Ramsay Young & Co.

expect in the commercial circumstances of the colonies. Both the population and the mercantile community were small. A large trading concern was, of necessity, one whose capital was distributed over a number of fields in none of which large-scale specialization was profitable. Successful trading and a large business implied the performance of whatever agency could be obtained—whether it was for a shipping company, an English distiller, or a milliner—and it meant an eye on every market. Until the forties it could also mean participation in the disposal of colonial wool.

To indicate the importance of general merchants as wool buyers, and to emphasize that the greater part of the capital which could be used for this purpose was in their hands, does not, however, imply their complete domination of the field. One might almost say, in fact, that wool purchasing appealed to all who possessed the means to buy it and access to channels of disposal. In Van Diemen's Land wealthy graziers are alleged to have bought the clips of their less wealthy neighbours,[8] while in Sydney T. U. Ryder was prominent among those who were not importers.[9]

The buyers' contact with the growers during the thirties and early forties was frequently on the main roads leading into Sydney, in the taverns on the roadside, and on the camping grounds at the Haymarket or the Quay. There they inspected the wool laden high on the bullock drays making their long annual journey into town to deliver the clip and take back supplies for the following year. Romantic accounts of the competition between buyers, and the haggling between buyers and draymen are sufficiently plentiful to make any elaboration of the selling procedure unnecessary here.[10] The essential point is that the sales were effected directly between buyer and grower, in an atmosphere of mutual distrust and without the benefit of a scale of values other than that imperfectly derived by the buyer himself from reports of the previous year's sales in England.

However, the geographical expansion of the industry increased the hazards, the difficulties and the expenses of transporting the wool to the cities. For some growers this problem was overcome by

[8] J. Bonwick, op cit., p. 224. Though reported second-hand from an unnamed work published in Calcutta in the thirties or forties, it fits the known pattern in N.S.W. well.

[9] He was a commission agent selling livestock and real estate. Some of his notices may be found in the *Sydney Herald*, 1 and 7 Jan. 1842.

[10] Cf. S. H. Roberts, *The Squatting Age in Australia, 1835–1847*, pp. 422-3 for a graphic description of roadside selling in the twenties and thirties, a description which is equally applicable to the years up to the mid-forties.

the addition of new links to the marketing chain. Following precedents established by the sporadic operations of Matthewman & Roberts and Charles Sims from the early thirties at least,[11] buying activities were extended to country towns. Growers were consequently able to dispose of their clips to firms like Syers Bros., who had establishments in both Sydney and Bathurst.[12] Most growers, however, turned to using public carriers who were located in the main rural centres. They began to employ the country storekeepers and stock salesmen as agents to arrange transport for them. In this capacity the country agent came to exercise a considerable importance, by the third quarter of the century, often providing the first link between the grower and the market.

In the thirties and forties, however, the important implication of the use of public carriers and transport agents was that it became less usual for the grower to accompany the wool to the city. The type of roadside transaction described above was essentially one of personal contact between the grower and the buyer. An intermediate agent was now needed in Sydney or Melbourne to undertake the sale for him.

In one way this simply meant the extension of functions previously undertaken by certain traders in those cities, for, when dissatisfied with offers made on the roadside, growers had been accustomed to placing their wool in the hands of storekeepers who conducted subsequent negotiations for them.[13] The increased demand for these facilities in the thirties and forties, however, led to a certain degree of specialization and the provision of more appropriate institutions. In Sydney, Samuel Lyons opened his stores for the auction of wool in the early thirties, offering free storage and an advance before the sale, and charging a commission of 5 per cent.[14] In 1844 the Australian Oxen Co. commenced auction sales of wool and pastoral property,[15] and in 1845 Sydney witnessed a veritable scramble to offer auctioneering facilities for wool. Lyons reduced his selling commis-

[11] Matthewman & Roberts operated in Bathurst (*Sydney Herald*, advertisement, 3 Sept. 1832); Charles Sims in Nepean, Bathurst 'and surrounding district' (*Sydney Herald*, advertisement, 8 Jan. 1832).

[12] *Sydney Morning Herald*, 14 Nov. 1842, advertisement. Later in the century small country buyers—storekeepers, commission agents, stock agents, etc.—assumed some slight importance as intermediaries between the very small-scale agricultural producers in parts of Victoria and the market in Melbourne (cf. Royal Commission on Agricultural and Pastoral Lands, 'Report and Minutes of Evidence', *Proc. Vic. Leg. Ass.*, 1879-80, vol. 3, *passim*).

[13] Roberts, op. cit., p. 423.

[14] *Sydney Herald*, 1 Jan. 1835.

[15] R. B. Skamp, *The Wool Trade: its history and growth in Australia and Tasmania*, p. 13.

sion to 1 per cent. Stubbs lowered his to $\frac{1}{2}$ per cent, an offer which was closely followed by the almost lyrical appeal of M. Pyric:

> To Wool Growers, Settlers, etc.
>
> The undersigned begs to intimate to the above that having for some time observed with deep regret how seriously their interests have suffered by the incompetence and general want of intelligence of the Auctioneers entrusted with the sale of their produce, he has been induced to come forward (his numerous other professional engagements notwithstanding) and offer those services which he flatters himself the public generally well know how to appreciate.
>
> In order to the more effectual accomplishment of the object he has in view, he proposes, not only to throw open for their gratuitous accommodation his Mart and Stores, but also to devote a large portion of his own dwelling to such of their body as may be desirous of availing themselves of his hospitability . . . and as the object of the undersigned is rather to protect and advance the interests of those to whom this advertisement is addressed than to derive immediate personal gain from their patronage
>
> *One sixteenth per cent*
>
> will be the entire charge made and he therefore anticipates that the Mart will be the channel through which their favours will abundantly flow.[16]

In Melbourne, Isaac Hinds and the Bakewells and Bear & Son were holding periodical auctions of wool during the mid-forties.[17] The significance of these concerns, which were in fact the fore-runners of the specialized wool-selling brokers like Richard Goldsbrough and T. S. Mort, lies partly in the fact that they did force, to some extent, a degree of regularity and orderliness into the transactions between grower and buyer and partly that, in the changed conditions of transport, they allowed this contact to be made at all.

It is unlikely, however, that wool auctioneering would have become so popular an occupation had this been the only basis of its expansion. There were also important changes in the demand for wool which reinforced its effects. The mercantile group of buyers already discussed was too small and possessed insufficient resources to operate on a scale appropriate to the augmented supply, even

[16] *Sydney Morning Herald*, 16 Oct. 1845.
[17] Skamp, op cit., p. 13. Messrs Bear & Son advertised the commencement of their private and auction sales of wool in the *Port Phillip Patriot and Morning Advertiser*, 11 Oct. 1845.

to that part of the supply which was offered locally.[18] The expansion of auctioneering accommodation was partially made possible by, and in turn itself facilitated, an influx of new buyers whose activities supplemented that of the merchants. It is possible to distinguish four groups of buyers in the late forties: professional wool dealers, professional wool speculators, professional speculators, and the mercantile buyers.

Increasing quantities of colonial wool of steadily improving quality had been one of the factors that enabled it to attain a most important position in the English wool textile industries. That position reinforced the speculative opportunities offered by purchase in the colonies for resale in England. Professional wool dealers purchased clips not suitably prepared for the English market. They processed them, either by scouring or by sorting and repacking together wool from a number of clips. James Johnson, Clissold & Hill, the Hon. Saul Samuel and the Yorke Brothers operated some of the scouring works in the Sydney district and helped swell the demand for wool in the colonies.[19] Apart from some very small and irregular purchases for manufacturing purposes in the colonies,[20] the only local processing to which wool was subject was that designed to increase its value at the London sales. This applies as much to those services of wool-classing, sorting and packing that were rendered to growers and woolbuyers[21] as to the activities of the processor-buyer.

There were also a number of professional wool speculators. Andrew Hinchcliffe, in addition to his interest in the scouring works at Waterloo, acted on behalf of principals in England.[22] For them he bought parcels for resale in England, where they became part of the general speculative holdings, purchased in England and on the

---

[18] It will be argued below that the growth of production far outran the expansion of facilities, and possibilities, for sale within the colonies, and that the inadequacy of the local market was one reason for the change to the consignment technique of export. Local sales, nevertheless, rose during this period.

[19] W. H. Chard, *Australasian Wool Markets*, p. 16. R. J. W[ithers] in a series of articles published in the *Sydney Daily Telegraph*, 20 Sept., 27 Sept., 10 Oct., 25 Oct., and 14 Nov. 1913, under the title 'The Romance of Wool Selling', recounts that Johnson in a two-year period handled over 8,000 bales and doubled the Sydney price on every lot but one when sold in London; on that lot the London price was two-thirds greater!

[20] See, for example, the advertisements for wool inserted by Uther's Hat Manufactory and E. Hunt's Upholstery Warehouse, *Sydney Herald*, 13 Feb. 1832.

[21] See ch. 4.

[22] Chard, op. cit., p. 16; H. Austin 'Recollections of the Australian Wool Trade', *Australian Country Life* (Sydney monthly), June 1906. This forms part of a series of the reminiscences of the then doyen of the Australian woolbuyers, which were published in this journal between May 1906 and September 1907.

Continent, in which they specialized. Similarly Rudolph Kummerer made speculative purchases on behalf of a group of Europeans resident in London.[23] James Sanderson, representing Sanderson & Murray of Galashiels, is not entirely typical of this group: though the major part of his purchases were resold on the London market, some was sent directly to the warehouses of his Scottish principals,[24] anticipating a type of purchase which did not become common for another twenty-five years. It is worth noting that in 1854 France made an essay of the colonial market which seems to have gone unnoticed: H. Noufflard announced that he wished to buy for resale by public auction at Rouen, and for this purpose had laid on a ship to transport the wool there direct.[25]

A further group of buyers were professional speculators, akin both to the general merchants and to the wool speculators, but not primarily or even largely concerned with wool transactions. As a group they comprised those who were able and willing to undertake speculative activities in any of the numerous fields which were available, and to them wool was merely one of those fields. One of them was James Milson.[26] A former partner in the general import-export firm of Robert Campbell Junior & Co., Milson was quick to take advantage of the opportunities offered by the discovery of gold, and during the fifties he made substantial profits by purchasing it for shipment to England. By 1856 he had extended his operations to speculative share dealings and was a member of the Sydney Stock Exchange. It was this interest in, and an eye for, a worthwhile risk that led him to woolbuying. In return for two-thirds of the profit, Milson provided the finance enabling John Chase to purchase wool in the country and resell it in Sydney. It is obvious that the opportunities created for Milson and Chase, as well as for T. U. Ryder,[27] to purchase in the country were the product primarily of the geographical expansion of the pastoral industry, for their clients were usually small growers who would have sold their clips in Sydney or Melbourne and who were easily persuaded to forgo the costs and responsibility of the carriage. Others with Milson's instincts keenly

[23] Austin, op. cit., May 1907. [24] Ibid.
[25] *Sydney Morning Herald*, 20 Dec. 1854.
[26] R. H. Goddard, *The Life and Times of James Milson*, p. 181 and ch. 17, *passim*.
[27] Cf. 'Black Papers': A. C. Dunlop to N. Black, 8 April 1851. The 'Black Papers' comprise an immensely valuable collection of letters to and from Neil Black between 1839 and 1880 housed in the Public Library of Victoria. I am indebted to the Librarian for permission to quote from them and for facilities which made it possible to examine the collection before the task of cataloguing it was completed.

followed the sales in Sydney and puchased for resale in England whenever the market held prospects of unusual speculative profits.

Despite the dynamic importance of professional wool processors and dealers, of professional wool speculators and professional speculators, the major group of buyers in the early fifties remained the colonial merchant and importing houses. It is indicative of their importance that Richard Goldsbrough was using the customary form when he addressed the announcement of the opening of his wool sorting and packing establishment in Melbourne to 'Merchants, Settlers Etc.'[28] In Tasmania, where the aggregate output was smaller than in the mainland colonies, a considerable proportion of the total clip was still being sold to merchants.[29] In Mebourne, firms of the stature of William Degraves & Co. and J. B. Were sought to buy wool.[30] Similarly in Sydney, merchant houses—Prince Bray & Ogg, Gilchrist & Watt, and Scott, Henderson & Co. are examples—provided a regular core of buyers at the auction sales, while others like Cooper & Hunt and Chris. Newton & Bro. bought occasional parcels.[31] In order to compete with the growing demand from specialized wool dealers they were forced to improve their own technical efficiency. Robert Campbell applied to a London wool broker early in the forties for help in securing a competent woolbuyer and sorter,[32] having already employed G. F. Dixon, one of the more noted of the early buyers.[33] Other firms, including Prince Bray & Ogg, Scott, Henderson & Co. and later Gilchrist & Watt & Co., strengthened their partnerships by the inclusion of a skilled woolbuyer.[34]

The motives actuating these merchant purchasers were a combination (inseparable probably) of speculation and a desire to acquire foreign exchange. At a time when the foreign exchange market was still very rudimentary, wool bought in the colonies and resold in London provided sterling funds which were otherwise obtained

[28] Melbourne *Argus*, 12 Sept. 1848.

[29] Cf. S. S. Smith, *Important Suggestions for a Better Development of Colonial Wool and Leather etc.*, pp. 39-40. Considerations peculiar to the island retarded the development of the consignment system.

[30] See their advertisements in the *Argus*, 12 Nov. 1852 and 18 Sept. 1852 respectively. Were Bros. & Co. bought wool from its formation in 1840—J. B. Were & Son, *The House of Were, 1839-1954*, p. 15; a decade later, as J. B. & G. Were, the firm extended its activities to Sydney.

[31] Austin, op cit., May and June 1906; Withers, op. cit., 10 Oct. 1913.

[32] T. Shaw, *The Australian Merino: being a treatise on wool growing in Australia*, p. 4. Shaw had been a wool purchaser for J. T. Simes in London before coming to Campbell.

[33] Withers, op. cit., 10 Oct. 1913. Dixon later bought for Gilchrist & Alexander.

[34] Withers, op. cit., 10 Oct. 1913. Bray bought for Prince Bray & Ogg; Scott for Scott, Henderson & Co.

only with difficulty. This certainly provided the main motive of the merchant buyers in the twenties and early thirties. The formation of Anglo-Australian banks and trust companies in the thirties eased the position slightly, but the relief was temporary and the banks were disinclined to participate widely in foreign exchange transactions.[35] Consequently the direct purchase of wool bills and wool was an essential incident to importing.[36] Wool bills were relatively cheap during the short exporting season, but they fell due in London within a similarly short period. An evenly distributed flow of cheap foreign exchange might be acquired by purchasing bills at their cheapest, buying wool at the height of the season and shipping it to arrive at staggered intervals after the bills fell due, and then buying more wool towards the end of the selling season to provide funds when exchange was most difficult to obtain. Not only importers but anyone with funds to remit to England found wool attractive as the vehicle.[37] Wool, as distinct from wool bills, had of course the added lure of the speculative gain. Even as late as 1855, when one might have expected that the export of gold would have had a considerable effect on the exchange facilities,[38] a Melbourne wool-selling broker issued the following significant report on end-of-season supplies: 'There have been many enquiries after full stout-bodied wools for shipment per *Marco Polo* by parties desiring such for remittances, which is certainly the most legitimate mode of disposing of this portion of our colonial produce . . .'[39]

By the middle of the century, then, that portion of the clip which the growers disposed of in the colonies followed a well-defined

[35] Cf. S. J. Butlin, *Foundations of the Australian Monetary System 1788-1851*, ch. 13 *passim*. The completion of the process of transferring the capital of these concerns to the colonies may provide one reason for the enhanced interest in wool auctioning in the forties.

[36] The extent may be gauged from the evidence of J. C. McLaren, L. Duguid, W. H. Mackenzie and A. Walker before the Select Committee on the Debenture Bill (*N.S.W. V. & P.*, 1841).

[37] Emigration bounties were remitted in this fashion (evidence of A. Walker before the Select Committee on the Debenture Bill); the proceeds of the Redfern estate were remitted to James Alexander, the widow's second husband, in the form of wool bought by P. B. Whitfield who was sent to N.S.W. for that purpose (Withers, op. cit., 8 Oct. 1913); Bonwick, *Romance of the Wool Trade*, pp. 224-5, quoting the Calcutta source already mentioned, reports that wealthy Tasmanian graziers had frequently had the proceeds of their clips remitted to them in the form of slops and station requirements which when sold in the island returned good profits.

[38] Gold, as well as tallow, wool and later silver, was of course sought by merchants as a source of exchange. Possessing a more stable and publicized value, however, gold was less attractive unless bought at the point of production from miners willing to accept a discount.

[39] P. N. Walker in the *Argus*, 21 July 1855.

course. The greater part was sent from the country to Sydney and
Melbourne where auctioneers offered it at periodic sales to merchants, speculators and processors. Some was still sold privately
either to buyers who visited the stations or in response to newspaper
advertisements in the towns.

(b) *Consignment, 1840–1900*

In the eighteen-fifties, however, the greater part of Australian
output remained the property of the growers and was held at their
risk when it left the colonies. It was consigned for sale on their
behalf at the London auctions. This system of disposal was the
dominant one between the forties and the nineties. During those
years the export organizations were refined and became more
efficient, as specialized concerns replaced general ones and as the
provision of financial services became more closely tied to the performance of exporting functions.

Basically, export consignment implies the employment of an
oversea agent to whom a shipment of goods is addressed and to
whom is entrusted their sale on the exporter's behalf. The Australian wool trade reveals few examples of this minimal form. Some
growers did arrange their own shipments to friends and business
acquaintances[40]—more commonly in the thirties and forties than
later—and large corporate producers like the Australian Agricultural Co., the South Australia Co., and the Van Diemen's Land Co.
made their own export arrangements. In general, however, colonial
wool growers used a local agent in whose hands they placed the
produce and to whom they delegated the whole function of making
the consignment. In addition the agent provided an advance against
the ultimate realization on the clip. Historically these two functions
were closely integrated, and they placed the functional middlemen,
whom we shall call consigning or exporting agents, in a crucial position in the wool export chain.

During the thirties and forties consignment services were provided
mainly by the same group of general colonial merchants who
figured as woolbuyers. In Sydney merchants like J. B. Montefiore
& Co. and Gilchrist & Alexander,[41] in the Port Phillip District

[40] Neil Black, a Victorian settler, consigned his wool to the Liverpool firm of
Gladstone and Sargeantson, lawyers. T. S. Gladstone was one of the three British
partners in Neil Black & Co., formed in Scotland in 1839. Black as managing
partner operated the pastoral property in which the concern's capital was
invested. Numerous account sales of Black's wool indicate that it was consigned
to the legal firm in its capacity as the representative of the partnership.
[41] A survey of the Sydney press reveals the following sample of firms conducting both consigning agencies and buying departments: C. W. Roemer,

Dalgety Borrodaile & Co., Bell & Buchanan, J. F. Strachan, Richard Goldsbrough, James Henty & Co. and Stephen Henty,[42] and in Van Diemen's Land James Henty and Kemp & Co.[43] provided facilities both for buying and consigning wool. Once again this should occasion little surprise for, in addition to commanding most of the working capital, this group had ready-made commercial connections with English concerns which could serve their consigning activities.

Nevertheless, just as merchants did not monopolize woolbuying, neither did they handle all the produce consigned. Some of the growers themselves offered consignment services to their neighbours.[44] The firm in which one of Neil Black's British partners was a principal wrote to him in 1841 that they would be 'very glad to get consignments of Wool from your neighbours providing that the advance is *moderate* and the parties known to you to be respectable'.[45] Black had visions of going beyond the occasional parcels he did in fact send, and was prevented only by the demands of his pastoral obligations from opening a large-scale specialized agency in Melbourne.[46] The main non-merchant consignment agents, however, were the banks.

Their position is difficult to determine with accuracy, for practices varied from bank to bank, and conclusions are hard to document.[47] Certain considerations imply an aversion to acting as con-

Learmonth & Sims, Aspinal & Brown, Thomas Steele, Buchanan & Co., R. Ramsay Senior & Co., W. C. Botts, Lamb & Parbury, Thacker, Mason & Co., Smith, Campbell & Co., Griffith, Gore & Co., John Rostron, Gilchrist Alexander & Co., and William Pickering.

[42] Cf. 'Black Papers': S. G. Henty to Black, 9 April 1846, Dalgety Borrodaile & Co. to Black, 22 Oct. 1846, Bell & Buchanan to Black, 3 Jan. 1848. See also H. M. Strachan, *Some Notes and Recollections* (Melbourne, privately published, 1927), pp. 23, 27.

[43] Henty's activities are outlined in M. Bassett, op. cit. Kemp & Co. have been characterized as the other major Tasmanian consigning agency; see R. M. Hartwell, *The Economic Development of Van Diemen's Land* (Melbourne, 1954), p. 121.

[44] In 1844-5 some growers even banded together in a sort of co-operative consignment group; see Billis and Kenyon, *Pastures New*, p. 96. The authors are misled, however, into a grotesquely distorted conception of the sequence of development of marketing forms and characterize this as the first organization of selling.   [45] 'Black Papers': T. S. Gladstone to Black, 11 May 1841.

[46] Ibid., A. McLachlan to Gladstone & Sargeantson, 18 Dec. 1845, a copy of which appears on the flyleaf of McLachlan to Black, 19 Dec. 1845.

[47] I am indebted to the Australia and New Zealand Bank Ltd for permission to make use of some of the early archives of the Bank of Australasia, and to Mr D. Merry of the Bank and to Professor S. J. Butlin for advice in their use. In these and other bank records extant (see Butlin, op. cit., Appendix 1, pp. 562-3, for an exhaustive list) consignment activities are of too mundane and everyday character to be recorded.

signment agents for the growers—the banks' prejudice against
settlers' bills, their initial lack of interest in foreign exchange transactions and their disinclination to engage in business not sanctioned
by the canons of current English banking practice.[48] The absence
of their names from the lists of Victorian exporters compiled by the
Customs House[49] and from the lists of English importers of wool[50]
seems to strengthen that impression.

Yet they did act as consignment agents.[51] In 1845 Black expected
that 'In the future the greater part of our own wool shall probably
be sent through the Bank'.[52] In the same year the Superintendent of
the Bank of Australasia wrote of 'Bills of Lading for Property
[which] have been sent to [the Bank Secretary] direct *with instructions to hand it over to a reputable party for sale*'.[53] Butlin, moreover, leaves little doubt that this was a normal function exercised
by the banks.[54] By 1860 the banks had attained a position of considerable, though unmeasured, importance in the import of wool
into England and, by implication, in its export from the colonies,[55]
and later in that decade their consigning role was taken for granted
by the South Australian Northern Runs Commission.[56] Their
activity was largely an involuntary consequence of their financial
relation with the growers. Merchant consignors were able to discount
their bills of exchange at the banks on the security of credits
established through London, their personal credit in the colonies,
or the bills of lading for the consignments themselves. In those
unusual circumstances when banks were willing or constrained to

[48] Cf. S. J. Butlin, op. cit., ch. 13 *passim*.
[49] Published by authority in the *Journal of Commerce* as the 'Victorian Customs Bill of Entry', these lists name both the real or apparent (shipping agent)
exporters and importers of all goods leaving and entering Melbourne by sea.
[50] London wool warehousemen and wool-selling brokers issued annual lists of
importers. In 1860 the Bank of N.S.W. and the Union Bank of Scotland warehoused 7 and 114 bales respectively with Browne & Eagle of London. I am
indebted to that firm for permission to use the abstracts of their own clients
('List of Wool Importers') and other mansucript records in their possession.
[51] It must be understood that our interest is confined to those exports arranged
by the banks for their clients and does not embrace the wool claimed in satisfaction of dishonoured debts and exported as the banks' property.
[52] 'Black Papers': Black to Gladstone, 25 June 1845.
[53] Bank of Australasia, 'Superintendent's Circular Orders', no. 63, 12 Feb. 1845.
The phrase I have italicized represents precisely the function of a consignee.
[54] S. J. Butlin, *Foundations of the Australian Monetary System*, pp. 507-8.
[55] Strachan, *Some Notes and Recollections*, p. 91, gives a list of importers of
Australian wool into England in 1860, noting that, although the names of the
banks do not appear, they 'imported considerable quantities'. Other, contemporary, comments tend to confirm this judgment.
[56] Commission appointed to enquire into the State of Runs suffering from
Drought, 'Report and Minutes of Evidence', *S.A.P.P.* 1867, vol. 2, paper 14. See
particularly questions 414, 1957, 3994 and 4327.

finance growers' exports directly,[57] they chose to protect themselves by taking control of the consignment in both formal and practical terms.[58] It is probable that they employed freight and shipping agents to arrange the actual transport and that it was therefore in the names of the latter that the customs officials recorded the shipments.

In the fifties the outstanding characteristic of the consigning agents—the generality of their commercial and financial activities—began to be replaced by some degree of specialization. In the previous decade the only specialized concerns connected with the wool trade were those which, like Edwin Bennett or Frederick Ebsworth in Sydney and J. & R. Bakewell in Melbourne, provided facilities for classing and packing. Even in 1858 only five wool shippers of the eighty named in the Victorian Customs Bill of Entry—that is, 6 per cent—can be reliably identified as conducting business primarily or mainly as consignment agents; but their exports comprised about 13 per cent of those covered by the lists. By the 1870–1 season, however, twelve of the ninety-five named were specialist wool or stock and station agents and they handled 40 per cent of the trade.[59]

These specialist houses grew from diverse origins and consequently exhibited different features which profoundly influenced their attitude to basic marketing questions. Each of them, of course, sought technical efficiency in their exporting services and the broad pattern of their consignment methods was the same. But because of their different natures they were destined to play very divergent roles in the development of wool marketing institutions during the last third of the century. Three general groups may be distinguished which, while not sufficient to comprehend all entrants to so profitable a trade, nevertheless abstract the major significant variations. There were firstly those which developed, either entirely or as specialized departments, from general colonial importing con-

[57] Bank of Australasia, 'Letters to London', no. 197, 27 Aug. 1844 (W. H. Hart to Court of Directors), paragraph 13, after commenting on the colonies' export surplus, draws attention to the fact that 'The usual purchasers of this produce [wool] or the Bills drawn against it, viz., the merchants, being unable to operate in them and the engagements of the Producers or those connected with them being in the various Banks and principally in this Bank and the Union, we have naturally been compelled . . . in order to obtain payment of these engagements, to purchase a larger amount of London Bills than we require for our exchange operations'.

[58] See pp. 116-18 for a discussion of the banks' attitudes to financing wool exports before the sixties.

[59] Analysis based on the lists in the *Journal of Commerce* for the relevant years.

cerns. Others were formed in the colonies specifically to engage in some aspect of the wool trade and to them consigning was the main, or one of the main, activities. Finally, some companies, incorporated in Great Britain, combined wool exporting from the colonies with large-scale investment of British capital in the pastoral industry as financiers.

Founded in Adelaide in 1840 to conduct general and commission merchanting, the firm that grew into the house of Elder, Smith & Co. played a leading role in many spheres of South Australian commerce.[60] The extensive pastoral interests acquired by A. L. Elder, together with the pastoral affiliations the family contracted by way of marriage, soon led to the provision of consignment facilities. This branch of the business became highly specialized and the main one for which it was known at the end of the century. Similarly, the vast Dalgety organization began as a general import- ing firm in Melbourne to which was added a wool consignment agency which rapidly became more important than the merchant- ing.[61] James Turner & Co. of Melbourne, one of the major private companies in the trade by the eighties, forsook general importing during the fifties and paid specialized attention to wool exporting and, in the sixties, to the sale and finance of station properties.[62] These firms tended to retain their merchanting interests which, in fact, were more or less integrated with their wool exporting and wool financing activities. While Dalgety and Elder, Smith & Co. con- tinued their general importing for a time,[63] they were ideally

[60] [A. G. Price and J. H. Hammond], *Elder, Smith & Co. Ltd.—The First Hundred Years*, provides a comprehensive picture of its activities.

[61] The dating of F. G. Dalgety's early activities is difficult to establish. Dalgety & Co. Ltd, *A Souvenir to Commemorate the Jubilee Year*, indicates that he arrived in Sydney in 1833, took a position with Messrs Montefiore & Co. for three years, and was then in the service of various other Sydney merchants until 1843 when he went to Melbourne to open Griffith, Fanning & Co.'s branch there (pp. 14-15). In 1846 he entered into partnership with Borrodaile & Gore as importers and exporters. Borrodaile retired in 1847 and Gore in 1851. On the other hand John Cotton (Billis and Kenyon, *Pastures New*, 'The John Cotton Letters') mentions Dalgety acting as agent for Griffith & Borrodaile in 1844, refers to Dalgety, Borrodaile & Son in 1845 and records the retirement of Borrodaile in 1846 (letters of July 1844, October 1845 and November 1846). In the following years the rapid establishment of associated concerns in Geelong, Tasmania, and New Zealand and the changing personnel of the partnerships led to a bewildering complexity of names which was resolved only by their amalgamation in 1884. (Borrodaile is the spelling used by Cotton; Dalgety & Co. use Borrodale; Joyce prefers Borradale.)

[62] Cf. H. M. Franklyn, *A Glance at Australia in 1880: or, food from the South*, pp. 219-22.

[63] Elder, Smith & Co. were very closely connected with South Australian copper mining, while Dalgety contracted to supply imported materials for the

situated to supply the whole range of goods required by pastoralists.[64] Their wool exporting provided foreign exchange; their agency functions placed them in intimate connection with growers who, for convenience, ran current accounts with them;[65] and they were well aware of the specifically pastoral needs of their constituents.

On the other hand, Richard Goldsbrough was trained in Bradford and commenced business in Melbourne in 1848 as a wool-classer, packer and broker.[66] Mort & Co., while initially general auctioneers, soon concentrated on pastoral property and graduated from this to wool consigning and selling in Sydney.[67] Other colonial produce brokers who also achieved some success in the consignment trade included J. H. Clough and Hastings Cunningham, who commenced business in Melbourne in 1854 and 1862 respectively,[68] and the Sydney firms of F. L. Barker and Maiden, Hill & Clark, both established in the mid-seventies. Although, in some instances, their consignments were very large, they were all primarily interested in the sale of wool in the colonies.

The most notable type of specialized wool house formed in the years after 1860, and the one whose characteristics, appropriated by the others, were to endure to the present day, was that formed specifically to provide extensive, long-term finance to the pastoral industry and to undertake large-scale wool consignment. The crucial feature of concerns like the London & Australian Agency Corporation Ltd, the New Zealand Loan & Mercantile Agency and others established later[69] is that they were formed primarily to provide

---

Melbourne Mt. Alexander Railway Company (Select Committee on Railways, 'Report', *Proc. Vic. Leg. Ass.,* 1856-7, vol. 2, paper D37, appendix D).

[64] Other consigning houses were similarly situated, of course, and did supply goods on occasion. In the same way all of them acted more or less as general agents for their constituents, paying rent for them, receiving and paying bills, etc., and they also held agencies for shipping and insurance companies. It was these two, however, in which the merchanting function was most developed.

[65] Neil Black, for example, ran current accounts with Bell & Buchanan, S. G. Henty, Dalgety, Blackwood & Co., and Younghusband of Adelaide as well as with the Union and Australasia Banks.

[66] Joyce, *A Homestead History,* pp. 111-17, provides an interesting portrait of Goldsbrough in the late forties and early fifties.

[67] R. J. Withers, 'The Romance of Wool Selling', 10 and 25 Oct. 1913.

[68] Clough was absorbed by the London & Australian Agency Corporation in 1866 and Cunningham by the Australasian Mortgage & Agency Company in 1880, each of the two British concerns being established for that purpose. A wool business subsequently opened by Clough was absorbed in the New Zealand Loan and Mercantile Agency in 1880.

[69] The A.M.L. & F., for example, was incorporated in 1863 with the intention, realized in 1865, of taking over the Melbourne firm of Gibbs, Ronald & Co. which in turn had been formed in the mid-fifties primarily to undertake wool consignments to the parent firm of Richard Gibbs & Co. in London. The connection

5 Wool barges on the Murray River in the seventies
6 Buyers examining wool before the sale, Melbourne, in the seventies

channels for the investment in Australia of capital raised in England and, from a strictly logical view, their provision of export facilities, though perhaps necessary, was essentially a subsidiary aspect of their operations. On the other hand, long-term financing was forced upon many consignment and local selling agencies organized in the colonies between the sixties and the eighties. It was then, however, a function which derived from their commitments as wool exporters.

At the end of the sixties the banks entered the ranks of those who could be termed specialized, or at least large-scale, wool consignment agencies. In the forties and fifties, as we have seen, they did occasionally consign wool for their clients, though with reluctance and without publicity. There is some doubt just how far those services went—whether they involved physical participation or merely nominal responsibility for the consignment and whether the London offices of the banks invariably assumed the full functions of consignees or merely passed the shipments over to London houses which specialized in that function. At all events, all ambiguity was dispelled after the Colonial Bank of Australasia announced in 1868 that it was prepared to undertake the consignment and sale of wool in London.[70] While it aroused bitter opposition from the general mercantile community and generated a momentary controversy,[71] it cleared the way for large-scale, direct bank participation in wool exporting. Within a year the Bank of New South Wales had followed its lead and soon became one of the most important consignment agents.[72]

Though they were all wool specialists, these houses distributed the emphasis of their policy among different aspects of their

with Gibbs gave it access to English funds. The N.Z.L. & M.A. was formed in 1864 to invest in, and export pastoral produce from, New Zealand. It commenced business in Victoria in 1874 and in New South Wales two years later. The North British Australasian Co. Ltd, the Queensland Investment & Land Mortgage Co. Ltd, and the South Australian Land Mortgage and Agency Co. are other examples.

[70] *Argus*, 13 Jan. 1869. See also A. Barnard, 'Wool Prices and Pastoral Policies, 1867-1875', *Economic Record*, vol. xxxi (1955), pp. 276-7.

[71] Barnard, loc. cit. It extended even to whether this was an entirely novel practice.

[72] Any worthwhile attempt to explain the banks' changed interests must wait on Professor S. J. Butlin's promised study of Australian banking after 1850. In the meantime it might be hazarded that the fall in wool prices at the end of the sixties, which threatened the securities covering the banks' direct and indirect advances to the growers, and the proportion of pastoral financing which, even at that time, was being provided by wool houses at the expense of potential bank business, and the conflict of equities which arose when the provision of short- and long-term capital was in different hands, together weighed heavily in the decision.

businesses. To them may be added a further group of consignment agents which could, in this context, be classed as at least semi-specialists. They were the merchant firms which, while reserving their main attention for general mercantile pursuits, nevertheless ranked high in the lists of wool exporters. Fanning, Nankivill & Co.,[73] which had been operating in Melbourne since the late forties and was prominent in the trade with the East was itself, through its principals, the owner of sheep stations in the eastern colonies. It used the export facilities it developed for that wool as the basis of a wide consignment business.[74] The consequences of this increased specialization and this growth of scale are evident in the way in which the consignment of wool was conducted through very specific channels. Statistics are not readily available to show how the total exports were divided between the different groups of agents or the extent to which a relatively few houses dominated the trade. Certain deductions may be drawn from the nature of the consignees in England.[75] Between 1880 and 1891 the proportion of Australasian wool consigned to banks rose from 6.9 per cent to 15.9 per cent; that received by the specialized wool and finance companies rose from 27.7 per cent to 39.0 per cent; while the proportion addressed to private firms fell from 65.4 per cent to 45.1 per cent.[76] These are not wholly indicative of the structure of the Australian consignment trade. In the first place New Zealand wool was less markedly exported through the banks and wool houses than Australian and its inclusion in these figures probably inflates unduly the proportion credited to private firms. Moreover, the identification of the English consignee does not necessarily identify the colonial agent. While no wool consigned through the banks or specialized agencies in Australia would have been received by private firms, a certain amount of that sent through merchants may well have been addressed to members of the other groups. Finally, the importance of the specialized houses is understated by the inclusion, among the private firms, of four very large specialized but unincorporated consignment

73 H. M. Franklyn, op. cit., p. 215.
74 Other firms, like Bright Bros. & Co., J. H. White & Co. and Macfarlan, Blyth & Co., appear in the customs lists as important wool exporters, but there is little doubt that the substantial proportion of the wool they handled was credited to them in their capacity as shipping agents, and is irrelevant and misleading in this context.
75 It is too dangerous to argue from the degree of concentration among English consignees (see section 2 below) to a similar structure among consigning agents.
76 *A.I.B.R.*, vol. 14 (1890), p. 166, and vol. 16 (1892), p. 181, gives lists of importers of over 500 bales of Australasian wool into England.

agencies.[77] It is clear, however, that, whatever the precise allocations, the importance of the wool houses and banks increased considerably after 1880. For the specialized houses it was a continuation of the trend that had begun in the fifties and sixties; for the banks the process had started at the end of the sixties.

That the private firms had been able to retain the largest single-group share of the trade was associated with a change in their composition. The banks and specialized houses gained at the expense of the merchant firms whose importance had been declining since the fifties. Even the trade of the semi-specialized merchant consigning agents suffered. Yet the period after 1880 in particular was one in which the sale of wool by auction in the colonies expanded rapidly. The place, in these lists, of merchants consigning on growers' behalf was taken by English woolbuyers, who arranged their own shipments either to the manufacturing centres or to London for resale. To these, who were most concerned with wool imported into England, need to be added those whose shipments were sent direct to the Continent or the United States. Between them these English and foreign buyers accounted for a large proportion of the wool shipped through private firms. Some indication of their importance may be gained from the fact that in 1882 the fifteen largest wool exporters appearing in the Victorian Customs Bill of Entry include five who were primarily woolbuyers. There were, in addition, a number of pastoral companies financed directly from England which, for special reasons, still used miscellaneous merchant firms as their consignment agents as late as 1891.[78]

(c) *Local Selling, 1855–1914*

In the period during which the use of the consignment system of export was most highly developed, an aggressive campaign to expand the size and change the nature of the local market was begun in the colonies. Specialized wool-selling brokers provided institutions on which an efficient trade could be based; colonial merchant buyers were replaced by foreign dealers and speculators and they in turn were succeeded by the representatives of foreign

---

[77] In 1889 Sanderson, Murray & Co. imported 73,818 bales, Robert Brooks & Co. 29,593, Redfern, Alexander & Co. 27,865 and Elder, Smith & Co. 27,640 (*A.I.B.R.*, vol. 14, p. 166). If these are added to the specialized houses the percentages read 12.4 to the banks, 43.7 to the specialized houses and 43.9 to private firms, instead of 12.4, 30.9 and 56.7 per cent respectively, as in the original compilation.

[78] The Australian Pastoral Co., for example, shipped through the offices of Gibbs, Bright & Co., ship agents and merchants of Melbourne and the company's managing agent in Australia.

raw wool consumers; wool consignment and finance houses were forced to abandon most of their consignment functions and transfer their operations to the colonies as wool-selling brokers.[79]

The increased orderliness and regularity imparted to local selling by Lyons, Hind, the Bakewells and others by the establishment of auction sales of wool and the provision of warehouse accommodation for it before and after sale, which was considered above, was further formalized during the fifties. T. S. Mort in Sydney and Richard Goldsbrough in Melbourne are the two to whom is attributed the provision of regular auction facilities (weekly at first and then more frequently as the demand increased) and of warehouses designed specifically for the sale of wool and consequently incorporating features enabling the wool to be shown to the buyers under the best conditions. This they did in the late forties and early fifties. It was they who, from the late fifties, sought to develop the local market rather than merely to provide facilities demanded of them. What concerns us here, however, is not why and how they tried to persuade the growers to sell their wool in the colonies rather than consign it and to persuade final consumers to operate in Australia rather than in England, but the fact that by their existence and that of their imitators they formed a new group in the chain linking grower to consumer.

Both Goldsbrough and Mort, as well as others like J. H. Clough, Hastings Cunningham & Co., Monkton D. Synnot, and P. N. Walker in Melbourne, Maiden, Hill & Clark and F. L. Barker in Sydney, the Guthries and C. J. Dennys in Geelong, and Elder, Smith & Co. in Adelaide provided dual facilities—either for sale in the colonies or consignment to England. Local selling formed their main activity—they styled themselves wool-selling brokers not consignment agents—and from the late fifties they specialized in this branch of business. Now, to the extent that this function represented no more than the provision of broking activities linking growers with colonial merchant buyers, colonial wool dealers, and speculators, their advent meant only the formalization of the selling arrangements that had existed between these groups in the forties. This in itself, it is true, was a most important development, for by acting as selling agent for the growers and providing centres where supplies were concentrated for the buyers, and by furnishing

---

[79] This chapter is devoted primarily to an outline of the marketing chain. For a discussion of the reasons for the changes—of Goldsbrough's attempts to expand the local market, of the factors inducing the foreign dealers and consumers to buy in the colonies and of the assumption of local broking functions by the large consignment houses—see ch. 7.

a means whereby sales could be effected efficiently and with probity, they immeasurably eased the contact between the two. Their main significance in this context lies, however, in the fact that by providing these improved institutions they made it increasingly possible for non-colonial buyers to operate in the market with skill, economy and profit.

Given the establishment of these selling institutions, it is in the nature of the buyers at the colonial auctions that the most important development in the local sale of wool after the mid-fifties is to be found. Already, in the forties and early fifties, we have noted the activities of such buyers as Kummerer and Sanderson, who bought for foreign principals at whose risk the wool was transported from the colonies. During the sixties purchasing on non-colonial account was increasing steadily, and it was primarily confined to English orders. The main buyers had, by that time, become full-time specialized wool-buying brokers accepting and executing speculative orders for such English wool dealers as Robert Jowitt & Sons of Leeds,[80] or speculating on their own account. Hinchcliffe, Hirst, Hick, Halliburton, Ebsworth, Johnson and Austin were between them able to conduct most of this business.[81]

During the seventies foreign buying increased greatly. Henry Austin, one of the leading buyers, in 1872 executed orders for merchants in Germany and Belgium and for Germans in England as well as for Englishmen. Colonial buying brokers, however, were not well situated to operate on Continental account. That demand came to be exercised through the branches of European dealer firms established in the colonies at this time. In the late sixties a tripartite alliance of Belgian, German and Dutch interests, Ostermeyer, Dewez & Co., and another Belgian concern, Renard Bros. & Co., opened offices in the colonies.[82] A few years later Masurel Fils et Cie, destined to become one of the most important forces in the colonial market, sent C. Maquet to Sydney as its first representative.[83] American purchases were made through Newell & Co. and other colonial firms.[84]

[80] Jowitts purchased irregular parcels through Thomas Holt in Sydney and Dodgshun & Austin in Melbourne from the mid-fifties. Cf. A. Barnard, 'Wool-buying in the Nineteenth Century: a case history', *Yorkshire Bulletin of Social and Economic Research*, vol. viii, no. 1 (June 1956). The information is derived from the 'Jowitt Records'.

[81] Austin, 'Recollections of the Australian Wool Trade', May and June 1907.

[82] I am indebted to Mr G. Dewez, of T. Dewez & Co. of Sydney, for many recollections of the early firm and its partners. See Renard Bros. & Co., *Antwerp versus London as a Market for Australian Wool*, for an indication of that firm's interests.   [83] Austin, op. cit., September 1907.

[84] Newell & Co. were merchants indenting largely from the United States; their wool trade was actively sought, initially, as a sideline to the merchanting.

Throughout the seventies and into the eighties most of the purchases on foreign account were made for dealers and topmakers. In
the eighties these two groups began to follow the lead set by Masurel
and other dealers, to establish their own buying branches in the
colonies and to end their dependence on colonial, and the few
foreign, commission buyers.[85] It was the establishment of these
branches on a large scale that elevated the colonial auctions to
something approaching world status, for it shifted the focus of
dealer purchases from the northern to the southern hemisphere.
They were followed, in the eighties and nineties, by branch establishments of manufacturing firms which bought both for their
parent concerns and, on commission, for other raw wool consumers.
By the end of the century, while many colonial buying firms were
still operating, most of the wool sold in Australia was purchased by
the branches of foreign firms and, while wool was still bought
speculatively, even for resale on the London market, the greater
proportion of it was bought directly by, or by commission agents
for, final consumers and intermediate dealers.

These changes in the composition of the buyers at the auctions,
and their effect on the prices realized there, are basic factors in the
growing utilization of this channel of disposal by the growers. In
the fifties and sixties it had been, generally, the small grower who
sold his wool locally. The specific attraction of local sale—quick
realization and finalization of accounts—appealed mainly to that
class and outweighed for them the lower prices obtained. The
enhanced prices offered by dealers and manufacturers attracted new
sellers to the market. They were deprived, however, of their full
potentialities by rigidities in marketing which attached growers
to functional middlemen bound to sell in London.[86] In fact, the
local market came to maturity only when the wool and finance
houses, such as Dalgetys, were forced both by the prompting of
their constituents and the realities of the situation to offer sales
facilities in the colonies in the eighties.[87]

The assumption by these firms of local wool-selling functions
completed the circle of change which marketing patterns in the

---

[85] The process is discussed more fully in Barnard 'Wool-buying in the Nineteenth Century: a case history'.

[86] See ch. 5 and pp. 139-46.

[87] The N.Z.L. & M.A. commenced selling in Melbourne in 1880, Dalgetys in
1887 and the Union Mortgage & Agency Co. in 1888. Of this move (which 'was
necessary to conserve the interests of the company') the Chairman of Dalgetys
said 'It may diminish our consignments to London, but not to the extent that it
will increase our business in the colonies' (3rd annual general meeting, reported
in *A.I.B.R.*, vol. ii, p. 777).

colonies had undergone by the end of the century. Local sales to general merchants and colonial speculators by primitive and un-ordered methods in the thirties had been largely replaced by consignment to England through the agency of the same merchants. Those consignment functions of the merchants had been taken over by specialized agencies; their place at the colonial auctions taken by specialized foreign wool dealers. Local sales had been made effective by the growth of a class of local wool-selling brokers whose ranks had been swollen by the specialized consignment houses that provided dual facilities. Local selling was patronized in the thirties by all classes of wool producers, in the sixties only by those with restricted means, and by 1914 attracted two-thirds of the wool produced.

2 MARKETING BEYOND THE COLONIES

In 1840 all Australian wool no matter how it was exported—whether by merchant or other purchasers, by merchant or other consigning agents, or by the growers—was consigned to agents in England who arranged for its sale at the periodic auction sales in London or Liverpool. There it was sold by wool-selling brokers to raw wool consumers in Britain and to dealers who, selling by private treaty, distributed it to other manufacturers in Britain and, to a slight extent, in Europe. The main change which this marketing pattern underwent during the nineteenth century lay in the extent to which the consignment technique of export and the London auction sales were partially replaced, from the mid-seventies, by distribution direct from the Australian auction sales. From that time, that is, we must consider not one but two perhaps parallel but competing patterns. This change, in its most simplified form, meant primarily that the source of some manufacturers' and distributors' supplies was changed, leaving largely unaltered the routes by which the dealers' wool was subsequently distributed. Within the sector of marketing which was centred on the London auctions the changes that occurred related primarily to the structure and nature of the agency firms acting as consignees, and to the composition and structure of the distributive trade. Despite the changes in the general pattern—despite the competitive growth of the colonial auctions—the broad principles on which the London section of marketing institutions was based remained unaltered.

The importing merchants[88]—the English consignees—provided

88 Strictly speaking the term 'importing merchants' is a gross misnomer for at no time did these firms trade in the wool consigned to them; the only title they

the link between the colonial exporters and the rest of the market system. Their function was to act as agent for the owner of the wool (colonial purchaser or grower) in all matters relating to its sale —to receive it in England, to supervise its landing and storage, and to arrange with a wool-selling broker to offer it at the auctions. This agency was secured for the grower by the colonial consigning agents; the importing merchant, in other words, stood at the second stage of remove from the grower.

In the early years of the trade the unspecialized nature of the colonial consignors was matched by the number and variety of consignees. Colonial merchants consigned their own and their clients' wool to those with whom they were in closest correspondence —the English merchants from whom they imported their goods and the agents who conducted their English business.[89] Emigrant growers consigned to their friends, relatives and partners.[90] Large pastoral and land companies, for example the Australian Agricultural Co. and the South Australia Co., banks, and other concerns incorporated in England consigned their wool direct to their head offices. The existence of so varied a group of importing agents was not simply a product of the limited range of correspondents to which the difficulties and paucity of communications condemned the colonist. English wool dealers manifested an extreme reluctance, in those years, to play any role in the import of Australian wool, preferring to enter the market only as buyers at the London auctions. Lacking their specialized knowledge and resources and, in particular, the concentrated application of working capital which specialization alone conferred, the importing agents formed a fragmented group. Part of their function was to accept bills drawn on them, against the wool, by the consigning agents and discounted in the colonies.[91] These acceptances represented a contingent liability, for they might fall due before the sale of the produce and, therefore, before the importer was in a position to meet them. This fact, together with the difficulty of determining the credit-worthiness of colonial agents, imposed a natural limit on both the quantity of wool for which an English agent could accept responsibility and the number of colonists from whom he might receive it.

---

had to it was the formal one vested in them in their role as financiers. The term is retained, however, because it is the one used at the time.

[89] The example of James Henty's connection with the firm of Henry Buckle & Co., general merchants of London (Bassett, *The Hentys*, pp. 205, 315, 488, 513, 514, 516) will suffice to indicate a type of relationship that was very widespread.

[90] E.g. Black's consignments to the firm of Gladstone & Sargeantson mentioned above. [91] See pp. 96-8.

The growth of colonial production, however, enforced some degree of specialization on importing functions and led to concentration among the importers perhaps earlier than among the corresponding class of colonial agents. By 1859 the process was quite clearly definable. In that year Browne & Eagle stored a total of 49,190 bales in their London warehouses, acting on behalf of 97 importing agents. Of these, 82 imported an average of 199 bales each; the remaining 15 provided the company with two-thirds of its business.[92]

The routes by which firms attained this specialization were various. Some merchant houses, to whom wool importing had been a subsidiary complication of normal exporting relations with colonial firms, allowed it to expand to consume the major part of their activities; of these P. W. Flower & Co. may serve as an example. Even by the sixties some wool dealers had entered the field and provided consignee services while also purchasing at the auctions in London and perhaps, through commission agents, in the colonies. F. Huth & Co., a wool-buying broker and dealer who played a large part in stimulating Continental demand for Australian wool, operated on the largest scale but others, like Jowitts of Leeds, received variable parcels.[93]

Developments of this nature occurring in English firms were important, but the two main forces lay in the formation of pastoral finance houses and the integration of English importing and colonial exporting concerns. The pastoral finance houses, designed to invest British capital in the wool industry, assumed wool marketing functions as a concomitant of that investment. The most prominent among them were organized on a large scale and soon became important, as we have seen, as colonial consigning agents. Possessing offices in England, to which their exports were naturally addressed, they acquired rank among the consignees with equal rapidity. Though it is not pretended that the figures below reflect accurately the growth of its business, some appreciation of the expansion of the New Zealand Loan & Mercantile Agency as an importer may be gained from the fact that the quantity of wool which it warehoused with Browne & Eagle rose from 73 bales in 1866 to 2,339 in 1868, 4,002 in 1869 and 5,859 in 1870.[94] The banks were similarly fortunate in possessing London offices. The integration of colonial exporting

[92] Browne & Eagle, 'Lists of Importers'.
[93] Jowitt's receipts of consignments varied quite widely. The 'Jowitt Records', Colonial Ledgers, suggest that minimal figures for the following years are as follows: 1855, 150 bales; 1860, 186 bales; 1865, 732 bales; 1870, 909 bales; and 1875, 5,386 bales. See also Barnard, 'Wool-buying in the Nineteenth Century: a case history'. [94] Browne & Eagle, 'Lists of Importers'.

and English importing firms was both a cause and a consequence of specialization. In some cases the initiative came from the colonies, and a dependent outlet for a firm's consignments was created in England. F. G. Dalgety went from Melbourne to London to form his own receiving establishment,[95] while Elder, Smith & Co. utilized the importing services of A. L. Elder, the founder of the firm, when he retired to England.[96] On the other hand Richard Gibbs & Co. attained stature as importing agents because of the success of its offspring firm Gibbs Ronald & Co. of Melbourne. Many other importing firms, including P. W. Flower & Co., were represented on the boards or in the partnerships of exporting agencies.

By 1880 three specialized firms—two pastoral finance companies and an importing agency—together provided Browne & Eagle with just over half the business they received from 146 importers.[97] This does not wholly represent the firm's good fortune in numbering them among their clients, for a complete survey of the importers of Australasian wool in 1889 reveals that the specialized houses and banks together handled 56.1 per cent of the total trade.[98] By 1898 the five largest specialized consignment houses between them accounted for more than one-third of the Australasian wool arriving in England for sale by auction.[99]

Yet despite their impressive share of that market, by the end of the century their function as consignees was of subsidiary import- ance. As soon as they were forced to provide selling accommodation in the colonies their English role was destined to decline. Their place in the trade in 1898 represented a mere survival, though an admittedly lusty one, of their former dynamic importance. Their mantle was assumed by the banks, which became the major outlet for growers still wishing to sell their clips in London (fourteen of them imported over 25 per cent of the total), by the large producing companies, and by the few merchant consigning agents who, with headquarters in London, were conservative survivals from an earlier era. These groups were all concerned with receiving consignments from the growers or their agents. For a time, however, it seemed that the continued vitality of the London auctions might depend

[95] Dalgety & Co. Ltd, *A Souvenir to Commemorate the Jubilee Year*, p. 19. He took with him F. A. DuCroz as partner in the London concern and left James Blackwood as the managing partner in Melbourne.
[96] [Price and Hammond], *Elder, Smith & Co. Ltd.*, p. 17.
[97] 'Browne & Eagle Records', loc. cit.
[98] *A.I.B.R.*, vol. 14 (1890), p. 166. See n. 78 above.
[99] Gooch, Cousens & Co., *Wool Importers* (an annual publication, London, 1899). These firms imported 332,510 bales in a total of 935,940.

on the wool dealers who imported considerable quantities of wool
bought speculatively for them by their colonial branches and who
placed it directly in the salerooms. The uncertainties of the market,
the ease with which manufacturers could supply themselves from
Australia, and the importance of the trade in tops soon forced
them out, and in the twentieth century the diminished London
market was served primarily by the banks and the large wool-
producing companies.

The importers' prime formal function, as we have said, was to
arrange for the sale of the wool at the auctions. The group in whose
hands the responsibility for the actual sale was placed were the wool-
selling brokers. Some of these firms were already, in the eighteen-
forties, of impressive age. As the import of colonial wool expanded
during the forties and fifties, new entrants appeared from other
textile occupations. W. H. Willans, for example, had been in the
Huddersfield wool trade before coming to London as a broker in
1855.[1]

A wool-selling broker's was in many ways a personal business in
which personality, success on the auctioneer's rostrum and an
intimate knowledge of the clients' requirements played a major part.
The mortality rate among them was consequently high—despite
the longevity of some individual concerns. This inherent instability
was aggravated, after the eighties, by the fact that the amount of
business to be shared among them first ceased to expand and then
declined as the auction sales in the colonies became the main
avenue for the disposal of the colonial clip.

This competition from the colonial auctions increased the tendency for wool selling in London to be concentrated into relatively few
hands. This concentration had been a noticeable feature in the
early seventies. At the first three series of sales in 1874 five brokers
offered 81 per cent of the total catalogued, while the remaining 19
per cent was divided among nine other brokers.[2] By 1889 the five
largest accounted for only 76 per cent of the offerings, but the
number of other brokers had dropped to only six.[3] Competition, in
other words, had forced some of the weaker firms out of the trade
altogether. Towards the end of the century the process was accelerated by the amalgamation of broking firms. The firms of W. P.
Hughes & Co. and Willans, Overbury & Co., which were joined in
1914, illustrate the part played by a declining total business. In
1888 Hughes sold 109,203 bales and Willans, Overbury 78,692; in 1913

[1] Cf. the *Wool Record and Textile World* (Bradford, monthly) 28 Feb. 1929,
p. 579.   [2] Brodribb, *Results of Inquiries . . .*, p. 46.   [3] *A.I.B.R.*, vol. 14, p. 166.

Hughes's business had dropped to 62,353 and Willans, Overbury's to 53,217 bales.[4]

The other group of functional middlemen through whose hands the wool could pass before reaching the consumers or dealers were the wool-buying brokers. Their role was to represent actual purchasers in the saleroom, bidding on their behalf and frequently taking delivery of the wool and forwarding it to the dealer's warehouse or manufacturer's mill. Their intervention was necessary for two reasons. In the first place they enabled foreign manufacturers and dealers to purchase in London without making the journey from their own countries (in the same way as the colonial buying brokers enabled English buyers to operate without being present in person). And secondly, they were possessed of skills and influence in the auction room which the buyers themselves lacked. It was felt, for example, that buying brokers in London were so well seated in the room and in close calls so often caught the auctioneer's eye that a buyer had far more chance of obtaining the lots he wanted if he made his bids through one of their number.[5]

They attained this enviable position simply because they bought far more, on commission, than most consumers and dealers bought. The large buying brokers operated, in fact, on a very large scale indeed. Two or three of the large selling brokers who also acted as buying brokers bought as much as they sold. Fully two-thirds of the purchases made in the early seventies were actually made through buying brokers.[6] As there were no restrictions on entrance to the trade there were many brokers, drawn from all sections of the wool trade. Many were manufacturers and dealers who agreed to buy on commission for others while they were obtaining their own supplies in London.[7] Others, like Paul Pierrard and Frederick Huth, were specialist buying brokers, acting mainly on account of foreign consumers and dealers. Others again, such as Helmuth Schwartze, acted both as selling and buying brokers, combining an intimate knowledge of buying clients with an extensive knowledge of the wool coming forward.[8]

---

[4] I am indebted to Hughes, Willans, Irwell & Co., London woolselling brokers, for permission to extract this information from their archives.

[5] The Joint Sub-Committees of Enquiry appointed by meetings in New South Wales, Victoria, and South Australia, *Report on the Sales of Australian Wools in London*, p. 21 (this work is henceforth cited as *The Sales of Australian Wools in London*). Also Brodribb, *Results of Enquiries . . .*, p. 25.

[6] *The Sales of Australian Wools in London*, p. 23.

[7] Robert Jowitt & Sons provide an example (cf. the arrangements recorded in the 'Jowitt Records', 'Jobbing [erased] Order Book', pp. 11, 13, 82, 135 etc.).

[8] *The Sales of Australian Wools in London*, p. 36.

4

THE FUNCTIONS OF THE MARKET

In bringing together the producer and the consumer, the middlemen and agents whose places in the marketing pattern were defined in the previous chapter performed certain services which form the fundamental features of marketing—the concentration, exchange and distribution of goods. Marketing means much more than this, however, for it includes all of those services which make the exchange possible and which are utilized by buyers and sellers to effect it to their respective advantage. Grading and packing, transport and communication, and the provision of finance are as much functions of the market as risk bearing.

From the wide variety offered by this definition it is intended here to examine a selection of the more important functions, to determine changes in the performance of the services through which they were expressed, and to relate those services, more closely than in the previous chapter, to specific agents in the market.

I MARKET INFORMATION

The distribution of information relevant to the actions of both buyers and sellers was of prime importance when those groups were separated by 12,000 miles over which communication was slow and not wholly reliable. Throughout the whole of our period after 1840 this service was provided mainly by the agents most closely connected with both groups—the wool-selling brokers.

At the close of each auction sales series the London brokers published the range of prices established at the series, the quantity offered and that withdrawn at reserve prices, and indicated the general sources of the demand. In between the sales series their market reports examined the short-term prospects of the market, remarking the current and probable state of manufacturing activity, the apparent offerings at the next series, conditions in the money market, and other developments likely to affect the formation of prices in the near future. These reports were designed as much for the sellers and their English representatives as they were for the buyers.[1] Those representatives, and the buyers', were themselves in a position to make their own observations which they frequently forwarded, in addition to the brokers' reports, to their constituents.[2]

Supplementing this information, both brokers and importing agents endeavoured to interpret trend developments. Their comments ranged from reports of the number of sheep, the state of the weather and of grazing conditions, expected and actual lambing results and the anticipated quantity and quality of a forthcoming clip to discussions of the developments in manufacturing techniques, changes in fashion and their impact on the demand for various types of wool. They provided consumers, speculators and even the growers with a basis on which some preliminary notions about future prices might be founded. At the same time, read in conjunction with the reports of previous sales, they offered the growers some indication of the probable permanence of existing price differentials between wool types and guided them, therefore, in their breeding policies.

At times the manufacturers themselves sought to influence the types of wool produced both in general terms, such as the support given by the Bradford Chamber of Commerce to the drive, initiated by the manufacturers, to increase the colonial production of long wool in the sixties and seventies,[3] and in the more specific instances of advice given growers by English and Continental manufacturers to whom samples were sent.[4] This was of episodic importance only, and the brokers and importing agents exercised a more direct and continuous influence on the growers. In addition to their advice on the general lines of breeding that were most desirable,[5] they made detailed comments on the breeding, the condition and the presentation of the clips committed to their care.[6] In this respect the colonial wool brokers, who rendered the same service, were more fortunately situated than their London counterparts. The possible imperfections of their knowledge of the manufacturing industries was compensated by a closer relation with sheep raising.

---

[1] The reports were distributed as circulars, sent to clients and reprinted in colonial newspapers and journals as commercial news.
[2] 'Black Papers': Gladstone and Sargeantson to Black, 4 Sept. 1855. On an account sale Black is advised of his consignee's estimate of the next sales.
[3] Cf. pp. 23-4.　　　　　　　　[4] Billis and Kenyon, *Pastures New*, p. 190.
[5] T. Southey, *The Rise, Progress and Present State of Colonial Sheep and Wools*, pp. 21-2.
[6] Neil Black's 1840 clip was characterized as 'generally a good middle quality —soft and contained a fair proportion of wool suitable for combing; but not well washed'. 'Black Papers', undated and unsigned report by the broker copied on a duplicate invoice for rams.

Necessarily, the utility and reliability of the market information made available through these sources varied. The range of the reports and the details they embodied expanded as the trade grew and as it encompassed wider geographical areas. Brokers and consignees were sometimes slow to appreciate the extent of some of the changes they chronicled and tended to view them, perhaps naturally, out of perspective; their forecasts were often incorrect; and their efforts were once castigated as 'gratuitous prophecies' and the 'promulgation of crude and hasty theories about production and consumption'.[7] Nevertheless, they bridged, as best they could in an age lacking speedy communication and a penchant for statistics, what would otherwise have been a crippling gap in the market.

2   GRADING

The quality of wool may vary widely from sheep to sheep and from one part of a sheep to another. Basically, grading wool means confining the wool packed in one bale to a certain standard. This simple fact was enormously complicated during the nineteenth century by changes in the provision of grading services and by the refinement of the concept of wool qualities and types.

In the thirties and forties, colonial wool came down to the ports in loosely packed bales. If it was to be shipped to England for sale on the growers' account, it was sorted there and repacked firmly enough to withstand the sea voyage and the port and warehouse handling. If it was to be sold in the colonies it was frequently offered in open bins and then repacked, perhaps with other wool, at the direction of the buyer. These services were performed either by specialized sorters and packers[8] or by the employees of wool-buying merchants, consignment agents or shippers. On occasion they were organized on most efficient lines,[9] but in general the standard of sorting was low.[10]

Three developments during the succeeding decades moved the site of wool grading back from the port to the shearing shed. The

---

[7] These phrases were endorsed by no less a body than the Melbourne Chamber of Commerce. See the *Argus*, 29 March 1872.

[8] It is worth emphasizing that Richard Goldsbrough started business in 1848 as a 'wool sorter, packer and broker'.

[9] See, for example, the description of the Bakewells' establishment in Melbourne at the end of the forties in W. Westgarth, *The Colony of Victoria: its history, commerce, and gold-mining . . .*, pp. 269-70.

[10] T. Shaw, *The Australian Merino*, p. 6, describes colonial wool-sorters as 'old fellmongers, weavers, hatters and porters to cloth warehouses who are simply imposters'. A few years later S. Smith, *Important Suggestions*, p. 11, felt that colonial fleeces were hardly sorted at all.

growth of colonial production, the vastly increased utilization of the consignment method of disposal, and the greater distances over which wool was carried to the ports (necessitating sturdier packs and tighter baling on the station) made unpacking, sorting and re-packing in the ports increasingly uneconomic. From the late forties and fifties professional wool-classers offered themselves for seasonal employment on the stations,[11] and wool-classing became an import-ant qualification for managers and overseers. As classing became more complex during the second half of the century, their function lay as much in superintending the separation of different wools from the same fleece—skirting the necks and pieces and removing the bellies and locks on the shearing board—as in ensuring a roughly even quality of wool in any bale.

In London and, after the fifties, in the colonial centres, selling brokers performed a further grading operation by assembling the packed wool from each clip into lots containing bales of even quality. Until the end of the century, it was not necessary for them to re-sort wool in individual bales. The poor classing characteristic of wool from small mixed farms in South Australia and Victoria, particularly in the eighties and nineties,[12] induced colonial brokers first to interlot bales of the same quality offered on account of different producers and later to offer binned and bulked wool.[13]

Sorting and blending wool from different clips, a central function of wool staplers dealing with English wools in the first half of the century, was not widely practised by dealers who bought colonial wool for resale direct to manufacturers.[14] Blending or sorting done by topmakers, by woollen spinners at the mill, or by worsted spinners preparing to have it combed on commission, carries grading a step beyond the limit of our interest, for it was concerned either with the manufacturing or the marketing of wool processed into tops and noils.

---

[11] Examples may be found in the 'Collaroy Papers', vol. 1: B. A. Kemp to R. J. Traill, 15 Aug. 1853 (I am indebted to the Librarian of the Mitchell Library for permission to quote from this collection) and in the 'Black Papers': T. G. Shaun to Black, 6 Oct. 1866. Shaun had been a manufacturer in Leeds and a woolbuyer in London.

[12] R. B. S[kamp], *Farmers' Wool* is a plea directed to small wool producers to class more carefully. It was published under the auspices of Goldsbrough, Mort & Co. Ltd.

[13] L. W. Bagley, *Efficient Wool Marketing*, p. 49, provides an indication of the complex patterns of classing services now available to the grower.

[14] 'Jowitt Records', 'Purchase Book, 1870-1', containing a bale-by-bale list of purchasers at the auction sales together with their weights, prices and marks, and the details of their resale shows that Jowitt, at least, habitually resold imported wools in their original state and packing.

Thus five groups, the specialized or semi-specialized sorters and packers, growers, itinerant wool-classers, wool-selling brokers and perhaps dealers, have at various stages of the marketing process contributed to the grading of the wool. To some extent the change in the performance of this function was associated with the problems of transport and with the organization of the export mechanism. It was also a product, however, of the changing nature of wool-classing itself.

The crudest and earliest differentiating description applied was a simple geographic one—'Botany', and later 'Van Diemen's Land' and 'Port Phillip' wool; the most sophisticated, the 1,536 types and subtypes on which appraisal for government purchase was based during the second world war. In between these lay a gradual evolution of finer and finer distinctions. In the twenties the Macarthurs, the colony's leading wool growers, simply ranked the fleeces from fine to coarse and packed them accordingly.[15] In 1856 Neil Black's wool was classed into first, second, and third combing and first, second, and third clothing, with rams' wool and some pieces in separate bales.[16] The Australian Agricultural Co. was advised, nine years later, to confine the distinctions to first and second combing, first, second and third clothing, and first and second hoggetts.[17] By the end of the century a few new descriptions had been added, generally, like the infrequently used 'carbonizing', in response to new manufacturing needs. Yet if the terms used did not change greatly during these sixty years, the gradually widening adoption of their use was a most noticeable feature, particularly in the colonies where the wool-selling brokers did not, perhaps, play a large part in grading as in London. For many years the insufficiently informative terms 'fine' and 'coarse' and later first, second and third ewes and wethers sufficed for many growers, but more specific terms incorporating reference to combing or clothing wool gained an increasing acceptance.

The basis of classing, then, was a primary classification of the wool according to the manufacturing use for which it was most suited. Black's separation of combing from clothing wools corresponded to wools destined for use in the worsted and woollen branches respectively. Within these two groups further subdivisions

[15] Macarthur Onslow, *Some Early Records of the Macarthurs of Camden*, ch. 12, *passim*. Sales catalogues of that period (one is reproduced opposite p. 440) do not attempt to describe the wool other than by source.
[16] 'Black Papers': Gladstone and Sargeantson to Black, 5 July 1856, enclosing Thomas Southey & Son's valuation of a shipment classed in this way.
[17] A.A. Co., 'Despatches from London', no. 201, 27 Feb. 1865.

embraced different grades expressed as fine or coarse, ranked numerically or later alphabetically. It is apparent that grading of this nature did not represent classification on the basis of objectively established standards. The finer distinctions, drawn in the shearing shed, embodied no more than the ranking of the qualities in any one clip. Wool of allegedly the same quality taken from different clips realized widely different prices at the same auction.[18] The broad division into combing and clothing wools postulated a difference in wool types rather than wool qualities. One could say, in fact, that wool-classing was no more than wool typing complicated by a subjective ranking from good to bad. That the descriptions applied were inadequate and of significance only to the individual stations is indicated in the fact that English buyers placing orders through colonial buying brokers ignored them and used general terms and references to previous purchases and samples.[19]

The subjectivity of wool-classing underlines the difference between the grading of wool and of most other primary products such as cotton and wheat. In those trades the grades are standardized, easily recognizable by initiates, and embrace qualities which are stable, which can be tested objectively, and on the basis of which transactions may safely be concluded without inspecting the actual produce. In the marketing of other raw materials grading secures, by a series of discontinuous unities, a measure of homogeneity among an otherwise essentially heterogeneous collection of goods. The very complexity of wool types, deriving from the wide variety of influences—genetic, edaphic, climatic, and human—to which wool production is subject, at once demanded the orderliness of grading and prevented the achievement of its purpose.

Yet wool-classing was a valuable operation. Developed initially by the sellers and their agents as a form of product differentiation designed to secure higher unit returns, the prime area for its

[18] At the sale held in Melbourne on 21 Nov. 1883 by R. Goldsbrough & Co. greasy merino wool described as 1st combing realized prices ranging from 9d. to 12⅝d. per lb.

[19] J. Raistrick's orders to W. H. Chard of Sydney provide an example of this lack of precision ('Raistrick Records', 'Letters to Colonial Purchasers', 1 Sept. 1875): 'The kind of wool I want is of a medium to better quality, but the bulk of our wool is faulty, that is burry moiety or seedy, if it can be bought cheaper than clean wool, we do not mean over burry. This kind of wool according to your letter ought to be bought very cheap ... Regarding the class of wool which will suit us are moiety fleeces, scoured or greasy, pieces bellies locks scoured or greasy ... etc. ... We give you the following marks which we have had and liked very well ...' (I am indebted to the Librarian of the Brotherton Library, University of Leeds, where this collection is held, for permission to use and quote from it.)

exploitation lay in the assembly of the lots to be offered at the auction sales. A lot which contained wool of an even quality commanded a higher price because a buyer whose needs it suited could depend on using it all. Even by the forties wool textile manufacturing had reached a stage such that the inclusion of other qualities, whether superior or inferior, represented for the manufacturer the inclusion of waste to be sorted out and disposed of in uneconomic quantities at a probable loss. Descriptive labelling may have saved buyers some time by enabling them to by-pass definitely unsuitable wool in their warehouse examination of the bales before the sales, but the success of the grading depended entirely on the extent to which each bale contained wool of one quality only and each lot contained bales of even quality.[20] In its effect, that is, grading provided only a guarantee of uniformity within a lot and not one of an objectively standardized quality.

Classing also carried its dangers. Some new categories were justifiably added by the growers in response to legitimate manufacturing needs. The increasing complexity and the needless use of fine distinctions during the last thirty years of the century, however, caused some concern particularly among the London wool-selling brokers.[21] It was necessary to balance the value of accurate classing against the fragmentation of lots to which an excess led. It was an established fact that a lot consisting of fifty to a hundred bales of fairly even quality excited even greater competition among the buyers than an equal number of bales meticulously classed into lots of five bales or less.[22]

3 TRANSPORT

Transport was provided for the wool market by specialized agencies existing ouside the market. Growers admittedly used their own bullock drays in the days before public carriers offered adequate facilities, and some of the colonial consigning agents owned shipping lines or were agents for English fleets. While in the latter case this no doubt gave them a competitive advantage in their consignment business, interests in transporting were, strictly, a separable and analytically separate department of their activities. What is of conse-

[20] Misdescription and false packing of bales were among the earliest things for which the buyers demanded means of redress.
[21] Colonial Wool Merchants' Association, *Report of the Sub-committee appointed to consider the communications received from the Chambers of Commerce, Wool Growers and others in the Australian Colonies relative to the management of the London Wool Sales*, p. 2.
[22] Ibid., pp. 13, 16, 18, 21.

quence in the present context is, therefore, the effects which developments in the provision of public transport had on wool marketing.

In the colonies the growth of railway networks, the clearance of rivers, and the provision of river-boat transport, together with the pattern of tariffs charged, not only speeded and cheapened the inland carriage of wool but directly influenced the direction in which the produce flowed. The service along the Darling-Murray system, started in the fifties, for example, was one of the factors which opened the extremes of the Western Division of New South Wales to pastoral occupation. River boats carried the wool from the ports as far up as Bourke down to Port Victor and Goolwa in South Australia where it was transhipped to England or, later, to Melbourne.[23] In 1864 the Victorian government offered a freight rebate for wool carried on the Echuca-Melbourne railway which had been brought upstream to Echuca—that is, for wool coming down the Darling which had been diverted up the Murray away from South Australian ports. It was undoubtedly felt, both in Melbourne and Adelaide, that some of the wool which followed this route tended to be drawn into the Melbourne auction sales, to which the discriminatory rates gave it access, instead of being consigned to England.[24] In the sixties produce from the Riverina district of New South Wales, which had very strong ties with Melbourne,[25] tended to be sent to that city by river, road and rail for local sale or consignment to England. The extension of the New South Wales railway system to the Murrumbidgee district diverted part of it to Sydney, fanning the intercolonial rivalry between the local selling brokers. Railway rates, which, at the end of the century, favoured wool coming from the north-west plains and tablelands to Newcastle rather than to Sydney for direct shipment to England, illustrate a final, rather different use to which discriminatory policies were put.[26]

There was a limit, however, to the extent to which these factors could influence the marketing pattern. Riverina wool, for example,

[23] See A. H. Morris, 'Echuca and the Murray River Trade', *Historical Studies, Australia and New Zealand*, vol. 4, no. 16, p. 340. A rather more romantic account may be found in Ernestine Hill, *Water into Gold* (Melbourne, 1937), ch. 2.

[24] Royal Commission on Railway Construction, 'Report and Minutes of Evidence', *S.A.P.P.*, 1875, vol. 2, paper 22, *passim*.

[25] Select Committee on the Riverina Districts, 'Report and Minutes of Evidence', *Proc. Vic. Leg. Ass.*, 1862-3, vol. 2, paper D42. See particularly the evidence of G. S. Lang, A. McCleary, and R. Youl.

[26] Standing Committee on Public Works, 'Report on the Proposed Railway from Narrabri to Walgett . . . with Minutes of Evidence', *N.S.W. V. & P.*, 1900, vol. 5, question 1865.

tended to return to Melbourne during the late eighties and nineties despite the ease and cheapness of transport to Sydney;[27] Darling wool continued to go to South Australia despite the rating policy of the Victorian railways in the sixties, much of it in fact being transhipped to Melbourne rather than to England.[28] The fact is that the direction in which these wools moved was as much affected by the decisions taken about marketing them as by the conditions of transport. As one shipping agent put it, 'it is dependent on this, whether it is intended to sell the wool in the colonies or not. If it is intended to sell it, then the [Darling] wool goes to Melbourne; if it is intended for shipment to some other market, then it comes to South Australia'.[29] This seems, after the long history of intercolonial mercantilist rivalry, to have been a just and sobering judgment.

One undeniable, though general, effect of the extension of railways in the colonies was the greater concentration of wool into the three main ports of Sydney, Melbourne and Adelaide. The potential attractions of those cities as major points of collection and, incidentally, as major centres at which auctions could develop were thus increased. Moreover, the provision of intercolonial transport facilities theoretically at least placed all three within relatively easy reach of the speculative buyer resident in any one of them and thus enhanced the demand exercised at the auctions. At the same time cheaper and speedier transport had a considerable effect on the state in which the wool was sent to the primary market. High freight rates over long distances compelled the growers, on the whole, to send their produce to the coast in a scoured or washed state which provided a more economic ratio of weight and freight charges to value.[30] Railways tended to induce them to send it to the saleroom in the grease.[31]

Changes in method and routes characterized overseas transport during this period. The development and growing use of steamships shortened drastically the time taken to carry wool from colonial ports to London and, to that extent, reduced interest charges falling on the growers. Until 1877 the only steamship service available was that of the mail ships, which did carry some

[27] Ibid., question 2228.
[28] Select Committee on the River Murray Traffic, 'Report and Minutes of Evidence', *S.A.P.P.*, 1870-1, vol. 3, paper 86, question 27.
[29] Royal Commission on the Land Laws, 'Report and Minutes of Evidence', *S.A.P.P.*, 1888; vol. 2, paper 28, question 365.
[30] Cf. Royal Commission on the Queensland Border Railway, 'First Progress Report and Minutes of Evidence', *S.A.P.P.*, 1890, vol. 3, paper 33, questions 57 and 720.
[31] Railways were, of course, only one factor in the change. See pp. 7-8.

wool among their cargoes. After that date the number of steam-ships on the colonial run increased rapidly and accommodation for wool was eagerly sought.[32] The choice of steam or sailing ship also permitted growers a speculative latitude they had not possessed before.[33] Speedier transport, however, meant that the date at which the colonial clip became available for distribution in England was advanced. The concentration of the delivery of the clip into a shorter period forced an alteration in the timing of the auction series in London and, more important, aggravated the difficulty of preventing seasonal gluts. Similarly, the opening of the Suez meant more than just a reduction in the time and cost of carriage to England. Though it was of use primarily to steamships, it opened a short and practicable route to consumers on the Continent. Considerable interest was stimulated in Australia, where selling brokers anticipated an increase in direct Continental participation in the colonial auctions.[34] In Europe itself projects were initiated for the establishment of direct shipping lines to Australia, an interest based on the prospects of direct wool imports as well as new export outlets. The Messageries Maritimes opened a direct service in 1883. The North German Lloyd line linking the colonies with Bremen was opened in 1887, and in the following year Sydney was linked with Hamburg by way of Dunkirk and Antwerp by Robert M. Sloman's fleet. These additions to the existing services between Australia and England, partly in response to the heavy demand for wool carriage between the colonial markets and the centres of Continental consumption, considerably influenced the European patronage of those markets.

The influence of railways tended to concentrate the movement of wool to the three principal cities. During the second half of the century the extension of English shipping lines to subsidiary ports let to a contrary tendency to decentralization. Lines to England from Moreton Bay and Newcastle,[35] for example, diverted produce from the North Coast of New South Wales and the Darling Downs in Queensland away from Sydney. The ease with which they allowed growers to ship direct to England tended to reinforce consignment

---

[32] See p. 185, n. 18. See also G. S. Graham, 'The Ascendancy of the Sailing Ship, 1850-85', *Economic History Review*, Second Series, vol. ix, no. 1 (August 1956).   [33] See pp. 88-9.

[34] See the London and Australian Agency Corporation's comment published in the *Argus,* 3 Jan. 1870.

[35] Standing Committee on Public Works, 'Report on the Proposed Railway from Narrabri to Walgett . . . with Minutes of Evidence', *N.S.W. V. & P.,* 1900, vol. 5. See the evidence of W. B. Sharp and M. March particularly.

patterns of export which had become habitual during the fifties and sixties. (At the same time, of course, the success of those lines was dependent on the degree to which the interested growers preferred consignment to local sale.) From a different point of view the interrelation between transport and marketing patterns may be seen in the extent to which the fact that Liverpool was a natural port for ships on the colonial run contributed to its efforts to develop a wool market similar to London's; in the reduction in the number of ships laid on from Liverpool after London's supremacy had been established beyond doubt; and in the diversion of ships from London to ports like Grimsby and Hull when the colonies replaced London as the major source of English manufacturers' supplies.

4 STORAGE

Storage, in London, was similarly provided by specialist agencies in, but not strictly of, the wool market. Accommodation provided by the London and St. Katherine Docks, by the East and West India Docks, by Browne & Eagle and Gooch & Cousens was not devoted wholly to wool. The wealth of London's warehouse accommodation (due to the volume of its trade), the continuous flow of wool imports throughout the year,[36] and the non-warehousing functions which were performed for the wool trade tended, however, to make them specialists in *wool* warehousing.

The London warehousemen were, in fact, an integral feature of the London selling mechanism, and their links with the wool trade were often intimate.[37] They attended to the weighing of the bales on their arrival in England and again before delivery to the buyer, and they struck the tare deducted from the gross bale weights to make an allowance for the weight of the woolpack. These were routine measures which it was obviously within their competence and convenience to take. It was also in the warehouses that the bales were set out for the buyers' examination before the sale, and it was the function of the warehouse-keeper to draw samples from each bale for the selling broker and to arrange the lotting of each clip in the manner determined by the broker after an inspection of the samples. Though they worked under the supervision of the selling

[36] In 1869 the distribution of imports was 165,000 in the first quarter, 289,500 in the second, 234,000 in the third and 60,000 in the last. See *The Sales of Australian Wools in London*, p. 36.

[37] G. E. Browne, the founder of Browne & Eagle, brought to the business the experience of fifteen years' employment with F. Huth & Co, woolbuying brokers and importers. A letter from B. Figdor to Messrs N. M. Rothschild & Son written in 1847 and recommending him in these terms is held by the company.

brokers, the warehousemen in fact performed the basic technical services on which the auction sales depended, and they provided the premises on which the wool was displayed.[38]

In the colonies, on the other hand, the wool warehousemen were generally identical with other functionaries in the market. Before the fifties, storage was required both before and after a local sale and while the wool was awaiting consignment shipment. As many of the buyers and consigning agents were wholesale importing merchants they were able to use their own mercantile warehouse facilities. Though the wool season was short, most agents found that the quantity they held at any one time was fairly small and any excess they were unable to house could easily be placed in general warehouses or in those which the wool-sorters and packers were obliged to erect.

Specialist consigning houses became an important focal point in the exporting system from the fifties. Those that had not grown from general colonial commercial pursuits were less fortunate than the merchants. The growth of colonial production, the size of the proportion of it which they handled, the seasonal nature of their demands for warehouse space, and their competition, as a group, with general merchant consigning houses made it difficult for them to utilize existing mercantile warehouses. To store the wool awaiting shipment and to house goods such as they imported for their constituents, they built their own warehouses. Colonial wool-selling brokers were under an even greater compulsion, particularly after the sixties, to build their own. They suffered the same disabilities as the consigning agents in securing access to existing warehouses, aggravated, perhaps, by a slightly higher rate of turnover than all but the very largest of the agents. In any case it was necessary for them to provide accommodation where the wool could be viewed by the buyers. This condition alone denied them the use of the normal ill-lit and badly ventilated commercial warehouse. It was because they had to construct their own, and because the growth of the local auctions forced them to keep enlarging them, that the colonial brokers could boast the most up-to-date and efficient buildings in the trade.[39] The functions which the London warehousemen

---

[38] The functions of the warehousemen are described in detail in their own words in Colonial Wool Merchants' Association, *Report . . . from the Chambers of Commerce* [etc.] . . . *relative to the management of the London Wool Sales*, pp. 7-10 (Appendices B, C and D).

[39] The only London warehouse built specifically for wool in the second half of the century—by the Millwall Dock Co. in 1870—incorporated the main features of design, lighting and ventilation which had been evolved in Australia.

performed for the brokers were in the colonies performed by the brokers themselves.

The storage needs of the buyers exerted less influence on the structure of the trade. In London the wool was taken direct from the warehouse in which it had been displayed for sale and placed on rail or ship for dispatch to the consuming centres or dealers' stores. The problem of buyers at the colonial auctions after the sixties and seventies was slightly more complicated. Those who chartered their own ships or who were not willing to accept the first freights offering were forced to store for some weeks at least. Unless, by virtue of the size of their operations or by the conduct of some other occupation such as wool scouring, they possessed their own warehouse, they made use of normal mercantile accommodation. This involved extra handling but did not seriously inconvenience them. It was forced on them by penal clauses in the conditions of sale (expressive of the brokers' desire to clear their warehouses rapidly to allow a high turnover), requiring them to take delivery from the brokers' store by the expiry of the third day.[40]

5 ASSEMBLY AND DISTRIBUTION

We have already reviewed the methods by which the supply of colonial wools was concentrated at the central auction sales in London, and have showed how later this centralization was splintered by the creation of competing auction organizations in Sydney and Melbourne. This multiplication was merely the prelude to the administrative unification, in the twentieth century, of the Australian centres into one focal point for wool sales. In this context, the essential feature revealed is that the aggregation of supplies to a point from which they might conveniently be distributed was for the most part a function of the growers. The exception to this was the organization of the colonial auctions between the forties and the seventies, when the basic function of the buyers was to provide a middleman link between growers, who were unable or unwilling to accept that responsibility, and the central market. Viewed in this way the colonial auctions during that period represented only intermediate collection points in the marketing system, in exactly the same way as the country storekeepers and the city wool merchanting houses did in the Cape Colony.[41]

[40] This was later extended to 14 days.
[41] See the description of South African marketing methods in F. B. de Beck, *Le Commerce International de la Laine*, pp. 114-16 and U.K. Ministry of Agriculture and Fisheries, Economic Series No. 35, *Report on the Organisation of Wool Marketing*, London, 1932, pp. 66-7.

As important as the *methods* of aggregation and distribution, however, are the economic processes and decisions which they represent —the decisions to sell and to buy. Both present an aspect of disconcerting simplicity.

The Australian wool grower did not generally seek out the buyer prepared to give him the highest price. Nor did he generally design to release his stocks when and where market prospects appeared brightest. He simply controlled a flock of sheep, which he shore, prepared the clip to the best of his ability or inclination, and sent it to 'the market'. The primary function of the auction was to find a buyer for him—a buyer from whom he was separated by the intimidating and incomprehensible flurry of the saleroom; and the vagaries of the weather and transport timed the offer of his produce. Lack of substantial liquid resources rendered him impotent before the impersonal forces of the market, and his decisions were taken blindly in a routine fashion.

Yet, within the limitations imposed by the financial framework (which were admittedly extensive),[42] the growers' behaviour was more rational and deliberate than the traditional accounts imply. The fact that they set reserve prices to their clips may well have been of formal importance only and not at all indicative of a design to set a lower selling price, for the limits set were strongly influenced by what the brokers thought the buyers would bid and, when set too high, it was the reserve and not the offering that was adjusted.[43] Growers were, however, able to exercise a choice between selling privately from the station,[44] selling privately through a selling broker,[45] or selling at the auction sales and, particularly before 1850 and after 1870, between selling in the colonies or in London.[46] These

[42] See pp. 92-5, 116-25.

[43] In many cases reserves were probably set by the brokers themselves (Colonial Wool Merchants' Association, op. cit., pp. 12, 15). The brokers' most frequent exhortation to growers who set their own limits was to 'show a desire to meet the market' (*Journal of Commerce*, 24 Sept. 1883, R. Goldsbrough & Co.'s market report). These facts, and the short time that elapsed before wool withdrawn under reserve bids was re-offered (only long enough for a revised reserve to be advised) indicate that the limits were not genuine notices of an intention to restrict offerings if bids were lower but merely formal restraints on the brokers' actions giving the growers a semblance of power and protection.

[44] T. U. Ryder in the forties and fifties and William Haughton & Co. at the end of the century are examples of the relatively few buyers who operated in this way.

[45] In the 1898-9 season Sydney brokers sold a total of 447,517 bales of wool— 348,062 at auction; 46,299 privately after being withdrawn from the sales catalogues; and 53,156 without having entered the salerooms at all. *Sydney Wool and Stock Journal* (Sydney, weekly), 7 July 1899.

[46] Cf. the deliberation given this question by growers like Cotton (Billis & Kenyon, *Pastures New*, p. 233, 'The John Cotton Letters', December 1843).

choices afforded, in effect, an element of discrimination between buyers and of determination in the timing of the sale. Private sale was, however, an essentially deviant policy, while the second choice was limited to one between a date in the near future and another about three months later.[47]

The choice between a local sale and consignment to London was nevertheless very real. From the fifties the colonial selling brokers, as a method of popularizing their services, undertook to consign to England wool bought in at the local sales under the growers' reserve.[48] Some of the growers grasped this opportunity to test both the markets at little extra cost,[49] and others consciously and rationally varied the place of their sale. In a falling market sales were made in the colonies; in a rising one, in England.[50] In the seventies and eighties, when wool prices were uncertain or falling, an even more common policy was to sell the coarser parts of a clip in the grease in the colonies and to send the remainder, scoured, to England.[51] (The value of those parts did not warrant the expenses of scouring, and the freight on their greasy weight was disproportional to the value.) A further type of choice embodied the same sort of considerations and was resolved on the same broad principles. Though generally this was a function of the consigning agents, some producers (for example a company which did not employ agents) sent their wool by steamship in a falling market and by sailing ship in a rising one.[52]

The art of buying appears similarly uninvolved at first sight. The

[47] The completion of the major railway networks in the colonies theoretically afforded the growers a further choice—that of varying the place of their local sales between Sydney and Melbourne. There is no evidence that any systematic advantage was taken of it.

[48] To a grower whose wool had been bought in under reserve bid Richard Goldsbrough wrote in 1863, 'As your ideas of price are above the colonial rates perhaps it would be as well to ship the wool, which would perhaps be more satisfactory as you would have the full advantage of a rise in England should such take place', and offered a cash advance 'to within a shade of value' (Goldsbrough, Mort & Co. Ltd, 'Unbound Correspondence', Goldsbrough to T. J. Gibson, 13 Jan. 1863. I am deeply indebted to Goldsbrough, Mort & Co. Ltd for allowing me access to their archives in which this collection is held and for permission to quote from them).

[49] About 1s. per bale was involved. Cf. Royal Commission on Railway Construction, 'Report and Minutes of Evidence', *S.A.P.P.*, 1875, vol. 2, question 758; also 'Black Papers': Sir Charles Sladen to Mrs Neil Black, 20 Nov. 1880.

[50] Cf. Royal Commission on Railway Construction, 'Report and Minutes of Evidence', *S.A.P.P.*, 1875, vol. 2, question 658.

[51] Cf. Royal Commission on the Necessity for Improved Facilities for the Trade of the South-East, 'Report and Minutes of Evidence', *S.A.P.P.*, 1906, vol. 2, paper 20, questions 636-7.

[52] A.A. Co., 'Despatches from London', no. 759, 19 March 1896.

interests of manufacturer-buyers were admittedly different from those of dealers and speculators. Within the limits set by the derivation of his demand, the buying habits of the small manufacturer were regular and predictable. His resources did not permit him to stock against lengthy future requirements and he was forced generally to supply himself from one sales series to the next, or over regular periods from a dealer; regularity of purchases and a clearance of stock between purchases was imperative.[53] The dealer, by definition, sought to match inventory movements against anticipated price movements, and exercised a far more flexible demand.[54]

The emergence of alternative markets in the colonies at first diminished rather than increased the flexibility of both manufacturers' and dealers' purchases. Manufacturers who had, in London, bid through buying brokers for wool which they had inspected personally[55] were forced, when buying in the colonies, to place their reliance on general description, reference to samples and the skill of the colonial buying brokers to procure the wools they desired within the price limits they stipulated. Their confidence was often misplaced,[56] and they consequently followed the prudent policy of retaining at least some of their orders for London where they were in full control of their outlays. To some extent this procedure was forced upon all buyers, including dealers, who wished to buy in the colonial market at all. Not only did it provide an element of safety in buying operations but it avoided concentrating purchases, which in London would have been made at quarterly intervals, into the four months (October to January) of the colonial selling season. (It was not until, among other things, the technique of shipping some purchases by fast steamers and some by slower sailing vessels was perfected that a more even spacing of supplies was achieved and a full localization of demand in the colonies permitted.)[57] This

<hr/>

[53] The Sales of Australian Wools in London, pp. 10-11.

[54] This question is considered briefly by Barnard, 'Wool-buying in the Nineteenth Century: a case history'.

[55] One of London's larger buying brokers purchased 25,872 bales at one series of sales in 1870. Only 1,537 of them were bought to order; the other 24,335 had been inspected by the principals before the sale. See Edward Stavenhagen's letter in the Argus, 23 May 1870.

[56] Cf. the 'Raistrick Records', 'Letters to Colonial Purchasers', J. Raistrick to W. H. Chard in Sydney, 8 May 1879: 'Competition is so keen and other manufacturers are buying wool in London so much cheaper than ours that it will place us in a very awkward position, and we consider that our loss on this season's importations will be over £1,000. Your purchases have amounted to 9 to 10,000£ and for such a large amount to be laid out at heavy loss is very depressing to us and we cannot bear to think of it'.

[57] This is discussed by foreign buyers in Australia in J. Leach, Australia v. London as the World's Wool Depot, pp. 23, 27.

tendency to divide orders between the two markets limited the ease with which buyers could vary their buying programmes. Telegraphic communication in the seventies made it possible to supplement or modify orders placed at the beginning of the season as changes in the comparative price levels of the two markets seemed to demand. Nevertheless the buyer, once the colonial order was executed, had to assume that it met his specifications and refrain from picking up parcels in London which could be substituted for it. If, when the shipment arrived, it was found unsatisfactory, his ability to replace it depended on his willingness to treat it as a speculation and offer it for resale in London.[58] In time these difficulties were overcome. Brokers acquired greater familiarity with the requirements of their main clients, and the provision of detailed up-to-the-minute news from the colonial markets in the consuming centres enabled buyers to operate with increasing confidence.

These considerations were complicated by the techniques and problems of buying imposed by the nature of wool itself. The suitability of any bale of wool for the particular needs of any manufacturer could be gauged only by a personal appreciation of its fineness, length, soundness, lustre, colour, etc. gained by handling and viewing it. An added difficulty was the necessity to envisage these properties as they would appear after the wool had been scoured by the manufacturer. As all wool, whether bought scoured or greasy, was subject to this further washing before processing, one of the most exacting of the buying broker's tasks was the estimation of the amount of clean wool each bale would yield.[59]

[58] 'Raistrick Records', 'Letters to Colonial Purchasers', J. Raistrick to W. H. Chard, 8 May 1879; 'Of the 67 bale lot marked "B" we have left 46 bales in the hands of Mr. Jacomb for sale in the present sales . . . His valuation is below the cost price so it seems there will be a considerable loss with them . . . '

[59] Clean landed costs formed an important indication of the success of a broker's operations but until the end of the century Continental buyers made more use of scouring yields in their orders than the English. Tables showing the clean cost of wools of varying yields bought at different prices were in use from at least the sixties (in 1866 J. T. Simes, a London wool-selling broker, sent the Australian Agricultural Co. a copy of 'A Table showing the cost of wool in the scoured state when bought at from 8d. to 3s. 4d. per lb. and wasting from 5% upwards'). It was to facilitate the estimation of yields that a French buying broker in London proposed the use of identically sized wool bales with net weights clearly marked. See P. Pierrard, *The Standard Wool-Bale and the Improvements Necessary in the Universal Wool Trade*, originally published in French in 1873. Hypothetical calculations illustrating the financial losses attributable to a 2 per cent misjudgment of the yield are given on p. 17. More complicated tables, stating the price to be paid in pence per pound in London and Australia to get one kilo of clean scoured wool from bales of varying yield to be landed in France at various prices in francs, comprise the sheet published by P. Pierrard under the title of *French Parities and Ready Reckoner for Purchasing Wool in London*.

6 RISKBEARING

The marketing of wool, as of any other commodity, was attended by risks, and the long distances which separated producers and consumers rendered it peculiarly liable to physical hazards. Some of these risks were, of course, insurable. Marine insurance was provided for all sea carriage, and cover against fire was taken out while the wool was in store either before the sales or awaiting distribution by dealers.

The protection with which the purchasers at the London sales provided themselves followed the customary commercial pattern and presents no unfamiliar aspects. On the other hand the methods by which the wool was insured on its journey from Australia changed considerably during the second half of the century.

In 1840, when all the wool was consigned to England on account of the growers or colonial purchasers, marine insurance was arranged in England by the importing agents, to whom the name of the vessel and the quantity shipped were communicated and at whose estimates the insurance was effected. It was cumbersome, for they had first to secure a general cover and later, on advice sent after the wool was loaded and received, perhaps when it was in or near England, declare the particulars.[60] Even when colonial insurance companies had grown sufficiently to offer their services to the consignors the pattern was not changed readily. The consignees preferred an English company with whom they might settle claims immediately; colonial premiums were slightly higher than those quoted in England; and, if colonial allegations were based in fact, the importers received either a commission of $\frac{1}{2}$ per cent on the cost of the insurance from the consignors or a rebate from the company.[61] Consigning agents arranged cover on inland and coastal transport and colonial storage with the local companies, the English companies declining this class of business from lack of local knowledge. This strict division of functions was broken down in two ways. The English companies established branches and agencies in

---

[60] Cf. 'Black Papers': Gladstone & Sargeantson to Black, 17 Nov. 1866.

[61] The allegation is impossible to verify, but see Sir Daniel Cooper's and Young and Ehler's letters to *The Times*, 16 March 1871 and 17 March 1871 respectively. Brodribb (*Results of Inquiries* . . ., p. 35) refers to the alternative practice of the agent receiving from the insurance company a fifteen per cent rebate of the premium of a policy under which no claim was made. In 1844 the Bank of Australasia was induced to give up to consignees 'the usual allowance of 10% discount on the amount of Premiums and 5% brokerage made by the Insurance offices' in respect of its own policies taken out on wool hypothecated to it ('Letters to London', no. 210, 14 Nov. 1844). It is quite possible that the consignees continued to receive this perquisite thirty years later.

the colonies which gradually led to a relocation of the site at which the insurance was effected;[62] and the acquisition of local knowledge, the competition of local companies, and the desire of the growers for comprehensive cover from the shearing shed to the saleroom,[63] respectively enabled and forced these branches to provide full-scale marine, local transport and fire cover. At the same time more and more of the clip was leaving Australia at the risk of foreign buyers and, after the eighties, much of it was being sent direct to the Continent or the United States. Those buyers were indifferent as to whether they insured with English or colonial concerns, for neither operated in the countries to which the wool was dispatched. Moreover, while English buyers tended to continue insuring their purchases in England,[64] it was then a case of the owner controlling his own insurance arrangements and not one where an agent dictated them to his principals.

The uninsurable risks derived from the market itself. They comprised all the losses (measured as the difference between actual realizations or expenditures and those that would have resulted from a different course of action) which were due to ignorance or misjudgment or to changes in anticipated supply or demand changing the relationship between prices in Australia and those in London or the manufacturing centres. For the growers this risk was inherent in their choice between a local sale and consignment to England, and between sailing and steam vessels. As we have indicated above, (and will investigate further below), both the actual area of choice and the proportion of growers to whom it was effectively open were small. Accordingly, while analytically it was, and must be treated as, a market risk, in fact it had little perceptible influence on their actions. Because they could take so few steps in adjustment, growers who recognized the risks tended to exclude it from their calculations. The risks and the possibility of adjustment, in fact, were unrecognized by the majority of growers, who consistently shipped their produce to the same market as quickly as possible each year.[65]

---

[62] The large pastoral finance and consignment houses found the insurance agencies a profitable sideline.

[63] This desire was sharpened by the violence of some of the shearers and transport workers during the 1890 strike. See *A.I.B.R.*, vol. 15, p. 935.

[64] 'The Letter Book of John Reddihough': H. K. Newsome to Hick, Martin & Drysdale (wool-buying brokers of Sydney), 4 Dec. 1891. I am obliged to the Librarian of the Brotherton Library, University of Leeds, for permission to use these manuscript records.

[65] Most growers would have recognized that there was a speculative element to their consignments, but it might be hazarded that their recognition would have been couched in vague and general terms. If pressed some would have

In a slightly different form market risks were most clearly appreciated and most keenly felt by those who financed consignments. On
the shipment of their produce, growers were able to take an advance
against its realization from the consigning agent. The agent in turn,
as we shall see below, secured a compensating advance from the
English importing agent. The risk which these financiers ran was
that an unexpected decline in values or a faulty valuation might
cause the realization to fall short of the original advance made to
the grower and that the deficiency might not be met by the grower
or the consignment agent. The hypothecation of the wool insured
against total repudiation and the limitation of the advances, generally, to below 90 per cent of its estimated value provided some protection against misjudgment of the market.[66]

The way in which woollen manufacturers, and (before the structure of the industry changed in the sixties and seventies) worsted
manufacturers, stocked themselves with colonial wools directly from
the London sales by buying small quantities at frequent intervals
suggests that the growers, whether unwittingly or unwillingly, in fact
bore a very high proportion of the risks for the rest of the trade.
Nevertheless the dealers—woollen staplers, topmakers and merchants or worsted spinners—were the specialized riskbearers. They
held the wool against an anticipated demand which might change
either in quantity or in quality.[67] Once purchases were made on a
large scale in Australia these same risks were also borne by all who
bought there, whether for resale or for direct consumption. To these
groups the concept of market risks was most real and most appropriately applied. Their attitude was not that of the growers blindly
hoping that realizations would cover 'expenses' and provide some
sort of income; it was that of merchants and manufacturers to whom

defended their consistency on the grounds that in the long run the losses would
have been balanced by the gains. Cf. 'Black Papers': Black to Gladstone, 23 Nov.
1865.

[66] Despite these protective elements Jowitts lost a total of £22,000 over five
years on advances made to four Australian consignors. The consignments were
consistently, though honestly, overvalued and the colonial firms were unable to
meet the accumulated deficits. It cannot be determined whether these consignments were made for growers or on the consignor's own account. 'Jowitt
Records': 'Colonial & Banks Ledger 1877-84', 'General Ledger F, 1872-81',
'Broker's Ledger 1872-81'.

[67] The riskbearing functions of twentieth-century wool merchants and dealers
are outlined in U.K. Ministry of Agriculture and Fisheries, Economic Series No. 7,
Report on Wool Marketing in England and Wales (London, 1926), pp. 51-5, and
P. Nettl, 'Some Economic Aspects of the Wool Trade: structure and organisation of distribution', *Oxford Economic Papers*, vol. 4, no. 2 (July 1952). Essentially they are qualitatively the same as those borne in the nineteenth century.

the wool represented an investment which could be reckoned exactly and about which a statement of profit or loss could be constructed.

There was no way in which they could completely avoid these risks, though normal business techniques could be used to minimize them. From the late eighties attempts were made to establish futures markets through the operation of which some of the risks might have been shifted to even more specialized agents. In 1887 a futures market for raw wool was opened in Le Havre, a city which imported large quantities of South American wool and which already had successful futures markets for cotton, coffee and leather. In the same year a futures market in tops was established in Antwerp, the success of which led to its imitation in Roubaix-Tourcoing in 1888 and Leipzig in 1890. In 1893 Antwerp added futures trading in raw wool. Though forward contracts became common in England,[68] the idea of organized futures markets in wool was never accepted there.[69]

It is significant that these developments took place at the end of the eighties, for there was an intimate connection between them and the shift of the main focus of French, Belgian and German purchases of imported wools from the European centres to the producing countries. The increased risks demanded new institutions. In general, however, their success at least before the first world war was limited. Raw wool cannot be standardized to the degree or with the assurance that is essential to the operations of an organized futures market. Antwerp soon abandoned its efforts, and while the market at Le Havre was fairly active at the end of the century it was never a powerful influence. Tops can be standardized with more success, so worsted merchants, topmakers and worsted spinners were able to hedge their purchases in the tops futures markets. Woollen manufacturers, who did not use tops, and growers still consigning to England (who were, in most cases, ignorant of the workings of futures sales) were excluded from the benefits of these markets.[70]

[68] Cf. U.K. Ministry of Agriculture and Fisheries, Economic Series No. 7, op. cit.

[69] The Colonial Wool Brokers' Association in London resolved in 1895 that 'the effects of the Terminal Market for Tops are prejudicial to the interests of the producer and consumer and affect adversely the entire woollen industry', quoted in G. T. Blau, 'The Theory of Futures Trading with special reference to the Marketing of Wool' (typescript Ph.D. thesis, London School of Economics, University of London, 1942), p. 36, from W. Senkel, *Wollproduktion und Wollhandel im 19. Jahrhundert* (Tübingen, 1901), p. 98.

[70] The history and problems of futures trading in wool are admirably treated

7 PROVISION OF CREDIT

The particular pattern taken by the demand for short-term credit in the export trade arose from the structure of the trade itself.[71] The inability or unwillingness of the large English wool dealers to extend their operations to the colonies before the last quarter of the century laid on the colonists the tasks of financing the time taken to transport the wool from the shearing shed to the manufacturing countries. As long as they sold in the colonies the problem did not affect the growers to any extent. Once the consignment system became widespread, however, it assumed formidable proportions.

In the forties and fifties the distances, and the slowness and inefficiency of transport, both between the pastoral properties and the colonial ports and between these ports and the English market meant that the physical process of delivering the wool and returning the realization took at least from four to seven months. To that period must be added the possibility of delay in effecting a sale in London. The auctions were held on a strictly periodical basis with few private sales being made between the series, and a clip might therefore lie warehoused in London for eight to ten weeks before being offered, and then a similar period might elapse if it was withdrawn from sale under grower's reserve. Though the time was gradually reduced during the century, the fundamental problem remained down to 1900.

This delay of up to nine or ten months before the remittance was received affected the growers with varying intensity. The wealthier could ignore it, shipping the wool without anticipating the realization in any way. Those who sold in the colonial markets avoided the worst of the delay. The vast majority of the growers who consigned their clips, on the other hand, were governed by the problems associated with a delayed 'harvest income'. Income was received many months after the year's production was completed; major disbursements fell due at inconvenient times throughout the year; their liquid resources were small in relation both to those expenses and to the value of their produce; and the opportunities for sideline production by which their funds might be augmented were limited. In the forties and fifties, when the consignment system was becoming general, they were restricted to the sale of surplus and fat stock

in Blau, op. cit.; F. B. de Beck, *Le Commerce International de la Laine*, pp. 79-80; R. Delaby, *Le Marché International de la Laine*, pp. 194-6; J. G. Smith, *Organised Produce Markets* (London, 1922), pp. 167-74.

[71] Long-term financing was extremely important in the development of the market but was not a function of it. It will be considered in chs. 5 and 6.

and the production of tallow. From the fifties mixed farming, and from the nineties frozen meat for export, widened the range.

For the grower who consigned there were two ways in which this period of delay could be financed. If he arranged the consignment himself, without the intervention of a colonial agent, he could draw on his English consignee and discount the draft, generally secured by the shipping documents, either with the banks or with merchants requiring sterling exchange.[72] This method of export, as has been indicated above, was already becoming unusual by the forties, and discounted growers' drafts therefore played only a minor role in financing exports. Alternatively, the grower could obtain an advance against the realization from a consigning agent, thus shifting the problem from the grower to the agent.[73]

This did not embarrass the agents before the forties, for their advances were made in the form of a long-dated bill handed to the grower who negotiated it as personal paper.[74] When these notes were replaced by cash in the early forties they transferred the burden by drawing on the importing agents and discounting the bill. Exceptions to this were provided by those agents who shipped wool for the growers mainly as a means of remitting funds to England (and who were not, therefore, seeking accommodation to cover their expenditure) and by those to whom remittances to cover the advances were sent prior to the beginning of the season.[75]

The English agents, then, secured the short-term export credit in the trade. Their names were used on the documents which

---

[72] E.g. 'Black Papers': Gladstone & Sargeantson to Black, 6 Jan. 1844.

[73] The security for the advance varied from lender to lender and changed as the century progressed. Notes of hand and liens on wool were the two most common, though notes became less common after the forties. A letter of authority was presumably taken by the agent to enable him to draw against produce which was not necessarily hypothecated to him.

[74] 'Black Papers': Black to Gladstone, 25 June 1845: 'You are already aware of the change that has taken place in the system of making advances on wool here; before I went home (1842) it was done by Bills drawn by the Mercht. or his Constituents or Connections at home. This bill he handed to the Woolgrower in exchange for his wool in the name of the advances, and the wool he consigned to his connection in London. Now the advances are made in cash.' The interpretation of this sentence depends on one word in the manuscript. The word 'or' in the phrase 'or his Constituents' may be 'on'. The second meaning is possible but less likely; it would imply that the bills were bills of exchange, founded on the wool, which were handed to the growers (without bills of lading?) to be discounted by him.

[75] 'Black Papers': Gladstone & Sargeantson to Black, 28 June 1845: 'We enclose Heywood's Bills for Five thousand pounds . . . and engage further to accept five thousand pounds . . . in all ten thousand pounds which we request you to use for the purposes of making advances on consignments of wool to our care'.

enabled the colonists, whether growers or agents, to acquire cash long before the realization of the wool; and they were the ones on whom fell the contingent liability of meeting the bills before the sale.

This liability was not one which they relished. The wool ships arrived fairly soon after the drafts, which were sent by speedier mail ships, and as the usance was sixty days[76] and the sales held quarterly, many bills did not fall due until after the importer had realized the consignment. If the bills were unencumbered he was, therefore, able to meet them from the proceeds. The importer's course was more complicated when the bill fell due before the sale or when the colonial agent was forced to attach the shipping documents to it before discounting it with the bank. The importers were often unable or unwilling to lay out their own funds. In the years before the trade became specialized the resources which each importer could earmark for the wool trade were small, and when the scale of enterprise and the degree of concentration had grown large, importers preferred to invest their funds at the higher colonial interest rates.

They consequently sought outside accommodation. When the bill fell due before the sale, overdrafts were obtained from the banks,[77] on the security of the importer's name or other assets, or advances were taken from a wool-selling broker in return, among other things, for an undertaking to use his services at the auctions.[78] Banks retained their security in discounted bills by witholding the bill of lading, without which the importer could not take delivery of the wool, until the bill had been met or they were satisfied it would be paid. Some importers may have enjoyed such good relations with the Anglo-Australian banks that the documents were released on their unsupported acceptance of the draft; they might have secured credit to the amount of the draft, that is, on their names alone.[79] Others obtained access to the wool after the drafts were endorsed by acceptance houses, for this enabled the banks to rediscount the bills

[76] In 1870 some Melbourne merchants suggested that it should be extended to ninety days, comparing the wool trade unfavourably with the China and India trades with their long bills and the continuous sale of their produce. A longer bill, it was argued, would mean that the wool could *always* be realized before the due date. The proposal was not endorsed by the Melbourne Chamber of Commerce to whom it was addressed. See *Argus*, 13 June 1870.

[77] Cf. 'Jowitt Records', 'Private Business Letters, No. 2', R. B. Jowitt to Manager, Bradford Old Bank, 24 Jan. 1901.

[78] *The Sales of Australian Wools in London*, pp. 131-2.

[79] There is no indication that the substitution of warehouse warrants for bills of lading, either directly or indirectly as security for bills of exchange, was possible before the end of the century.

on the London short-term market. Failing these two avenues the importers could re-finance the shipments by borrowing either from their banks or wool-selling brokers, on the security of the wool, their names or other assets.[80] It was obviously better, however, if they could avoid the supplementary interest charges of a loan and have to meet merely the commission charges of an acceptance house or the bank. The ability to do this increased with the scale of the importer's business and the degree to which he was specialized in receiving wool consignments, and this pressure provides part of the explanation of the concentration of the trade in England after the fifties. In fact, by the third quarter of the century the links between specialized importers and the banking and acceptance houses were sometimes very close indeed.[81]

At the same time, not all discounted bills did have the bills of lading attached to them. The policy of the banks in the colonies varied in the thirties and forties. In 1836 the plea of the Hobart Branch of the Bank of Australasia that it might buy bills of exchange on London without taking the shipping documents was refused by the Inspector and Court of Directors, despite the support urged for it by Jacob Montefiore who thought that Sydney merchants would also object to surrendering them.[82] On the other hand the Commercial Bank, whose twelve local directors were all interested in wool shipments,[83] may well have permitted the practice to at least a select group of favourites. In at least the early years of their foreign exchange operations the banks discounted bills guaranteed under letters of credit from the head offices without taking security over the bills of lading.[84] In other cases consigning agents' discount accounts, through which the proceeds of negotiated

---

[80] When importers borrowed from wool-selling brokers or others against the bills of lading (cf. 'The Letter Book of John Reddihough': H. K. Newsome to Willans & Overbury, 6 March 1890) they appear to have used the normal sixty-day bills and not the sight drafts nowadays associated with re-financed shipments.

[81] The London Board of the Australasian Agency & Banking Corporation Ltd, with which R. Goldsbrough & Co. amalgamated, included J. C. Dimsdale of the banking firm of Dimsdale, Fowler, Barnard & Dimsdale; James Alexander of Redfern, Alexander & Co., was a director of the Bank of Australasia; F. J. Sargood, associated with Sargood, King & Sargood, was a director of the Consolidated Discount Co. Ltd; A. L. Elder and J. L. Montefiore were both on the London branch board of the Queensland National Bank; and Edward Hamilton was Governor of the Australian Agricultural Co. and a director of the Bank of Australasia.

[82] Bank of Australasia, 'Letters to London', 12 March 1836; 'Inspector's Letter Book', 13 Dec. 1836.

[83] Bank of Australasia, 'Letters to London', 18 Feb. 1845, para. 6.

[84] Ibid., 16 Nov. 1844.

drafts were passed, were occasionally partly secured in bulk by the deposit of liens on wool, stock mortgages, or the growers' personal notes, leaving unattached the individual shipping documents.[85] Another important exception to the bank's general rule was their willingness to discount drafts without hypothecating the produce, providing they were endorsed with two good colonial names.[86]

The specialization and concentration of the agency business after the fifties enabled large firms to operate discount accounts secured by other assets or perhaps by their names alone. This development supplemented the similar one in England in the solution of the problem of providing funds for the colonists' advances without at the same time embarrassing the English importing agents. The large specialized English concerns whose colonial correspondents included large numbers of relatively small concerns were able to utilize their connections in the London money market to meet the banks' demands for satisfaction. Large colonial firms were able to discount clean bills which taxed the consignees only if they fell due before the sale.

The provision of finance for woolbuyers in London was less complex. Dealers operating at the sales operated on credit made available by their local banks,[87] London discount and acceptance houses,[88] and wool-selling brokers,[89] to all of whom the transactions represented merely normal commercial procedures. Manufacturers who bought directly from the saleroom were similarly provided for by financial institutions and, especially in the case of European buyers, were also able to obtain credit from buying brokers through whom they purchased.[90] Other manufacturers bought from dealers at lengthy credit.[91]

When we turn from wool exported under consignment to wool sold in the colonies the same parallelism between financial services to the grower and marketing services remains characteristic. In their capacity as the growers' marketing agents the local wool-selling brokers made them an advance before the sale. The instruments on which they lent were generally wool liens or promissory notes,

[85] Ibid., 22 June 1844, para. 15 and enclosure.
[86] Bank of Australasia, 'Inspector's Letter Book', 13 Dec. 1836, and 'Letters to London', 12 March 1844.   [87] E.g., Jowitt with the Bradford Old Bank.
[88] Cf. 'The Letter Book of John Reddihough': H. K. Newsome to Hubbard & Co., 8 July 1890.   [89] Cf. *The Sales of Australian Wools in London*, pp. 132-4.
[90] Ibid., p. 25.
[91] Jowitts of Leeds gave credit terms varying from fourteen days to six months; with regular customers they were individually negotiated. The whole question is examined in A. J. Topham, 'The Credit Structure of the West Riding Textile Industry in the Nineteenth Century' (M.A. thesis, Department of Economics, University of Leeds, 1953).

although the distinction drawn between security for marketing and longer-term credits tended to become blurred and frequently no explicit security was taken for the advance.[92] At first they were made available from general funds lent to the brokering firms by the banks on the security of mortgages, liens, etc. taken from the growers and deposited with them, and the general assets of the brokers. Later, from the seventies and eighties, they were made directly from the broker's own banking department, the funds in which formed part of the firm's capital (and were even augmented sometimes by deposits)[93] and which were perhaps backed by a non-specific bank overdraft.

Colonial purchasers at the local auctions who sent their wool to England for resale at London on their own account were financed in exactly the same way as the grower or consigning agent. Complications arose only in the case of purchases made on behalf of non-residents. The problem was basically the same as the one that vexed the relations between consigning and importing agents. Wool-selling brokers demanded payment before the wool left their stores and, unlike their London counterparts who could accept bills endorsed by acceptance houses, they insisted on cash. The wool-buying brokers through whom the non-residents purchased had insufficient resources of their own and commanded insufficient credit, at least before the end of the seventies, to meet any extensive purchases without aid. Their initial problem, therefore, was to find enough funds to cover the operations of the first fortnight or so of each selling season. Subsequent purchases might then be made with the proceeds of the drafts negotiated against those early shipments. For the branches of English and foreign buying houses which operated in this fashion the problem was solved by the dispatch of remittances. Australian firms buying for foreigners were forced to seek remittances from some of their customers or to use for this purpose the proceeds of goods consigned to them by their customers for sale in the colonies.[94] By the time the colonial auctions had become firmly established in the eighties and nineties the buying firms were able to rely more on their internal resources and bank credit to tide them over the first of the season's purchases.[95] It was not

---

[92] See ch. 6.
[93] Many of the large pastoral finance and wool broking concerns like R. Goldsbrough & Co. advertised for deposits in the eighties. See pp. 162-4.
[94] W. H. Chard, woolbuying broker of Sydney, for example, sold cloths for J. Raistrick, a woollen manufacturer for whom he bought. See 'Raistrick Records', *passim*.
[95] Nevertheless some firms found it necessary to obtain credit from other

until pre-shipment finance under letters of credit was developed towards the end of our period, however, that this difficulty, and the expenses of a remittance, were completely overcome.

To finance subsequent shipments the buyer had to depend on discounting drafts which were drawn, almost universally, under letters of credit established by the non-resident through the London office of an Australian bank.[96] This proved as embarrassing to the overseas client as it had to the agents who received the growers' consignments. To obtain access to the wool the support of acceptance houses, banks or other institutions was needed. While they were specialized financial riskbearers these bodies were, at first at least, less intimately connected with the affairs of wool textile manufacturers than the English dealers and London wool-selling brokers. In addition, Continental buyers were forced to transact their exchange operations through London where, whatever their size and importance in their homeland, they were known only to wool-buying brokers.[97] The central role played by the Australian and Anglo-Australian banks in the techniques of financing wool purchases led eventually to their acquisition of an unrivalled, highly detailed, and specialized knowledge of firms importing wool from Australia. Another problem arose from the fact that the drafts, being sent by mail ship, fell due before the wool could undergo any extensive processing. This proved a handicap and deterrent, particularly to those smaller woollen manufacturers who preferred to pay the bills out of the proceeds of the maufactured goods, and to a slighter degree to topmakers and worsted spinners. It was overcome, to some extent, by the development of techniques which substituted other securities for the bills of lading and extended the credit beyond the currency of the bills of exchange.

It is evident, then, that the form in which export credit was provided depended on the method of marketing. As long as the growers con-

---

sources. D. & W. Gibb, who bought in Melbourne for speculative resale in London, obtained cash credits from Jowitts (to whom they consigned) through Jowitt's Melbourne branch, 'Jowitt Records', 'Private Business Letters No. 2', R. B. Jowitt to T. S. Beaumont, 21 Dec. 1900.

[96] Letters of authority drawn on London acceptance houses served the same purpose as a letter of credit and were used occasionally. See 'Raistrick Records', J. Raistrick to Chard, 1 Sept. 1875.

[97] The operation of the Comptoir d' Escompte de Paris benefited French buyers only. See the directions given to prospective Italian buyers in F. Gagliardi, *L'Australia*, p. 13. Japanese buyers were placed in an even more unfortunate position and their letters of credit had to be ironclad. See the arrangements made by Okura & Co. of Tokyo with Jowitt's Melbourne branch, 'Jowitt Records', 'Jobbing [erased] Orders', p. 116.

signed their clips to England the provision of finance had to follow the consignment pattern, for at every stage at which credit was given the wool formed the security. Thus the grower took his advance from the consigning agent and the consigning agent took his advance, through a bank or some other discounter, from the importing agent. London, in other words, provided both the growers' marketing credit and that required to carry the wool to the manufacturing country in one process. The process was divided, however, when the colonial auctions became primary distributive markets. The growers' marketing credit was provided by Australian sources within the colonies, while the task of financing the transport was left to organizations overseas. In this case the growers' wool was the security for the marketing credit, and the buyers' wool for the transport. Only in the case of terminal credits—those given to importing agents, to buyers at the London sales, and to importers—was financing in the wool trade diffused and absorbed in the general stream of commercial financing.

If, however, London remained the focal source of marketing credit as long as it remained the focal point of the consignment system, it is also true that it retained its marketing importance only as long as it was the only source from which that credit could come. An essential condition of the development of the colonial auction system was the ability of colonial institutions to provide finance on the spot. That ability was one product of the large-scale import of capital into the colonies in the eighties.

5

COMPETITIVE PRACTICES IN THE MARKET

COMPETITION in the markets for the services required by the sellers when disposing of their produce was limited by price stability and standardization, frequently associated with price leadership and governed through trade associations and commercial organizations; and it was limited by the overriding obligations imposed by the debt structure of the pastoral industry and the financial structure of the export trade. The wool auction sales of the nineteenth century lacked the full degree of free competition attributed to them, while the distribution of wool from the auctions to manufacturers was only imperfectly competitive.

These features of the marketing system were of direct and immediate significance in the determination both of the growers' net realizations and of the delivered prices of manufacturers' raw wool supplies. It is evident that imperfections in the market for wool will affect the price of wool. In addition, the contingent weight of the costs of the multiplicity of marketing intermediaries was of great importance. The chain linking producer and consumer was long and complicated. From the grower the wool passed either through the hands of a consigning agent to an importing agent, to a selling broker and then perhaps through a dealer or buying broker to the consumer, or through a colonial selling broker to buying brokers, dealer or consumer. Efficiency and economy in the trade, and consequently the minimization of those costs, depended partly on the ability of the various agents to effect economies of scale and specialization, and partly on the freedom and fullness of competition between them. During the second half of the nineteenth century business was concentrated into fewer, more specialized, hands at each stage of the market. This made it possible for them to pass some savings in costs on to the growers and manufacturers, but at the same time it tended to reduce price competition among them.

Those areas of imperfection in the markets for agents' services that are dealt with in sections 1 and 2 below were also of major significance in subsequent developments of the marketing structure, for they both implied and created rigidities which tended to consolidate the existing structure and place obstacles in the way of change. These specifically structural implications will be discussed at length subsequently;[1] here the practices will be examined mainly in terms of their effects on wool prices and marketing costs.

I AGENCY CHARGES

The determination of prices in the different markets for the services of agents in the wool trade varied considerably. The rewards of woolbuying brokers fluctuated, and the rates charged to different clients varied with the respective bargaining power of the participants; commissions charged by English importing agents similarly varied from client to client, but the differences were confined to a relatively narrow range and the rates were altered much less frequently; colonial exporting agents did not all receive the same commission but again the rates were fairly stable and each agent treated all his own constituents alike; London warehousemen charged standardized rates which fluctuated readily; non-discrimination, stability and uniformity characterized the commissions due to selling brokers both in London and in the colonial centres. In some of the markets price competition between the agents was severe; from others it was absent. Wool dealers, whether in England or the colonies, fall into a separate category, for payment for their services in creating time and space utilities was implicit in the very variable profits they obtained from the sale of their produce.

Buying wool to order was an extremely highly skilled task calling for considerable experience. Individual firms and buyers were therefore able to command different prices for their services. Moreover, these characteristics were so clearly the attributes of individuals, and the differences in returns based on them so clearly indicated the personal worth of the buyers, that no move was ever made to try to standardize their charges. Their very skill, however, tended to diminish competition among them. Having accustomed a buyer to his particular needs over some years, and having had satisfactory service from him, a manufacturer was wary of discarding him and going through the same process with another. Each buying broker, in other words, was able to retain the major part of his clientele in most circumstances. To expand his trade, therefore, each was forced to attract clients from the pool of uncommitted manufacturers who purchased directly in the saleroom or from dealers

[1] Chs. 6 and 7.

rather than from rival brokers. One consequence of this was that the rates charged by any one buying broker could vary widely. Agreements made when the manufacturing industry was prospering could be maintained when conditions were less favourable. Further, by not publishing their rates they were able to discriminate between their clients and maintain those discriminatory rates even under adverse conditions. At the same time, particularly valuable contracts might be made and maintained at rates favourable to the manufacturer. The manufacturers' dependence on the technical skill and knowledge of the brokers may have been of more consequence in the case of colonial buyers than in England, where the manufacturer could always attend the sales and inspect the wool himself before bidding for it through the broker. It was, nevertheless, an important feature of the English trade.

The records of Robert Jowitt & Sons illustrate the extent to which the rates could be varied.[2] Some of the clients who retained the firm as a buying broker were charged on a commission basis, the rate ranging from $\frac{1}{2}$ to $2\frac{1}{2}\%$ plus a forwarding charge of $\frac{1}{4}$ or $\frac{1}{2}\%$. To some extent the differences in these charges reflected different credit conditions attaching to the transaction. Terms of payment varied from cash within the 'prompt' period allowed by the selling broker to three, four, five and six month bills with interest specified in advance or set at $\frac{1}{2}\%$ above the bank rate at the time of each purchase. Clients were sometimes given the option, for example, of paying 1% commission and 5% interest on three months' credit or of paying $1\frac{1}{2}\%$ commission and the same rate of interest on up to six months' credit. Not all the instances of unusually high or low commissions, however, can be traced to this source, and the remainder represent true differences in the pricing of the firm's services. This is shown more clearly in the cases where the firm did not charge on a commission basis but stipulated that the client should accept the purchases at specified advances above the price paid in the saleroom. A typical example specified that on all wool up to 12d. per lb. in price the principal paid an additional $\frac{1}{2}$d., and on all over 12d. an additional 1d. A detailed examination of some of the rates charged by Jowitt is instructive. A sample of twelve agreements, six made between 1879 and 1884 and six in 1885, all operative in 1886, indicates very wide variations in the rates that clients paid.[3]

---

[2] The following discussion is based on the 'Jowitt Records', 'Jobbing [erased] Order Book' and 'General Ledgers'. Specific individual references would be confusing and unnecessary.
[3] See Appendix, Table XV.

On wool worth, for example, 7d. per lb. Jowitt's return varied from $\frac{1}{4}$d. to $\frac{3}{4}$d., and $\frac{1}{2}$d. was earned on wools varying in value from 7d. to as much as 28d. In the selection of the sample examined, care was taken to ensure that the rates themselves were independent of the terms of payment, so that the extent of the variation cannot be attributed to credit arrangements. Nor can it be attributed to the different times at which the agreements were concluded, for the 'control group' of contracts made in 1885 reveals the same characteristic. Clearly, the relative bargaining power of broker and client was a critical factor producing a differentiated scale of charges.

A similar discrimination is evident in the rates which Jowitts charged for purchases made for clients by their colonial branches. Agreements were made in 1888, 1889 and 1890 to buy in South Africa at rates of 2, $2\frac{1}{2}$ and 2 % respectively. To a Japanese buyer in 1893 the Melbourne branch charged 4% on the first £10,000 worth, 3% on the second £10,000 worth and $2\frac{1}{2}$% on all subsequent purchases; in 1896 its normal rate was only $1\frac{1}{2}$%. At the same time Jowitts paid different rates to other colonial brokers who acted for them. In 1886 agreements were made with two South Australian firms to buy wool for Jowitts' Leeds stock, one at 2% commission and the other at the same figure less a rebate of $\frac{3}{4}$% to Jowitts. In 1885 a New Zealand broker acted for the firm at a commission of 2% together with the 5% primage on the freight as a perquisite.

An equally wide range characterized the commissions charged by English importing agents in the first half of the century. In the forties they varied from the 4% levied by Gladstone & Sargeantson on the clips which Neil Black sent to them[4] to the more normal rate of $2\frac{1}{2}$%. By the seventies the differences had narrowed, but within that range most of the large importing agents seem to have charged different rates to the constituents of different consigning agents. Normally, gross commissions varied from 2% including the selling brokerage of $\frac{1}{2}$% (paid to the selling broker in this case by the consignee) to $2\frac{1}{4}$% including brokerage and $2\frac{1}{2}$% excluding brokerage but sometimes subject to a rebate to the seller.[5] In the twelve instances in which, between 1876 and 1893, Jowitts acted as consignees for clips shipped through colonial consigning agents their gross commission fell between the 2 and $2\frac{1}{2}$% levels.

These commissions were not, however, determined by negotiations directly between the importing agents and the seller. They were

---

[4] 'Black Papers': A. McLachlan to Gladstone & Sargeantson, 18 Dec. 1845, copied on the fly-leaf of McLachlan to Black, 19 Dec. 1845.
[5] Brodribb, *Results of Inquiries* ..., p. 19.

negotiated between the colonial exporting agents and the English importing agents, and the gross commission settled upon was quoted to the owner of the wool by the former. From this the consignee rebated a commission to the colonial agent. The net commission received by the importing agent and the consigning agent's commission were therefore dependent on the relative bargaining strength of the two parties (into which entered the future advantages which each would derive from trading with the other, as well as their present relative positions). The dependent relation in which many growers stood to their consigning agents (a subject to be pursued below in section 2) and the nature and closeness of the links between the latter and the consignees created a situation in which some of the growers might easily have been exploited by discriminating tariffs. On the advice of the colonial agents, importers may have charged higher rates to some selected growers and then divided the spoil. By its nature this is a most difficult proposition to investigate. It seems, however, that differential rates were applied by the English agents not to different clients of the same colonial agent but to all clients of different colonial agents.

As importing agents, Jowitts made individual arrangements with each of the twenty-two Australian concerns from which they received consignments between 1876 and 1893. The variety of conditions incorporated was very wide. Only twelve of the consignors were acting as agents for other colonists, the remainder being speculators who resold their wool in London and who arranged their own consignments. Though Jowitts' return varied from $\frac{1}{4}$ to $1\frac{3}{4}$ per cent, and the colonial agents' commissions from $\frac{3}{4}$ to $1\frac{1}{2}$ per cent, in only two of those twelve instances were unusually high commissions paid to both by the one owner.[6] In other words, not only was there no discrimination between the clients of any one consigning agent, but it appears highly unlikely that there was any bulk exploitative discrimination against all the clients of one agent as compared with the clients of other agents.

One essential feature of the charges was: that while the commissions of importing and consigning agents varied greatly, the gross commission from which they were taken did not vary much. Gross commissions were largely standardized between 2 and $2\frac{1}{2}$ per cent. When the importer took a larger commission than usual it was at the expense of the colonial agent, and vice versa. There were advantages, then, in the fact that growers, unlike the manufacturers, were unable to participate in a bilateral determination of the rates

<hr />

6 See Appendix, Table XVI.

they were to be charged and that, instead, they were quoted a specific comprehensive rate by each colonial agent which they could either accept or decline.

Standardization and stability, in fact, were very important in pricing the services of all agents employed in marketing a grower's clip. The composite rate charged by consigning and importing agents was virtually standardized; the London selling brokers all charged the same commission, and the colonial brokers did the same; the incidental charges made by selling brokers and consigning agents were similarly standardized.

In most cases this practice had some sort of organizational support. In the colonies the Chambers of Commerce represented the common meeting-places and accepted authorities of the consigning agents and wool-selling brokers. As part of a wider scheme they approved scales of charges which their members might legitimately make, and acted to regulate general relations among them, to settle disputes among them and to arbitrate on the propriety of their actions.[7] Commissions for paying freight, securing insurance cover, making advances against shipments of produce, and selling wool in the colonies, the selling brokers' receiving charges, and the allowance for tare and draft on wool sold locally were all governed in this fashion.[8] All the charges that a grower had to meet directly when selling or exporting his wool and that were levied in the colonies were covered by these regulations.

There was no formal organization among the colonial wool-selling brokers until 1890, but the influence of the Chambers of Commerce and the Stock and Station Agents' Associations,[9] to which most belonged, helped to maintain uniformity in the rates charged in (but not between)[10] the main centres. Formal organiza-

[7] The Melbourne Chamber of Commerce, for example, reprimanded a selling broker for improper conduct and exorbitant charges when, as consigning agent, he had salvaged consigned wool from a sunken vessel, scoured it and sold it at the grower's expense. See the *Argus*, 7 Nov. 1860.

[8] Cf. the Melbourne Chamber of Commerce's commercial charges approved on 30 Oct. 1856, in the *Journal of Commerce of Victoria*, 9 Jan. 1858, and the comprehensive Australian list in E. Greville (ed.), *The Official Directory and Almanac of Australia, 1884* (Sydney, 1884).

[9] A report of a meeting of the Stock and Station Agents of Melbourne held on 29 June 1866 is preserved in the archives of Goldsbrough, Mort & Co. Ltd. Attended by twelve agents, including representatives of the three main wool-broking houses, the meeting fixed the rates of commission which could be charged on the sale of stations, and bonds of £250 each were deposited as guarantee that that scale would be adhered to.

[10] There was keen competition between selling brokers in Sydney and Melbourne, particularly for the trade of the Riverina district, in which the difference in rates between the two centres played an important part.

tion was unnecessary and perhaps impossible until the local markets had become firmly established, for the brokers' common interest in popularizing the local institutions overshadowed their individual desires for short-term competitive gains. The Wool Selling Brokers' Associations were formed in response to a similar move by the buyers who sought to alter the conditions on which the wool was sold.[11] Once in existence, the selling brokers' organizations in each selling centre had dual roles. On the one hand they became regulative trade associations through which the brokers negotiated with buyers, and which, above all, maintained the auction form of sale.[12] At the same time they served as a means of managing auction sales which were brought together in a central salesroom[13] and later, in conjunction with the growers' organizations, of broadly controlling the quantities offered for sale.[14]

In England the colonial wool trade was regulated primarily by the New South Wales and Van Diemen's Land Association. This body was formed in 1836 to promote wool growing in those two colonies by assisting emigration and distributing information. Its membership gradually narrowed so that it consisted mainly of wool importers and importing agents, and its direction was undertaken by a self-perpetuating committee (drawn from the same groups) which was originally appointed in 1846 at the last general meeting before the Association was dissolved in 1871. A colonial desire to

11 A manifesto issued by twenty leading Melbourne woolbuyers in October 1889, pledged the signatories 'not to buy . . . any wools which may be offered next season 1890-1, by any of the selling brokers of Melbourne, so long as the present delivery charge remains one of the conditions of sale'. The formation of the Victorian Wool Buyers' Association two years later followed directly from this manifesto. (Victorian Wool Buyers' Association 'Minute Book no. 1', unbound MS. sheet prefacing the minutes. I am obliged to the chairman and committee of the Victorian and South Australian Wool Buyers' Association for permission to make use of their minute books from 1891 to 1914.)

12 The committee of the Victorian Wool Buyers' Association were anxious to comply with repeated requests that Association members should buy only from members of the Selling Brokers' Association, that they should not buy in the country, and that purchases by private treaty should be restricted to the winter months when no major auctions were held (e.g. 'Minutes', 26 Jan. and 31 Oct. 1905).

13 In Sydney, sales were centralized from 1863 to the eighties (see pp. 154-5); the task of arranging the roster of brokers' sales and solving similar problems was left to a special committee appointed by brokers as private individuals. It proved impossible to maintain this system but, after a decade of separate selling, centralization was made effective in 1892 under the control of the brokers' association. The opening of central salerooms in Geelong and Melbourne in the same year largely resulted from the insistence of the buyers. (Victorian Wool Buyers' Association, 'Minutes', 4, 24, 25 and 26 Nov. 1891, 30 Jan. 11 Feb. and 4 Oct. 1892.)

14 This control resulted in a significant restriction of supplies only in the late 1920s and early 1930s, when the market was subjected to unprecedented pressures.

7   Wool sale, Messrs Harrison, Jones & Devlin, Sydney, 1881

have direct representation in London to supervise the sale of wool, first expressed in 1869, led both the Sydney and Melbourne Chambers of Commerce to request a widening of the Association's constitution so that it could include colonial merchants and represent all their interests.[15] When it was in fact re-formed as the Colonial Wool Merchants' Association in 1871 none of the colonial bodies was informed of the intention, and the only liberalization in form lay in the admission of all wool importers and importing agents handling more than 1,000 bales a year.[16]

Because the consignees formed the pivotal section of the trade in London, dealing directly with—hiring, in fact—the selling brokers and wool warehousemen, the Association on behalf of its members 'took under its care the whole trade, regulating the sales, warehouse charges and so on'.[17] Its control over the charges made by selling brokers and warehousemen was admittedly imperfect. Rates were fixed by negotiation between the respective trade associations. In formal terms the broker's commission of 1 per cent was set and enforced by the Selling Brokers' Association and sanctioned by the importers.[18] Similarly, even before the warehousemen openly agreed to charge standardized rates and form an association to regulate them,[19] the New South Wales and Van Diemen's Land Association merely approved their charges after they had been formulated by the warehousemen in informal collusion. Nevertheless, however restricted the Association's role may have been in formal terms, in practice it held the superior bargaining position and was able, when it chose, to force concessions from the other two groups of agents in London. In 1865 the warehousemen were forced to give up to the importers the proceeds of the wool left lying on the floor of the showrooms after the buyers had inspected the bales;[20] and in 1870 and 1871 the insistence of the Association forced a reduction in both brokers' and warehouse charges.[21] Moreover, in demarcation disputes with the brokers it preserved for the importers

[15] *Sydney Morning Herald*, 2 Nov. 1869; *Argus*, 13 June 1870, 17 April 1872.
[16] Colonial Wool Merchants' Association, *Report . . . from the Chambers of Commerce* [etc.] . . . *relating to the management of the London Wool Sales*, p. 1.
[17] *The Sales of Australian Wools in London*, p. 62.   [18] Ibid., pp. 18, 137.
[19] At a preliminary meeting of the Joint Committee of the London and East India Docks and the other wool warehousemen held on 1 Oct. 1889 it was formally resolved that 'between the warehousekeepers and the Joint Committee rates and charges should be the same in every respect . . . [and] . . . that frequent meetings should take place . . . to discuss any questions that may arise' (MS. note attached to a scale of warehouse charges in the possession of Browne, Eagle & Co.).
[20] *The Sales of Australian Wools in London*, p. 58.
[21] On the warehouses see the *Argus*, 14 April 1870, and the Colonial Wool Merchants' Association, op. cit., p. 3. J. Hoare, wool broker, announced in his

the monopoly of their important function;[22] and on behalf of the
consignees it determined the conditions on which the wool might
be treated for by the buyers.[23] In both these fields no doubts could
be entertained about the force of the Association's decisions.

On the other hand, it was not sufficiently representative to exercise effective regulation of the charges made by, and the relations
among, the importing agents themselves. We have already seen that
importers' commissions were not standardized. Their treatment of
incidental expenses and returns[24] and the conditions under which
they were prepared to accept and finance consignments also often
differed widely. Moreover, the colonial banks engaged in the consignment trade stood outside the formal organization of the Association. In the early seventies their position was that of competing
interlopers, and the commissions at which they advertised their
willingness to operate undercut the established agents and were,
in fact, instrumental in forcing a reduction in those rates.[25] Once
they had become accepted as participants in the trade, however,
their aggression faded and they tended to conform to the scales of
charges made by the large English importers.

In fact, the control over the charges made by members, which
was exercised not only by the New South Wales and Van Diemen's
Land Association and its successor but also by the Chambers of
Commerce and other commercial organizations, was largely nominal.
As organizations they were either too limited in their membership
or clothed with inadequate powers to set and maintain rates in their

circular of 20 Jan. 1870 that 'to meet the wishes of many of the large Colonial
Importers . . . henceforth the commission for all wool entrusted to my care for
sale at Public Auction will be one half per cent'. Attached to a copy of this
circular held by Browne, Eagle & Co. is the manuscript note that according to
information given by H. Schwartze, a broker of rather more importance than
Hoare, 'There was no definite time when brokerage was altered from 1% to ½%,
but was altered at different periods at Brokers' option—but just prior to 1870
they made their charge universal to ½%'. This does not agree with the brokers'
evidence before the 1870 committee of enquiry (see *The Sales of Australian
Wools in London*, pp. 18, 131; Colonial Wool Merchants' Association, op. cit.,
p. 12; also a letter from Sir Daniel Cooper reprinted in the *Argus*, 13 May 1871,
from *The Times*, 16 March 1871). The note is of interest in indicating that though
the brokers bowed to the wishes of the importers it was not made binding by
their Association.

22 *The Sales of Australian Wools in London*, p. 147.   23 Ibid., pp. 62-3.

24 The disposal of the proceeds of 'sweepings' from the salesroom floors, of
rebates on freight and insurance payments and occasional charges for entry
documents, were among the issues on which importers' policies differed and
which angered the colonists in 1869. See *Sydney Morning Herald*, 3 Nov. 1869.

25 See *Sydney Morning Herald*, 3 Nov. 1869, also W.A. Brodribb, *Recollections
of an Australian Squatter* (Sydney, n.d.), p. 19; and Sir Daniel Cooper's letter,
Argus, 13 May 1871.

own right. They 'sanctioned' charges which in practice formed a maximum, but not always a minimum, level to which the agents adhered. Essentially their function was to formalize rates determined by price leaders.

It is significant that although importers' net commissions could vary quite widely, the gross charge to the sellers did not vary greatly from importer to importer. In this case what was standardized was not the commission as such but the range within which variation was permissible. Leading importers differed in their own charges and were unwilling to bind themselves to a single rate. Their influence in the importers' associations, however, enabled them informally to impress on other importers the same range of variation as they themselves collectively encompassed. Similarly, the Melbourne Chamber of Commerce did not decide on an arbitrary figure of $1\frac{1}{2}$ per cent as the commission appropriate to wool-selling brokers in that city. It accepted and endorsed the current rate which was, in turn, set in collusion by Richard Goldsbrough, J. H. Clough (later the London & Australian Agency Corporation) and Hastings Cunningham, and adhered to by the smaller brokers.[26] At the end of the century when all colonial selling brokers were members of their local associations this process may well have been obscured. There was by then no single outstanding brokers; rather, four or five giants shared the bulk of the trade between them. Proposed changes in the rates were discussed within the Association and announcements made simultaneously by all brokers. The only essential changes from the earlier days were the substitution of four or five for the original leader and his associates and the removal of the discussions from the dining-room to more formal surroundings.

The formal organization of the London selling brokers was similarly not an essential element in the maintenance of standardized rates. The association existed mainly for reasons of technical convenience, for selling from a central saleroom made it necessary to have some mechanism to allocate the times at which each broker took the rostrum. It also treated with the New South Wales and Van Diemen's Land Association in the bilateral monopolistic regulation of relations between the brokers and importers, and governed the brokers' relations with the buyers. The brokers acted uniformly in their charges to importers and buyers and in the conditions on

[26] Even in the matter of supplementary charges and the conditions of sale the Melbourne Chamber of Commerce was forced to endorse allowances for tare and draft at the local auctions of which it did not approve. See the *Argus*, 11 July 1860.

which they extended credit to them. These uniformities were designed to prevent unnecessary and damaging competition among them, and being protective they were restrictive. But they were in evidence before the formal organization was established, and may be seen, from an early date, in the unanimity of the printed conditions of sale which prefaced each sales catalogue. Delivery of the wool was to be taken within a specified time and cash had to be paid before the warehouse would release it, etc.[27] As it happens, they were of a limited value. No matter how formally the Association may have stated them, the more important regulations were surreptitiously evaded in practice—a clear indication that the Association and the brokers themselves were concerned only to eliminate *excessive* competition. The only ways they could increase their individual returns were by raising the average value of the produce they sold (and therefore their commission on it) or by increasing their turnover. The first could be achieved by improving their selling techniques, by influencing individual buyers to bid more freely by giving them advance information about favoured clips,[28] by waiving the conditions of sale by delivering before payment was due, or by accepting drafts as payment.[29] The second depended on the extent to which a broker could influence more importers to patronize him, a process in which both personal relations and the provision of financial accommodation played a large role.

Throughout the greater part of the nineteenth century changes in the rates charged for selling and importing services occurred infrequently and only under considerable pressure. The commission which John Macarthur paid to William Young as consignee in 1819 was $2\frac{1}{2}\%$;[30] in the mid-seventies $2\frac{1}{2}\%$ was still considered a normal charge. For selling the wool Macarthur paid his broker 1%; that rate was changed for the first time in the early seventies.[31] In 1863,

[27] Many of these catalogues from the first half of the last century are still in existence. Those the author inspected were held by Messrs Hughes, Williams & Irwell and Messrs Kreglinger & Fernau of London. Uniformity in the sales conditions, at least among the main brokers, dates from the early forties.

[28] Cf. *The Sales of Australian Wools in London*, p. 48.

[29] See p. 100. The relative ease with which buyers could find credit to conduct their purchasing rather contradicts the thesis advanced by J. H. Clapham (*The Woollen and Worsted Industries*, p. 94) and others that because the conditions of sale demanded cash payment only strong buyers were able to patronize the London sales.

[30] Cf. the account sales reproduced in S. Macarthur Onslow, *Some Early Records of the Macarthurs of Camden*, opposite p. 352.

[31] The New South Wales and Van Diemen's Land Association's sanction for the 1 per cent charge was given in 1838! See *The Sales of Australian Wools in London*, p. 137.

Richard Goldsbrough's charge to the growers for receiving wool for sale was ⅛d. per lb. and for selling it 1½%, while for delivering it to the buyer he also charged ⅛d. per lb. In 1889 those rates were still unchanged.[32] The motives behind this stability varied. On the one hand, the commercial charges proper—the importers' and selling brokers' commissions—bore little relation to the volume of trade. The level at which they were set provided a profit, whether a firm handled 500 or 50,000 bales. Secure in the power which a 'truck'-like financial relationship with their principals gave them,[33] and complacent in the knowledge that their smaller rivals were incapable of competing with them effectively, the price leaders saw no reason to alter their charges. On the other hand, the colonial selling brokers derived positive advantages from stability. The unvarying nature of their charges was rewarded with the accumulating goodwill of both buyers and sellers—a goodwill which, until the local sales had become established on a firm and popular basis in the eighties, was essential to their operation and expansion. Moreover, these commercial charges were not appreciably affected by such changes in the agents' own costs as were beyond their control. In addition to increasing much less rapidly than the volume of their business, their demand for labour and fixed capital resources was so small that changing wage rates, etc. were not reflected in their profits.

These costs did, however, bear a direct, apparent and important relation to the business of the warehousemen, for whom the expansion of the trade meant greater labour employment and the construction of new premises and for whom every change in wage rates held significance. Consequently, the warehouse rates changed far more frequently than commissions for importing and selling. Between 1867 and 1889 they were altered no less than nine times, as increased economy in handling and falling wages allowed, and as the threat of competitive price-cutting by one of their number forced, their reduction, or as increased labour costs forced their increase.[34] By contrast, it required the organization of the growers'

[32] Although there is insufficient evidence to construct a continuous list of charges between 1863 and 1889, the identical quotations in the four specific instances known (1863, 1881, 1883, and 1889), strongly support this conception of a long-term stability. For these dates see Goldsbrough to T. J. Gibson, 12 Jan. 1863 and the duplicate invoices made out to R. Hogarth (31 Oct. 1881) and M. D. Synnot Bros. (24 Oct. 1881), all of which are in the possession of Goldsbrough, Mort & Co. Ltd; the Royal Commission on the Tariff, 'Report and Minutes of Evidence', *Proc. Vic. Leg. Ass.*, 1883, vol. 4, question 23, 879; and the manuscript manifesto, filed with the Victorian Wool Buyers' Association, 'Minute Book no. 1' (see n. 11, above).   [33] See pp. 116-25.

[34] The Millwall Dock Co. opened in the early seventies boasted warehouses of a superior design and announced its intention of undercutting the other ware-

discontent to change the rates charged by the importers and London selling brokers. During that agitation and its aftermath, the New South Wales and Van Diemen's Land Association forced both the selling brokers and warehousemen to reduce their charges, and the action of the colonial banks forced the importers to make some concession in their own rates.

2 FINANCE AND WOOL AGENCY AS JOINT SERVICES, AND DISCRIMINATORY MONOPOLY

A grower's freedom to choose between competing consigning agents in the colonies was limited, in practice, by his obligations to one of them arising out of past and current indebtedness. The provision of credit was very frequently made conditional upon the grower's willingness to use the lender's services as a consigning or selling agent for his wool, and sometimes as a general mercantile agent for his other interests. This feature of the trade, which was a product of the pattern of the colonies' commercial and financial development, became one of its essential characteristics and a cornerstone technique in the business tactics of wool consigning firms.[35]

It originated in the fact that the merchants were forced, until as late as the forties and fifties, to provide the bulk of the day-to-day finance by which the growers operated. This was partly due to the fact that banks rarely established branches outside the main cities until the fifties so that the growers did not have any banking facilities at hand. The main reason, however, was that quite apart from the location of banking businesses there was no group but the merchants to whom the growers could turn for financial assistance. The banks were generally disinclined to deal extensively direct with the pastoralists, and were unwilling to discount 'settlers' bills' on the grounds that they were notoriously unpunctual in meeting their obligations.[36] The merchants were expected, partially in the belief that 'the merchants are better acquainted with the resources of the settler than the Bank can possibly be',[37] to afford the pastoralists

---

housemen. For some years it remained a disturbing element and forced some competitive price reductions. On the other hand, the reason chosen by the warehouses in 1889 to justify their open collusion was labour and wage trouble.

[35] Essentially similar features may be found, of course, in many other trades, e.g. the export of tobacco and cotton from the southern states of America in the eighteenth and nineteenth centuries.

[36] See S. J. Butlin, *Foundations of the Australian Monetary System*, pp. 508-9, on the question of the growers' relations with the banks.

[37] G. R. Griffith, director of the Union Bank of Australia, giving evidence

the credit they needed and in return to receive their own accommodation from the banks. This attitude forced the growers to seek direct from the suppliers whatever credit they needed to purchase nearly the whole range of their requirements. As nearly all the merchants carried stocks, or would import stocks, of most of these goods, there was a tendency for a grower to choose one as his main agent and thereby consolidate the debt respecting most of his purchases.

In return for this accommodation, at least a certain amount of informal pressure was, or could have been, exerted on the grower to direct to that merchant the consignment of his clip.[38] This possibility assumed even more formidable proportions when financing of this nature required the grower to maintain a current account with the firm.[39] The only types of formal security the growers could offer until the forties were mortgages on real estate, personal notes and shipping documents respecting exported wool, and in practice their circumstances restricted most of them to the last two. Borrowing against a shipment of wool, however, was not a satisfactory answer to the problem of getting day-to-day credit. Personal notes were, therefore, the most common way of securing the debts if, indeed, they were secured at all. As the wool was the grower's main asset, the merchant's main form of protection lay in keeping a hand on the disposal of the proceeds of the clip and in being able, if necessary, to use them to offset the debits in his own books. This he could do by handling the consignment, a process which in effect put him in control of the shipping documents.

Legislation on preferable liens on wool and mortgages on stock, in the forties, provided the growers with legally acceptable security for loans, which enabled them to anticipate shearing and organize their finances with greater confidence and flexibility. Superficially, borrowing against this type of instrument might be expected to diminish the importance of merchant financing, for the registration clauses reduced the element of risk and rendered the banks' reasons for avoiding settlers' accounts less convincing.[40] In fact, however,

before the Select Committee on Monetary Confusion, 'Report and Minutes of Evidence', *N.S.W. V. & P.*, 1843.

[38] The various Dalgety companies carried the process further, exerting pressure on the pastoral clients to patronize their mercantile departments.

[39] Current accounts with merchant firms were common up to the sixties at least. Neil Black, for example, operated them with Bell & Buchanan, S. G. Henty, Dalgety Borrodaile & Co., Younghusband & Co., as well as with the Union and Australasia Banks.

[40] The Bank of Australasia ('Letters to London', no. 316, 6 Nov. 1845) indicates that the Bank found the registration clauses 'most beneficial'.

following their long practice of discrimination, the banks were unwilling to accept liens direct from the growers. Though liens
afforded a first-class security, they still preferred 'not to bring our-
selves into direct contact with the security; we always have a person
between us and the settler'.[41] Just as, in the past, when a grower did
succeed in having a bill discounted it was only after he had bought
the name of a second party to act as guarantor,[42] so now liens were
more readily considered if they were endorsed by one acceptable to
the bank—that is, by a merchant. Consequently, while liens were
reluctantly accepted by the banks, it was far more common to find
that they were taken as security by merchants, who sought their
own funds from the banks. They were taken as protection for credit
granted prior to the shearing and for advances made against a
consigned clip. Again, the merchant could best protect his investment by overseeing the export and realization of the wool on which
his payment depended.

Irrespective of the other profits which the consignment business
might be made to yield, this protection afforded a very convincing
reason for a merchant to make past and current debts conditional
upon being given the agency.[43] In this way many growers became
tied to the services of the particular consigning agents.

The colonial wool-selling brokers and the specialized consignment
houses adopted the same measures to secure the adherence of their
constituents. While the logic was the same, the emphasis was rather

---

[41] L. Duguid, in evidence before the Select Committee on Liens and Mortgages, 'Report and Minutes of Evidence', *N.S.W. V. & P.*, 1845.

[42] S. Lyons, in evidence before the 1843 Select Committee on Monetary
Confusion.

[43] Overdramatized, and not entirely just, summaries of the merchants' role
and motives found their place in colonial fiction of the last century. The law of
the sheeplands was handed on by a squatter to a 'new chum' in these words: 'You
must have an agent. Bankers not yet being present in the flesh, a merchant, if he
is a dealer in hob-nails and shoe-leather, answers quite as well. An institution
through whose hands your wool and tallow and fat sheep may pass; the former
finds its way to England, getting in return stores such as flour, sugar, tea and
tobacco, and a keg for shearing and a stray cheque to view the lions in Sydney
. . . If those on whom you confer your favour under the exigency of the money
market debit your drafts on Sydney . . . then there needs be a debit to cover
booking and other trifles which may bring the percentage to over 30 per cent.
Why man, you'll learn to bear it like a squatter should . . . If driven to bay in fear
of that overdraft, why man alive, shear twice a year. Never mind the law, logic
or equity of the thing, but do it. All laws are liable to bend to circumstances.
When your merchant gets hard up and needs to balance twice a year, as a cause,
the effect being to double the percentage, wait for your revenge when the wheel
of fortune turns, in a wet season . . .', J. Mouat, *The Rise of the Australian Wool
Kings—A Romance of Port Phillip* (London, 1892), pp. 77-8. Himself a squatter
in 1846, Mouat draws widely on his own experiences in this tale.

on securing the agency than on taking additional security. Moreover, once the practice was established it was necessary for new entrants and agents in alternative channels of disposal to adopt it. By the end of the sixties at the latest, lenders on liens and stock mortgages, whether those instruments were re-discounted at the banks or not, had taken upon themselves the legally enforceable right to oversee, if not actually to handle, the consignment or sale of the produce hypothecated to them.[44]

Short-term general finance of the nature described in the preceding paragraphs was, of course, separate in form and implications from the advances made on the shipment of wool. The latter was a formal recognition of the fact that an agent *had* handled the consignment; the importance of the former lay in determining who was to be the consigning agent for an as yet unshorn clip.

The specialized consignment houses and colonial wool-selling brokers also extended the concept of 'promised produce' to cover the wool grown on stations mortgaged to them. They were able to do this because their facilities for providing long-term credit, apart altogether from any considerations of prudence, forced the growers to accept the conditions which they attached to mortgage finance. The banks' stated policy was 'to avoid locking up the capital of the company in any security from which we are not likely to derive quick returns',[45] and this determination was strengthened by the difficulty with which they realized properties to which they had fallen heir during the forties. In many cases, too, they were legally restrained from lending on the security of land which was the most suitable basis for long-term finance. Restrictions of this type did not always weigh heavily with them, for short-term instruments like wool liens and stock mortgages were in fact renewed from year to year to form what were in effect long-term loans, against which mortgages were taken as collateral security. This was especially so in the seventies and eighties,[46] when the scale of bank participation

[44] In 1865 the prospectus of the New Zealand Loan & Mercantile Agency Co. Ltd indicated that it was proposed 'to make advances on the growing clip of wool, secured by registered liens . . . the wool to be transmitted to London for sale by the company' [*The Bankers' Magazine and Journal of the Money Market and Commercial Digest* (London, monthly), vol. xxv, p. 658]. A letter from J. Walker, Inspector of the Bank of New South Wales, to the manager of the Bank's Melbourne branch, dated 18 June 1870 (in the possession of Goldsbrough, Mort & Co. Ltd) and the law case involving the London and Australian Agency Corporation Ltd (reported in the *Argus*, 25 Oct. 1872) also indicate the lenders' legal rights.

[45] John Lamb, chairman of the Commercial Bank, in evidence before the 1843 Select Committee on Monetary Confusion.

[46] Cf. the evidence of W. McMurtrie before the Royal Commission on the

in pastoral finance increased very substantially.[47] (This expansion reflected both their share of the capital imports from England and their greater complacency with the course of economic development.) Before the sixties at the earliest, however, their lending on mortgages was not extensive, and the task of providing long-term pastoral finance fell to other groups.[48] The merchants were among the first to participate, investing their own surpluses and acting as agents for local and English investors. Later, specialized pastoral finance houses, using English capital, and other wool marketing agents became involved to varying degrees.

It seems highly probable that merchants and other private mortgagees, and later the banks, frequently reserved the right to stipulate the channel by which the wool was disposed. Large-scale pastoral financiers, such as Dalgety or Mort or the London & Australian Agency Corporation, went further and expected, as a matter of course, that wool from stations under mortgage to them would be consigned to or through their houses. The potential conflict as between short- and long-term financiers inherent in this situation is obvious. It was partly to overcome that problem that the large specialized agencies sought to raise capital on the English market during and after the sixties, for with suitable financial backing they were able to fulfil both functions and minimize friction. One consequence of this, however, was that many growers were bound to consigning agents or local wool-selling brokers by the ties both of past and present short- and long-term debt in an association which, in realist terms, could be broken only by the transfer of the debt to a different firm with whom a similar bond was established.

The implications of this method of providing finance meant more than a practical restraint on the growers' freedom to change their consigning agents. In general, each colonial agent carried on his wool business with only one, or in rare instances two, of the English importing houses, and would not accept consignments addressed to

Banking Laws ('Report and Minutes of Evidence', *Proc. Vic. Leg. Ass.*, 1887, vol. 3, paper 65, particularly questions 1234-7). He agreed that 'fully three-quarters of the business of advances by the banks in this colony rests on freehold or landed security of some sort', but emphasized that it was 'only collateral to other business' and presumed that banks 'would not go into that business direct'.

[47] The extent of the banks' interests in pastoral properties is revealed in the analysis of mortgage registrations in N. G. Butlin, 'Company Ownership of N.S.W. Pastoral Stations, 1865-1900', *Historical Studies, Australia and New Zealand*, vol. 4, no. 14 (May 1950).

[48] Cf. S. J. Butlin, *Foundations of the Australian Monetary System*, pp. 501-2 and 504-5, for an account of the mortgage market and the banks' place in it prior to 1851.

others.[49] To some extent this was a normal feature of colonial commercial activity as such, in which conservatism born of habit and previous good relations tended to consolidate, and distance to preserve, the exclusiveness of initial contacts. To a greater degree it was a product of the mechanism by which specifically export finance was provided. As long as the importing agents remained organized on a relatively small scale, as they did until the middle of the century, and possessed relatively limited capital resources from which to finance the trade, it was inevitable that the contacts which each of them was able to make should be restricted. Moreover, as they bore the risk of repudiation in the event of the bill drawn against the wool by the consigning agent exceeding the realization, it was natural not only that they should have been cautious in dealing with unknown firms but that the ties already linking them with colonial agents should have been strengthened and possibly formalized. Similarly, the colonial agent's dependence on a regularly available source on which to draw bills implied a close attention to maintaining existing connections.

Naturally, both the strength and formality of these links varied considerably. At one extreme stood the vast Dalgety network which carried consignments to the London firm from partnership branches in Melbourne and Geelong, in Tasmania, New South Wales and South Australia. The Adelaide firm of Elder, Smith & Co. consigned to the firm established by its retired founder, A. L. Elder, specifically to act as the London agent for its extensive and varied interests. In other cases, English firms established interlocking partnerships with existing colonial concerns; P. W. Flower & Co. of London, for example, were connected with Flower, Salting & Co. of Sydney; and Parbury, Thacker & Co. with Lamb & Parbury. Others were connected by the emigration to the colonies of one of the family, a type illustrated by Donaldson, Lambert & Co. which received consignments from Donaldson & Co. of Sydney and Moreton Bay. Even in less formal, though regular, contacts such as those existing between J. B. Were & Co. of Melbourne and F. Huth & Co., between James Henty and Buckle & Co., or between W. C. Botts and Ellice, Kinnear & Co., the strength and dependability of the financial arrangements were increased by the closeness of the personal and non-contractual relations between the London and colonial personnel.

This policy of exclusive trading connections was not, however,

49 'Black Papers': Black to Gladstone, 26 Dec. 1840, details his difficulty in securing an agent to consign his wool to Gladstone & Sargeantson.

rigid or invariable. No formal or lasting agreement seems to have governed, for example, the consignments sent to Robert Jowitt & Sons by the Sydney firm of Mackintosh & Hirst, and despite Neil Black's early pessimism he was able to find an agent to consign his wool to his Liverpool correspondents. In Sydney, various agents in the mid-forties gave a choice of consigning either to London or Liverpool.[50] Moreover, the more specialized and highly capitalized firms which developed after the fifties and sixties were willing, in the case of importers, to receive shipments from a wide variety of consignors and, in the case of exporters, to address them to a variety of consignees.[51]

Nevertheless the practice was sufficiently general to introduce a significant area of restriction into the market for the importers' services. It meant, on the one hand, that a grower bound by debt to a consigning agent was committed also to the services of a specific importing agent. On the other hand, the automatic determination of an importing agent by the choice of a particular consigning agent confused the process by which an unfettered choice of the latter was made. This complication to the grower-consigning agent relation-ship raises the question of the extent to which the growers' choice was based on an appreciation of the consigning agents' own services and how far it was determined by the fact that each agent repre-sented a given English agent. In other words, was the choice dictated by a consideration of the exporting agent's competitive position in the granting of advances, the facilities he provided for classing and packing the clip, the ease with which he could secure choice freight accommodation and the terms on which the business could be

[50] See, for example, the advertisements of Buchanan & Co., Eccleston & Hurst and Gilchrist & Alexander in the *Sydney Morning Herald*, 1, 6 and 9 January 1845, respectively.
[51] In 1882, the consignees to whom (as well as to their own London office) R. Goldsbrough & Co. shipped wool included some of their main business rivals—Dalgety, DuCroz & Co., Young, Ehlers & Co., and the Australian Mortgage, Land & Finance Co.—as well as smaller ones. The quantities sent to them were, of course, small; of the 4,000 bales against which advances were still outstanding on 30 Sept. 1882, 2,000 were addressed to Goldsbrough's office, 700 to the five main rivals and the remainder to 'Sundries' (R. Goldsbrough & Co., 'Balance Books', Advances on Shipments, 30 Sept. 1882).
Consignors could, and did, of course, occasionally change their importers. D. & W. Gibb, for example, proposed to ship to Jowitts instead of to Sanderson & Murray unless the latter followed their selling instructions more closely—'Jowitt Records', 'Jobbing [erased] Order Book', p. 63. In the unsettled period following the agitation of the early seventies various small importers endeavour-ed to attract new trade (cf. W. A. Brodribb, *Recollections of an Australian Squatter*, pp. 195-7). These incidents do not invalidate the general picture pre-sented above.

arranged? Was it made irrespective of the identity of the consignee? Was that identity weighed against the relative merits of this and that consigning agent or was the agent chosen because he represented a particular importer?

It appears that, when debt obligations did not dictate behaviour, the choice was made primarily on the basis of the services of the local agent. John Cotton, for example, selected Griffith & Borrodaile and later Dalgety & Borrodaile as consignors partly because of their pre-eminence in the field and partly perhaps because of past business connections with the firm and personal relations with the partners, without any apparent consideration of the identity of the English agent.[52] It is perhaps easy to underestimate the importance of personal friendship and recommendation in business affairs in early colonial days; the commercial equivalent of patronage, so potent a factor in political and administrative preferment, cemented many a contract which otherwise appears irrational. Even Neil Black, with a multiplicity of agents and merchants already acting for him, found employment for Dalgety & Borrodaile after Gladstone had written to him that Borrodaile was 'a most highly respected gentleman and connected powerfully on this side of the water, so that if it should suit you or appear to our interest you may do business with him in the utmost confidence.'[53] A more general explanation may, however, be sought in the growers' relative ignorance about the market in England for importers' services in which they were, theoretically, participating. It is likely that, despite the growers' voluminous correspondence and their thirst for conversation, the finer distinctions of the facilities offered and services rendered by the different English agents were largely unknown to them. Even when they were known they were frequently ignored, for they were considered part and parcel of the process of selling, and over that the growers felt they had no control.

Yet a further limitation of the grower's freedom to choose his agents arose when an importing agent sought accommodation from a wool-selling broker in London to meet bills of exchange and in return undertook to sell the produce through that firm. In practice this may not have been a significant restriction.[54] It illustrates, how-

[52] Billis and Kenyon, *Pastures New,* 'The Cotton Letters', *passim.* This was in the forties, before Dalgety's London concern was established.
[53] 'Black Papers': Gladstone to Black, 26 Oct. 1840.
[54] A bitter critic of the importing agents said that 'in some cases the wool reaches London, and is sold, before the drafts are paid; if not they get money readily from the brokers, with an understanding that they will sell the wool' (Brodribb, *Results of Inquiries . . .*, p. 17). The significant thing here is that in

ever, the way in which the provision of credit established, at each stage of the market, a dependence on the next and also the way in which credit that was conditional on handling the wool tended to rigidify the market organization. The main danger inherent in brokers' advancing to importers lay in the ambiguous position in which each party was placed. The brokers, selling produce in which they were financially interested, could be subject to conflicting pressures: to sell it at any price which would cover their advances; or to follow the mandate theoretically given by the growers and accept only its maximum realizable value. The importers were subject to a similar conflict of loyalties: to sell as soon as possible and extinguish their own debt with the broker; or to carry the wool, and the debt, should auction bids fall below the growers' reserve prices.

Perhaps more important than this formal obligation to sell through a particular broker was the fact that, because growers rarely exercised their right to give specific directions about the disposal of their wool, importers tended, in any case, to utilize almost exclusively the services of a particular wool warehouseman and a particular selling broker. Again the choice of one agent involved the automatic choice of others.

A grower could, therefore, be deprived of, as well as cut himself off from, active participation in the market for many of the services which he utilized. From his point of view this situation stemmed from his relationship with the colonial consigning agent. Loans were made dependent on the grant of the agency to conduct the consignment. Burdened with past debt, the growers could not easily change their consigning agents. There was, it is true, a slight movement between financiers, but its importance was generally slight.[55] The only periods when this assumed any significance were when highly capitalized new entrants made a determined effort to capture part of the pastoral financing business—notably the banks in the seventies and eighties—or when the financial capacity of existing firms grew at grossly divergent rates, making some of them more willing and able to accept transfer business. Finally, the choice of a colonial agent involved also the automatic choice of importing agent and sometimes of warehouseman and selling broker also.

---

making the strongest case he could, he was forced to rely on the device of contrasting the occasions on which this happened with the *implied* infrequency of the 'some cases' in which it did not.

[55] Superficial inspection of the detailed accounts of R. Goldsbrough & Co.'s debtors in the eighties suggests that very few large accounts were transferred to it from other financiers.

This was an obvious case of imperfect competition and one that could have been conducive to discriminatory exploitation. As we have indicated, no advantage was taken of this opportunity. On the other hand, the standardization and stability of the gross importers' commissions were at least partly derived from this situation. To the extent that these charges were maintained at unnecessarily high levels—a fact indicated by the reductions effected, under pressure, in the seventies—then those restrictions did mean that the growers *as a whole* were exploited. The corollary to this is equally important: competition between agents was focused on the financial field. While a core of clients fettered by debt could broadly be depended upon by each agent there was no incentive to attract new trade by price competition. Only when new competitors like the banks entered this field was price competition likely to acquire a new importance for a short time—as it did in the seventies when the rates were reduced in this way.

3 COMPETITION IN THE AUCTION ROOM

We have been concerned in the preceding pages with the freedom of competition in the markets for the services of agents concerned with assembling and distributing wool. Those imperfections that existed affected the structure of the wool growers' realizations. This they did, however, primarily by their influence on the growers' selling costs. Only to a minor extent did they increase the buying costs to consumers or distributors in such a way that the prices they were prepared to pay in the saleroom were reduced. There were, however, other imperfections that could affect price formation.

In the first place, market offerings did not always equal the supplies available in first hands and speculative stocks. The New South Wales and Van Diemen's Land Association, and later the Colonial Wool Merchants' Association, held back from the periodic London sales series (which were held only four or five times a year) all wool that had not arrived in London a specified number of days before the opening sale. In the same way wool was offered, as far as possible, in the same order as the ships on which it arrived were docked in London.[56] These were simply wise, and on the whole fair, mechanical restrictions which facilitated the conduct of the sales. The significant restriction lay in the importers' practice of withdrawing some of their clients' wool from the sales if it appeared that the

[56] Colonial Wool Merchants' Association, *Report . . . from the Chambers of Commerce* [etc.] . . . *relative to the management of the London Wool Sales*, p. 11

market would be glutted.[57] Although to set an example committee members sometimes withdrew portions of their own individual holdings, one of the unknown factors here is just how they determined which clips were to be held over. The colonial brokers' organizations also sometimes sought to bring forward only that quantity which they deemed the market capable of absorbing, although because of the much closer contact between grower and broker it occurred much less frequently than in England.

The effect of this was that sometimes average prices were slightly bolstered for a short time at the expense of increased warehouse and interest charges to some of the growers. In the saleroom, the price of each lot was determined by the buyers, subject only to the owners' reserve prices. Among the buyers themselves competition was not always as free or as full as the advocates of the auction system maintained.

While protection from and aggression against the selling brokers was historically the first and most frequent issue upon which the Victorian Wool Buyers' Association acted, at least of equal importance as a rationale of its existence was the underlying protection of buyer from buyer that it afforded. Among its early resolutions were proposals for reform in auctioneering procedures which would have enabled buyers to identify rival bidders and thus make clear to each his competitive position and minimize the danger of the price being forced up *mala fide*.[58] Protection against dilettante buyers was sought in the attention paid, in Melbourne and Adelaide,[59] to the amount in which raising bids might be made.[60] The first rule passed by the Victorian association, the 'last bidder' rule,[61] sought to protect and encourage low bidding. It implied the expectation that growers' reserves would frequently be above the top bid and that lots would be bought in for which the buyers were in reality prepared

[57] *The Sales of Australian Wool in London*, pp. 12, 34, 66.

[58] It was resolved that 'Loud bids have a most decided preference' ('Minutes', 18 Dec. 1896). (The story is still told of the buyer who had a standing arrangement with a broker that his willingness to top preceding bids was to be signalled by the position of his hat!) Auctioneers were to pause before the fall of the hammer and name the buyer in a close call (27 Oct. 1891, 26 Nov. 1891, 12 Dec. 1891, 10 Oct. 1893).

[59] The South Australian Wool Buyers' Association was formed in 1892 and immediately affiliated with the Victorian association. The minute books from 27 Jan. 1892 to 6 May 1921 are held by the present Victorian and South Australian Wool Buyers' Association.

[60] The maintenance of the ½d. raising bid was justified on this ground at an even later date. See A. Sinclair, *A Clip of Wool, from Shearing Shed to Ship*, p. 66. This work has considerable interest and value as a general survey of the formal rules of the market in the first decade of the twentieth century.

[61] 'Minutes', 12 Oct. 1891.

8 Sorting and restoring waste wool after the sale, Melbourne,
in the seventies

9 Shipping wool, Circular Quay, Sydney, 1880

to pay more than they bid. To encourage low bidding and at the same time ensure that the top bidder (whose desire for the wool was signified by that attribute) should not be deprived unjustly of the benefit of his restraint by someone topping his bid privately afterwards, he was granted, immediately after the sale, the sole right to treat for it within a given period. This definite, if tacit, agreement not to force prices up 'needlessly' did not extend as far as formal rings or open collusion among the colonial buyers. In London, rings were occasionally formed, particularly among the smaller buyers, who, by sharing the purchase afterwards, were able to secure wool offered in lots too large for their individual use. This practice probably had little effect on prices.

There were serious dangers, however, in any auction room where the 'last buyer' rule was applied. It provided an opportunity for two or more buyers acting in concert to claim wool at a lower price than was possible otherwise. As a hypothetical example,[62] suppose there were four buyers, A, B, C, and D of whom B and C were in secret accord, and suppose that three lots of four, fifty and sixty bales appeared consecutively in the catalogue. Buyer B wants the fifty-lot bale so he bids high enough to secure the first of the three lots— that of four bales. When the second lot is offered he remains silent; when no other bids are being made and A appears to have the call, B then claims the lot at A's price under the privilege of last buyer. Buyer C wants the third, sixty-bale, lot and signals his desire to B. The latter, acting as before, secures the lot from D, who appears to have the call, and afterwards makes an adjustment with C.

There was also another, less deliberate, way in which competition was reduced. Differences in function and purpose tended to create non-competing groups among the woolbuyers. This is most evident among the buyers at the colonial auctions in the last quarter of the century. The broadest distinction was between those buying brokers, dealers and local processors who bought only low qualities of wool or purchased wool only below certain low prices, and those who sought quality. This received the trade's recognition and approval in the institution known as 'star' sales. Lots of three bales or less were marked in the sales catalogues with an asterisk or maltese cross (the star) and sold in special 'star' salerooms. In broad terms the 'star' lots consisted of the least attractive wools offered, although occasionally small parcels of very superior qualities were included. Wool from small holdings on which little attention was paid to

---

[62] This example is drawn entirely from the anonymous comment on the rule appearing in *A.I.B.R.*, vol. 10, p. 655.

breeding or classing and preparing the clip for sale and the very inferior wool from station clips formed the greater proportion of them, and they realized prices considerably lower than the bulk of the clip. In this context the main point about the separate 'star' sales is that in the colonies they were held concurrently with the sale of the rest of the catalogue. Consequently, while some buyers were represented in both rooms, in general the 'star' and main sales attracted buyers with different aims. In London the 'star' sales were held after the main catalogue had been disposed of. They started therefore at seven or eight in the evening and again were avoided by the majority of the buyers.[63] The separation of the two sales was based on a very real distinction between two non-competing groups, both of whom found some of their time wasted before the catalogues were divided in this fashion.

In the main saleroom many colonial buying brokers tended to concentrate on buying for the manufacturers and dealers of particular consuming countries or for a particular branch of the wool textile industry. Those who bought primarily on American account confined their attention to the limited range of light greasy combing wools to which the tariff restricted them. Those buying for French manufacturers and dealers sought other varieties which suited the peculiarities of the French industry, while Belgian purchasers were interested in still another group of wools. Brokers specializing in executing orders for the worsted industry, or for a special section of it, did not compete widely with those buying for the woollen industry or for other worsted sections. While their competition overlapped, local manufacturers and scourers, foreign manufacturers and processing representatives, English and French dealers all had relatively specialized demands. Similar divisions were undoubtedly also present in the London market but its extent was diminished by the fact that there were fewer buying brokers and each, consequently, served a wider variety of clients.

The real dangers of collusion among the buyers lay in the possibility that overlapping sections of these groups might informally apportion, before the sale, wools in which they had a common inter-

---

[63] In London buyers were faced, in 1870, with catalogues of up to 6,000 bales stored in five or six different warehouses. They started inspecting them as soon as the light allowed them—eight or nine in the morning—and scarcely had time to finish before the sales commenced at four in the afternoon. It required a strong constitution, therefore, to stay for the 'star' sales. When buying firms did require representation in the 'star' room the task could, of course, be delegated to a junior buyer to widen his experience and improve his technique in the saleroom.

est. It is quite impossible to estimate the extent to which this happened. The only evidence to indicate that it existed at all, indeed, depends on an interpretation of a buyer's notations in his copies of some sales catalogues. These particular catalogues were used, in the saleroom, to record the prices and buyers of the lots offered for sale.[64] In them were also recorded, before the sale, the buyer's coded price limits for many lots. Now it happens that in some cases those price limits exceeded the actual prices at which the wool was sold to other buyers—an indication that he may have refrained from bidding against them. In addition, a pencilled notation made before the sale occasionally records the name of the buyer who was the successful bidder.

The broad isolation of the groups from one another in the saleroom bidding was greatly facilitated by the development of wool classing and grading by the sellers. The fact that wools of the same quality were classed in different groups by different sorters and that one grade name could embrace a variety of qualities did not matter in this context.[65] As long as the lots consisted of bales of even quality, woolbuyers could specialize, and purchase lots of fifty or more bales secure in the knowledge that these could, if necessary, be shared among their clients without waste. Consequently they encouraged the development of the art. At the same time, as the success of their specialization depended partly on the accuracy and honesty of the sellers' classing, they guarded themselves carefully. One of the major preoccupations of the Victorian Wool Buyers' Association was the proportion of bales from clips of varying natures and sizes which they required the selling brokers to open for inspection.[66]

---

[64] The catalogues, used in Melbourne between 1883-4 and 1900-1 by Thomas Beaumont & Son, are held by the Australian National University.

[65] See pp. 79-81.

[66] The printed rules of the Victorian Wool Buyers' Association (inserted between the leaves of the minute book for 1894 and presumably formulated in this form about that time) laid down, as one of the conditions on which its members were willing to do business, the following proportion of bales to be shown (Rule 7):

For Station Clips

Lots of 200 bales and over, 9%, say 18 bales.
,,   ,,   75   ,,   ,,   ,, 15%   ,, 11   ,,
,,   ,,   25   ,,   ,,   ,, 30%   ,,   7   ,,
,,   ,,   5   ,,   ,,   ,, 60%   ,,   3   ,,

For Spade-packed (i.e. farmers') Lots

Lots of 200 bales and over, 9%, say 18 bales.
,,   ,,   25   ,,   ,,   ,, 40%   ,, 10   ,,
,,   ,,   15   ,,   ,,   ,, 60%   ,,   9   ,,
,,   ,,   7   ,,   ,,   ,, 80%   ,,   5   ,,

From large station clips they required only a small percentage in the belief that from a large flock the classer could hardly fail to arrange lots of even quality, while from small farmers' clips they sometimes demanded a full showing. Each buyer came to know particular clips very well and could depend on the uniformity of the classing from year to year to guide him in his choice. The same characteristics could not be attached to wool bought by dealers, repacked, and offered for sale again. For many years the buyers therefore sought to have these lots especially marked with the dealer's name so that they should not be misled by the mark of the original grower.[67]

At least in the Melbourne market there was an extremely loose market-sharing type of arrangement which tended to keep approximately stable the relative sizes of the business handled by each buying firm. This may, to some extent, reflect both the nature and the power of the executive and committee of the buyers' association. Its composition was remarkably stable and during the first twenty-two years of its existence the ten places on it were filled by only thirty-two members. These members, moreover, were among the strongest in the market. From this committee emanated the suggestion, followed throughout the nineties, that saleroom seats should be allotted on the basis of the quantities bought by each firm at the previous season's auctions, due consideration being given to their seniority and standing.[68] Although the salerooms were designed to place each seat within the field of the auctioneer's vision, in fact those buyers seated in the centre just in front of the rostrum caught his eye more readily than others when a close call had to be decided. This method of seat selection placed the largest and most powerful buyers in those positions. At the end of the nineties, as prosperity returned, some of the smaller buyers and more recent entrants to the trade began to rebel,[69] although they had still achieved no success by 1914.

The total influence of these practices on price levels was small. They slightly distorted the transmission of demand from the manufacturing mill to the saleroom and reduced infinitesimally the average prices realized at the auctions. On relatively rare occasions, when

---

[67] See Victorian Wool Buyers' Association, 'Minutes', 22 Dec. 1899, 19 Feb. 1900, 13 Oct. 1902, 21 Nov. 1903, and 30 Sept. 1907. See also the *Sydney Morning Herald*, 26 June 1907, for an account of the Sydney buyers' boycott of dealers' wool.

[68] Victorian Wool Buyers' Association, 'Minutes', 19 Oct. 1897, contains the recommendation that the practice should be followed in the coming, as in past, seasons.

[69] Ibid., 22 Oct. 1897, 22 Jan. 1904.

the last-buyer rule was abused, for example, they may have meant an appreciable difference in the prices obtained for a few particular lots. It is doubtful whether price falls were averted when the English importers' committee or the colonial brokers withheld supplies from the saleroom. The trade as a whole knew the quantities of wool that had been received at the London docks and were able to estimate roughly the size of the current clip still to be sold. It knew, that is, when supplies were being withheld, and it knew that they must come forward at a later stage. The expectation of those future supplies therefore influenced their bidding for current offerings.

6

CENTRALIZATION OF THE MARKET IN LONDON

UNTIL late in the nineteenth century London was the central market for colonial wool. Most of the wool exported in 1850 was sent there direct on the growers' account. That portion of the clip which was not shipped in that fashion was forwarded by colonial speculative buyers operating in various colonial centres which became, in effect, intermediate collection points.

I THE ORIGIN OF CENTRALIZATION

The explanation for that centralization is not difficult to find. Given the fact that, in the early years of the trade, the intimate economic, social and political bonds between the colonies and the mother-country dictated that Britain was to be the consumer of colonial wools, this concentration of the supplies, and its location, were the product of two fundamental facts.

Firstly, the English wool dealers were unable or unwilling to undertake the function of distributing the wool from a point in the colonies, and the consumers were unable to deal directly with the producers. Before 1828 there was, admittedly, no attraction in colonial transactions for the wool dealers. The trade was a limited one, with a mere handful of scattered producers serving an equally small number of manufacturers.[1] But even after 1828, when the quantities of colonial wool were expanding and when its utility in English manufacturing had been widely recognized,[2] the dealers were unwilling to assume the risks and inconvenience of assembling supplies from 12,000 miles away. The wool, therefore, had to be brought to them in England.

Secondly, the scattered mills which comprised the early consum-

[1] Cf. the difficulties which Macarthur had in convincing the manufacturers that he had a worth-while product. Macarthur Onslow, *Some Early Records of the Macarthurs of Camden*, especially ch. 13.
[2] This recognition was willingly given by manufacturers and dealers appearing before the Select Committee of the House of Lords on the Wool Trade, 1828. Their evidence is indicative of a generally changed attitude to the colonial product.

ers were small, and the scale of their production and resources made it difficult for manufacturers to travel far or frequently to obtain their raw materials.[3] Though some of them employed agents to attend the English fairs and negotiate on-the-farm contracts with English wool growers to secure the supplies of home-grown wool they required, most of them used the services of the wool staplers who specialized in this task. Wool staplers were not interested in the imported colonial produce—which at first they were not, in any case, qualified to judge—and the manufacturers were forced to conduct their selection and purchasing themselves. One central point of sale rather than a number of scattered points proved a convenience and provided dealers and manufacturers alike with the choice of the whole clip at a minimum of cost.

That London happened to be the point of centralization was due to its position as the first port of England, to the supremacy of its financial institutions, to its central location in the British transport system, and to its possession of institutions which could be adapted to the trade. For a time, in the forties and early fifties, its monopoly was slightly infringed by the efforts of Liverpool merchants to establish sales of colonial wool on a comparable basis. Liverpool was also an important port on the colonial shipping runs and its merchants held a considerable interest in colonial trade and property. Colonial consigning agents, particularly those who were general import-export merchants, and who were therefore in contact with English firms represented in both cities, offered consignment facilities to both London and Liverpool in the forties and early fifties.[4] For a time there were even short-lived attempts to commence competing auction sales in Bristol and Leeds.[5] None, however, could provide sales facilities equal to London.

2   THE CENTRALIZATION OF GROWERS' SALES

From the point of view of the trade as a whole, then, London was the central point right from the beginning. From the narrower point of view of the growers, London represented the place to which the

[3] Macarthur Onslow, op. cit., ch. 13.
[4] Many examples could be selected from the Sydney newspapers. As early as 1835 Aspinal, Brown & Co. of London and Aspinal, Brown & Aspinal of Liverpool were offered as alternative consignees by Aspinal, Brown & Co. of Sydney. In 1845 the colonial firms of Eccleston & Hurst, John Rostron, and Gilchrist & Alexander all offered the two destinations. In 1854 Crawley & Smith were willing to consign either to Antony Gibbs & Co. of London or to Gibbs, Bright & Co. in Liverpool.
[5] Roberts, 'The Australian Wool Trade in the 'Forties', p. 365.

market was relocated during the forties. Growers like Macarthur had always consigned direct to England. Most growers in the thirties, however, sold their clips in the colonies, and the risk of the consignment fell on the speculative purchasers. The abandonment of local selling and its replacement by consignments on growers' account meant, in effect, that for the majority of growers the market was moved from Sydney and Melbourne to London or Liverpool.

Essentially this change in marketing form and the related change in the market place in the thirties and forties were changes in the incidence of marketing risks and in the provision of marketing finance.

The merchants in the colonies acted as wool purchasers and then they changed to consignment agents.[6] They surrendered their role as purchasers, and by implication their riskbearing function, reluctantly. This is evidenced by their continued willingness, both at the time and after the new pattern was firmly established—even as late as the seventies, indeed—to purchase wool as well as to provide consignment facilities. Further, even before consignment on growers' account became at all common, the merchants themselves consigned their purchases; consignment channels existed, that is to say, to which the merchants denied the growers access. That they were *forced* to admit them in the thirties and forties suggests four hypotheses.

Their unwillingness would have been an appropriate response to a fairly long period of rising prices. This would have induced both merchants and growers to covet the (negligible, and, by definition, physical) risks of selling in England. To some extent this does characterize the period, for British manufacturers were at last appreciating colonial wool, and its quality was improving. A general trend of this nature, however, was less important to speculators than much shorter movements, and the fall in wool prices during the forties means that these considerations cannot have provided adequate motivation for either growers or merchants.[7] There is little documentary evidence to support a second hypothesis: that, irrespective of price movements in England, colonial merchants discounted too heavily the risks they ran, and that the disparity between the colonial and English prices was consequently wide enough to encourage the growers to assume the risks themselves.

6 See pp. 49-50, 57-8.
7 The development and popularity of colonial auction sales in the forties, which seem to contradict this thesis, were the product of the immediate distress among sheep owners and of a shortage of foreign exchange among the merchants rather than of the lower prices realized as such.

It is more likely that willingness of one party and reluctance of the other may best be explained by two other sets of factors. On the one hand, growers sought responsibility for the sale of their clips in England as an incident of their changed status during the period of pastoral squatting expansion. During the thirties and forties the sheep owners, as a class, acquired financial support in England which enabled them to evade some of the difficulties which formerly led them to seek a quick sale in the colonies. At the same time their financiers preferred that the wool come to England at the growers' risk, for they were then in a position to handle the receipts. They assumed that responsibility, that is, for reasons unconnected with price movements and price levels—in fact, without a clear appreciation of the risks inherent in it. On the other hand, merchant interest in woolbuying was not wholly, or even mainly, based on speculation. Wool and wool bills provided an excellent means of obtaining foreign exchange.[8] This motive, too, was one that provided a driving force irrespective of price movements.

It is suggested that changes in the financial structure of the pastoral industry—the creation of direct financial links between the growers and England—encouraged growers to participate directly in the marketing process. The fact is that the squatting movement of the thirties and forties was based on new, relatively large-scale capitalist foundations and that it was essentially, particularly as it gained momentum, a movement of relatively wealthy immigrants— surely one of its most neglected aspects and one that has become submerged in romantic myth. The mania for sheep certainly produced the settler who started with nothing but the credit obtainable on his note of hand, but the gulf which had formerly separated the few Macarthurs from the many emancipists was blurred by a multiplication of the former. What is significant in this context is not the circumstances that produced this transformation, but the way in which these capital resources were made available and the other facilities which that method incidentally afforded.

While the individual investor undoubtedly remained an important figure, an increasing number of pastoral ventures were financed in the form of partnerships of varying degrees of formality joining colonial investor-operators with British absentee investors. Raising capital in England, a by-product of the importance of the immigrant squatter, enabled some of the growers to draw bills on the English concerns. Discounted locally, these drafts afforded a means

[8] See pp. 55-7.

not only of transferring capital for long-term investment but also for securing short-term finance after shearing.

Typical of this development are the arrangements made by Neil Black with his British partners. Neil Black & Co. was formed by four partners in Scotland in 1839. The funds were to be invested in pastoral activity, initially for a period of five years, and Black emigrated to Victoria to act as managing partner. The main accounts of the firm were kept in Liverpool by Gladstone & Sargeantson; proceeds from the sheep station were to be credited there; the British partners were to purchase many of the station requirements in England and forward them to Black, and to arrange and pay for the transport of Scots shepherds and other labourers;[9] and, to provide funds for colonial transactions, Black was authorized to draw bills on the Liverpool firm and discount them locally. As it was generally cheaper to realize the wool in England rather than to sell it locally and remit the proceeds, it was an easy step for the firm to associate the bills which Black drew with the wool exported from the station, and to make the occasion of the shipment an opportunity to complete the documents and to make the wool the security on which they were accepted. In practical terms, of course, there was no question but that the drafts would be associated with the wool, but from the standpoint of the firm's internal arrangements there was no compelling necessity that they should. The essential point was that Black possessed English connections on whom he could draw.

Even where no formal partnerships or shared capital arrangements existed the new class of pastoral occupiers, coming in so many cases direct from Britain, were able to arrange similar facilities with friends and acquaintances in whose hands the conduct of their English affairs was placed and on whom discountable bills could be drawn on the shipment of wool. The merchants' monopoly of suitable English financial connections, based on their commercial relations, was broken. This meant that growers possessed a method by which they could, theoretically without explicit reference to their clips but generally on the security they offered, anticipate their realizations. The remittance delay was not avoided, but the period could be covered by the techniques which this financial structure made possible.

[9] 'Black Papers', 'Messrs Neil Black & Co. in account current and interest account to 24th December 1842 with Gladstone & Sargeantson' (covering period from 22 April 1839) debits the company for payments made by Gladstone and Sargeantson for a hand flourmill, bulls, sheep and lambs, passage money, clothing, etc., for ten men.

These developments, that is to say, made the intervention of merchant buyers in the wool export process largely unnecessary, for one of the basic features of that system had been the transference of the financial burden of that period of delay from the growers to the merchants.

At the same time, the pastoral expansion created conditions to which merchant marketing became increasingly inappropriate and unadaptable. The very magnitude of the quantities to be dealt with posed problems with which mercantile resources were incapable of coping. Only a small proportion of the clip could be bought for exchange purposes as this involved an outlay which yielded no return for several months, and the colonial mercantile wealth was not inexhaustible. When they purchased as speculators pure and simple they were in a position to discount drafts against their shipments, but even this did not wholly overcome the problem. On the one hand, the purchase of the entire clip would have involved discount accounts for each of the few merchants far in excess of the levels the banks would have accepted, for beyond a certain point the risk of overvaluation of the produce and failure to meet deficiencies increased rather than diminished. On the other hand, the purchases involved cash payments,[10] and the proceeds of the discounted bills did not, in many cases, quite equal those payments. The result was that on each shipment the merchants bore a proportion of the financial burden themselves. This did not matter so long as their operations were on a relatively small scale, but to have purchased the whole clip would have drained off too large a proportion of the resources of merchants to whom wool was but one of many commercial ventures.

The re-entry of the merchants into the wool trade as consignment agents developed as a matter of convenience to the growers. The farther settlement spread from the main ports the more difficult it was for the growers themselves to attend to the completion of the shipping documents and the bills of exchange, to the problems of finding freight accommodation for the wool, and to the other vexatious details of arranging the consignment.[11] Their surrender of these functions was conditional, however, on the receipt of an advance from the agent comparable with that which they them-

[10] Until the early forties payments for wool purchases and advances on consignments were made in the form of bills and notes; cash payments were then substituted. See the 'Black Papers': Black to Gladstone, 25 June 1845.

[11] Cf. Billis and Kenyon, *Pastures New*, 'The Cotton Letters', November 1845 (p. 252), for an account of the inconvenience to which arranging his own shipments put John Cotton.

selves could secure by discounting their own drafts. At the same
time the consignment system fitted well the merchants' desire to
retain some control of the growers' means of meeting debt obligations incurred previously.[12]

3   THE RATIONALE OF CENTRALIZATION IN LONDON

It is possible to view this change in mercantile functions in a
broader context. The success of any exporting system depends on
its efficiency in providing the credit by which it operates. Merchant
purchasing declined because it was no longer able successfully to
finance the export trade; it was replaced by the consignment system
because through it that finance was made available. Individual
exporters found sufficient credit because of the closeness of their
contacts with the financier-consignees; it was adequate for the
industry as a whole because the large number of small financiers
to whom the growers and consigning agents had resort, initially at
least, collectively possessed more resources and were able to accept
greater quantitative risks than the small number of mercantile firms
to whom the colonial merchants turned.

It was primarily for this reason that London remained the central
market until the seventies and eighties. The development of specialized importing agencies in England which had close ties with exporting agencies in the colonies served to strengthen the ease with which
credit was given both to the growers to cover the period between
shearing and receipt of the realizations, and to consigning agents
to cover their advances to growers. None of the alternative possible
forms of marketing or market location, on the other hand, offered
an efficient formula for financing the period during which the wool
was being transported from Australia to the place of consumption.
Auction sales in the colonies could not expand to a significant size
during the fifties and sixties because the manufacturing consumers,
on whom such an expansion depended, were not able to finance
imports from a distant market. A scattered distribution system based
on numerous auction sales in Europe could not readily reimburse
the consigning agents or merchants on whom transport would have

[12] The temporal sequence of development has been deliberately distorted
here to highlight the motivation of the change. Before 1830 wealthy pastoralists
consigned on their own and their friends' account (Fitzpatrick, *The British
Empire in Australia*, p. 85), and during the forties a wide variety of exporting
techniques existed side by side: purchase and export by merchants and others;
growers' direct export by consignment; consignment through merchants,
wealthy growers and other agents. The analytical sequence presented in the
text, however, seems the best way of representing the essential features of the
change.

depended,[13] because financial relations between those areas and the colonies were relatively undeveloped and a cumbersome intervention of the London money market would have been necessary.[14] In addition, the London sales organization served the growers' interests well, at least until the end of the sixties, and the concentration on London accorded well with the prevailing sentiments—of 'Home', of empire and of imperial relations.

4 STRESSES IN THE CENTRALIZED STRUCTURE

The centralization of the market in London and the operation of the consignment system were, from the practical point of view of the growers, interdependent. There was no value to be derived from consigning to any other potential market, for only in London was there that concentration of buyers specialized in colonial wools, and there was no large-scale practical means of getting the wool to London except by consignment at growers' risk. The growers' attitudes to the London market and the consignment system were, therefore, very closely interwoven.

Up to the sixties the growers were, on the whole, fairly satisfied with the location of the market and with the services of those who marketed their wool there. It was assumed by lay theorists that the fact that marketing agents were paid in the form of commissions strengthened the bonds which linked them with their principals and assured a community of interests throughout the whole of the selling process.[15] Determined in this fashion, the commissions encouraged all to seek the highest realizations. In fact the groups that were concerned with supplying the primary market were defined from one another not only by the functions they performed but also by the attitudes engendered by those functions, by their relations to the whole market process, and by their relation to the provision of the short-term credit by which the trade operated. In normal times the relations between the various groups of agents, and between them and their principals, were based on and reflected a necessary and obvious identity or intersection of interests. Submerged in this pedestrian harmony, however, were dissonances which

[13] In fact this type of system did develop after the seventies when Continental dealers offered wool bought in the colonies at regional auction sales in their own countries. Its success depended on a changed set of conditions. See pp. 166-8, 175-7.

[14] See pp. 101-2; see also the arrangements proposed by Gustave Ebell, a Berlin wool broker, for the receipt of consignments from Australia in the seventies, (Brodribb, *Results of Inquiries* . . ., pp. 8-10).

[15] Cf. James McBain's letter in the *Argus*, 4 Nov. 1869.

more faithfully represented the fundamental interests and attitudes of each group. These were most vividly revealed at the end of the sixties when, under the stress of a disastrous fall in prices, the growers and others became dissatisfied with the London sales organization and with the consignment system.

The fate of the colonial agitation between 1869 and 1875, the shifting alliances and the divergent interests of the pastoralists and their agents, form an object study in the implications of the centralization in London and provide an insight into the change in market institutions which occurred in the last quarter of the century.[16]

The movement for reform was started by meetings of colonial merchants (as growers, financiers and commission agents), colonial bankers and growers late in 1869. The two themes which ran through their considerations were the weight with which the marketing costs of the consignment fell on the fast depreciating returns from wool, and the suspicion that the fall in prices and realizations was in some way due to the organization and practices of the London selling trade. So great was colonial ignorance of the conduct of the sales, however, that committees were appointed by the meetings in Sydney, Melbourne and, considerably later, in Adelaide, to investigate the actual conditions in London and recommend ways in which they could be reformed. Early in 1870 their representatives met jointly in London and delegated their investigatory function to a sub-committee.[17]

The personnel of the joint committees was a mixed one, including growers resident in London, importing agents and wool merchants. The sub-committee of inquiry, on the other hand, carried a disproportionately heavy weighting of importing agents. That merely indicated a harmony of interests between the growers, the consigning agents, the speculators and the financiers in the colonies and the importing agents and financiers in England. It arose from their common interest in the level of realizations on which their livelihood, commission incomes and interest receipts were based, and was apparently underlined by James Blackwood's declaration in Melbourne that his firm (Dalgetys) realized the need for reform and sympathized with the colonial discontent.

16 The discussion in the following pages is based on Barnard, 'Wool Prices and Pastoral Policies, 1867-75', *Economic Record*, vol. xxxi, p. 275. I am indebted to the Editor for permission to incorporate this material here.

17 It was this sub-committee whose proceedings were reported in *The Sales of Australian Wools in London,* and however unsatisfactory its inquiry may have been to the colonists at the time, the evidence it took now forms a major source of information on the trade.

The first rift in the community of interests appeared when F. G. Dalgety accepted the task of convening the Melbourne representation in London. He made plain his reluctance to accept, unmodified, his colonial mandate, and did so only after obtaining reassurance that a public inquiry was really desired. At first he suggested that it could serve no useful purpose as the action of the New South Wales and Van Diemen's Land Association in increasing the number of sales series in the year and (unsuccessfully) asking for reductions in warehousing charges and selling brokerage had already secured the colonists' objects. That this was the view of the importers as a whole was made clear by the complacent, almost perfunctory fashion in which the inquiry conducted by the sub-committee they dominated was carried on. Though a show of thoroughness and enthusiasm was made, and the opinions of all sections of the trade sought on specific proposed reforms, no attempt was made to come to grips with the heart of the colonial demands. The colonists had certainly expressed a desire to have investigated the technicalities of the trade —questions relating to warehouse procedure and the weight of wool sold, the brokers' policy of lotting bales for sale and the frequency with which sales were held—but they also evinced a certain uneasiness about the whole organization of the London sales. The President of the Melbourne Chamber of Commerce doubted 'whether it was desirable that London should have a monopoly of the wool sales' while others considered that the sales organization was outdated and incapable of handling the trade.[18] This fundamental question, and those relating to the charges made by the importing agents and the selling brokers, received scant attention at the inquiry, which was concerned almost exclusively with peripheral issues. The conclusions of the committee reflect its prejudices and preoccupations: 'Your Committee are unanimously of the opinion that the mode in which wool sales have for very many years past been conducted, has been that most conducive to the best interests of the flock-owners; and that those interests could only be imperilled or sacrificed by disturbing that policy or substituting an experimental one'.[19]

This divergence of opinion between colonists and importing agents was fundamental. The fact that the importing merchants had been asked to reduce their own incomes; that they were the ones ultimately responsible for the sale of the wool and that criticism of selling

[18] See the report of the Melbourne meeting which established its London committee, *Argus*, 3 Nov. 1869.
[19] *The Sales of Australian Wools in London*, p. iv.

organization reflected on their management of their own and the growers' business; and the charge that they had grown complacent in their long undisturbed control of the trade—these were of deep personal but slight structural significance. Their distance from Australia and the infrequency of any deep or prolonged contact with colonial constituents contrasted sharply with their proximity to other members of the London trade. Primarily they were men with businesses in London, not the representatives of colonial clients, and their interests and sympathies were centred in London. They held, moreover, a vested interest in the existing organization of the sales, an organization to which their whole business was attuned and on which their commercial existence depended. Nothing could be more widely separated than the colonists' unsettled desire for *any* more efficient method of disposal and the importers' willingness to seek higher net realizations *within* the existing market framework.

The views of the colonial mercantile community were expressed more soberly and with greater caution than those of the growers. Nevertheless the Melbourne Chamber of Commerce frankly disbelieved much of the evidence on which the committees based their report, disparaging 'judgments and opinions [which] must . . . take a very strong bias or colour from the situation in which the witnesses find themselves placed'. It spoke of a 'highly artificial organization . . . perhaps now unparalleled in the methods of disposing of any other commodity' and characterized the control of the sales organization as monopolistic.[20] It seriously considered tentative inquiries received from England and France about the possibilities of direct trade by-passing the London salerooms,[21] and later, in 1872, was led to wonder 'whether this artificial arrangement is not in some respects unsuited to modern circumstances and whether the violent oscillations of the price of wool during the last two years . . . may not be reasonably attributed to some extent to the artificial restriction of the sale of the article'.[22] It attacked, in other words, the periodicity of the sales series which was one of the basic features of the London organization and approved, by implication, the colonial practice of selling right throughout the period wool arrived in port. Less restrained growers, who were becoming increasingly articulate and availing themselves of the polemical opportunities of the newspaper columns, showed even less enthusiasm for the London organization. They adopted the theme of Sir Daniel Cooper's dissenting report on the London inquiry: '. . . if you rely on aid from this [English]

[20] *Argus*, 13 June 1870.   [21] Ibid., 17 Aug. 1870.   [22] Ibid., 27 March 1872.

side, you may expect much but will obtain little'.[23] It was they who fanned the embers of the agitation once again in 1871 by presenting a memorial of repeated and new demands to the Colonial Wool Merchants' Association.

Once again the difference in attitudes stemmed from a fundamental variance of interests. The merchants had taken the initial steps in the agitation in 1869—the public meetings in Sydney were convened by a group of merchants, and in Melbourne by the Chamber of Commerce. Their participation in marketing problems arose out of their interests as consigning agents in commission earnings and therefore in the gross realizations at the sales, from their interest as growers and speculators in the net realizations, and from their interest as financiers in the ability of the growers to meet their long-term debt obligations. Consequently, the aspects of the London market which, above all, attracted their attention were the number of sales series, warehousing, taring and weighing, lotting and sales techniques—that is, those practices that could be adjusted either to lower the (narrowly defined) selling costs or to stimulate bidding at the auctions. Part of their interest in market reform evaporated with the recovery of wool prices in the 1871-2 season. But even at the height of their indignation, in 1870, it was evident that a strong, even if temporary, antagonism to the conduct and nature of the London sales was repressed, if not rendered impotent, by some deeper overriding commitment to it.

In fact, the colonial mercantile community *was* committed to the London market system however much verbal dissatisfaction it expressed and however longing the glances cast at possible alternatives. As speculators buying at the local auctions, their contacts lay almost exclusively with the London auction sales; as consigning agents their contacts lay in England, and their very existence depended on the continuance of some method of overseas disposal at the growers' risk; and as intermediaries in the provision of short-term export credit they realized that only from or through London could that credit be secured.

To the extent of that fundamental dependence on London the merchant consigning agents shared a common interest with the specialized consignment houses with English offices. It is significant, however, that the leadership of the colonial agitation rested in the hands of the former. The specialized houses were, of course, even more deeply committed to the existing system than the merchants, and after the initial appearance of Blackwood at the 1869 meeting

[23] *Sydney Morning Herald*, 23 May 1870.

in Melbourne they played no further part. Their businesses were directed, even more explicitly than those of the merchants, to London. The banks, similarly, held aloof from the movement. Some, as branches of English concerns which acted as importing agents, were unable to take any independent attitudes at all for all their relations with other consigning agents and other groups interested in marketing were determined by the attitudes taken in London or by what was appropriate to the interests and conditions of the London office. Others, Australian concerns, sought a reduction of selling costs—particularly warehouse charges and brokerage—but their profits were dependent on the continued use of London as a selling centre.

The growers continued their movement for market reform until the middle years of the decade. They included among their activities, however, exploratory moves of a more revolutionary nature. W. A. Brodribb, as president of the Pastoral Chamber of the Riverina, made extensive enquiries about the possibility of consigning wool direct to auction sales in Germany and Belgium.[24] Belgian interests in Australia made use of the opportunity to try and popularize the Antwerp sales,[25] and in the colonies themselves some pastoral figures like Brodribb were making trials of the local auction organizations.

The predominant interest of the colonial selling brokers, the group which stood to gain most from the agitation, was partly hidden during these years. Their basic objective was to increase local sales at the expense of consignments to England and they were therefore fundamentally opposed to the interests of the importing agents and the colonial consignment agents. Their use of the opportunities which the agitation provided for them was, however, limited to intermittent propaganda avoiding explicit reference to the causes of the dispute and drawing attention only to the general advantages of colonial auctions. Towards the end of the interchange of memorials and reports which constituted the agitation they did, it is true, attempt to attract growers by abolishing one of the conditions of sale to whose inclusion in London exception had been taken. The reactions of the colonial buyers to this move provide an interesting commentary on their attitude to marketing questions. They had joined in the initial movement for reform in London because, as speculators, they were disturbed by the low prices and the heavy marketing costs. When, however, the same approach was applied to

[24] Brodribb, *Results of Inquiries* . . ., pp. 8-14, 21, 27-30, 43.
[25] Renard Bros. & Co., *Antwerp Versus London as a Market for Australian Wool.*

the local market in which they appeared as buyers they were not content with a compensating variation in the conditions of sale which reduced their costs; instead, they struck a year later to have the reform revoked.

The reasons for the timidity of the local selling brokers during this period are to be found in their still divided nature. Though their historic role lay in developing the local auctions, at this time the largest of them—T. S. Mort in Sydney, R. Goldsbrough, the London and Australian Agency Corporation Ltd, and Hastings Cunningham Ltd in Melbourne—still consigned a large quantity of wool to England for their constituents, and to this extent their interests were those of other consigning agents. They did not depend wholly on the London market, but the local sales organization was still insufficiently developed for them to display the antagonism to London that their broking role logically demanded.

The picture that emerged during these five or six years, then, is of widespread dissatisfaction with the London sales organization, with London as a centralized market, and even with the consignment system. The degree of the dissatisfaction varied with the nature and basic interests of the market participants. The particular divergences of attitudes revealed were partly those which were appropriate to a time of stress. At other periods they were submerged or distorted by other tensions and preoccupations. The differences between the views of the growers and most of their marketing agents, it is submitted, however, were ones that remained real and significant even after harmony between them had apparently been restored.

5 THE PRE-CONDITIONS OF MARKET RELOCATION

The essential lesson of the market reform movement, however, was that no matter how anxious growers may have been to change the marketing methods and alter the channels of wool disposal, they were powerless to break out of the framework of the London sales based on growers' consignments. In the process of making the centralization effective and efficient, groups had emerged which had a vested interest in maintaining the existing institutions. These groups, moreover, held all the power.

The major specialized consignment and importing agencies were also the main sources of both short-term export credit and long-term developmental credit for the pastoral industry. Being dependent on them, the growers were obliged broadly to follow their dictates in the disposal of the wool which secured the credits. These concerns were centred on London. Their finance and the wool trade provided a two-way complementary flow, into the orbit of which the merchant consigning houses were pulled even against their will. The banks that engaged in the consignment business did so partly to acquire a foreign exchange more readily, and partly to gain the consigning agent's commission. Like the banks which were English concerns, with their financial roots in England, they too centred their trade on London, and even today continue as the largest importing agents.

The development of the colonial auctions and their ability to compete effectively with London—the possibility of a relocation of the market back to the colonies—was dependent therefore on a basic readjustment of the financial structure of the wool trade. It was necessary that institutions should develop which could finance, within the colonial framework, the growers' demand for pre-sale credit; that credit, that is to say, had to be divorced from the necessity of drawing discountable bills on foreign importing agents. At the same time changes in financial organization, communications and the structure of textile firms were essential to enable buyers to operate in the colonies with efficiency, a minimum of risk, and the ability to finance the transport of the wool from the colonies to the consuming countries. Without these changes and without the development of efficient and firmly established selling institutions in the colonies, no amount of willingness would have sufficed to bring producers and consumers together on a large scale within Australia.

These changes and that relocation did occur in the last quarter of the century, and to their discussion the following chapter is devoted.

7

THE RELOCATION OF THE MARKET IN AUSTRALIA

REGULAR, frequent, auction sales of wool began in Sydney and Melbourne in the late forties and early fifties; by the end of the century half the Australian clip was sold through auctions held in Sydney, Melbourne, Geelong, Adelaide and Hobart. By the beginning of the first world war nearly 70 per cent of the output—1,703,744 bales—was disposed of in those cities and in Brisbane, Perth, Launceston and Albury, and the various selling centres had been welded into a homogeneous national market controlled, in respect of broad policy questions affecting supply and demand, by a federal administration.[1]

The process of relocation began effectively in the seventies. At that time sales in the two Victorian selling centres, Melbourne and Geelong, began a long and pronounced upward movement. From an annual average of forty to fifty thousand bales in the late sixties and early seventies sales jumped to one hundred thousand bales in the middle of the decade, to two hundred thousand at the end of the eighties and to over three hundred thousand in the nineties. The development did not consist, however, of quantitative growth alone. In the half-century before the end of the sixties the local markets had depended on the activities of speculative intermediaries who formed a link between the growers who sold there and the London salerooms, where the wool textile industries sought their raw materials. In the early seventies conditions were established that enabled consumers and dealers to buy more easily and efficiently in the colonies. This changed the nature of the Australian markets from that of collection points on the route to London to primary markets, though small at first, in their own right, and it permitted the growth which followed.

From the late seventies and particularly in the early eighties the Sydney sales expanded rapidly and, by the end of the decade, rivalled those in Victoria. By the end of the eighties these three

[1] See Appendix, Table XVII, for details of Sydney, and Melbourne and Geelong wool auctions, 1859-1900.

selling centres were offering a serious competitive threat to London. They had attained a certain maturity by the nineties and that decade could be characterized as one in which they were consolidated, in which the detailed institutions and regulations appropriate to that status were evolved in their day-to-day operation, and in which growth continued as a snowballing effect induced by the weight of numbers and the power of competition and imitation among raw wool consumers.

In terms of the preceding discussion three sets of changes were necessary to bring about this movement of the markets. Selling institutions of known integrity, efficiency and reliability had to grow to provide the basic setting for the market. It was essential that the form of sale be by auction, for Australia's wool country was too wide to permit extensive on-farm treaties even by resident distributive firms, and the growers had become too accustomed to the London auction system to entrust their clips to city agents for regular private sale. Embryonic auction organizations were created by Stubbs and Lyons in Sydney and by Hind and the Bakewells in Melbourne, but through the fifties and sixties private sales retained their significance. It remained for Thomas Sutcliffe Mort and Richard Goldsbrough to popularize the auction system in the colonies, and to give the lead in providing facilities attracting both sellers and buyers.

Developments had also to take place to encourage and enable the growers to dispose of their clips in the colonies rather than consign them to England. The growth in the number of small flock-owners played a part in this for it was generally the small producer who most desired to make a quick sale. Once the spread between colonial and London prices began to narrow as a result of the activity of manufacturers and dealers in Australia, the saving in marketing costs which could be made by selling locally began to exert an increasing attraction for all classes of wool growers, particularly as prices were declining. Full advantage of this could not be taken, however, until the industry was substantially free of financial pressure to market in London. This freedom was acquired in two ways: firstly, the selling brokers in the colonies sought incorporation in England and tapped the English capital market for funds with which to provide the finance; and secondly, specialized pastoral finance houses, domiciled in England and engaged in the consignment trade, shifted their location and became colonial selling brokers.

The third set of changes necessary was that which would encourage and enable consumers and dealers to incur the risks and inconveniences attendant on obtaining their supplies from the other side of the world. Obstacles were swept aside by the completion of the telegraphic link between the colonies and Europe in 1872 and the introduction of faster transport on shorter ocean routes, while the changing structure of the European textile industries made it easier for manufacturers and dealers to finance the transactions and carriage. The actual shift in their buying habits was to some extent part of a general movement of world wool markets back to the producing countries and partly the result of specific competitive pressures which led groups of consumers of Australian wools to seek cheaper sources of supply than London.

1 THE DEVELOPMENT OF SELLING INSTITUTIONS IN
THE COLONIES

The two figures who dominated the process of creating the selling apparatus in the colonies were Richard Goldsbrough and Thomas Mort. Mort had commenced his colonial career in the services of Aspinal, Brown & Co. in Sydney in 1838,[2] and in 1843 he established his own auctioneering concern. Until well into the fifties the sale of stock and station properties was the most important of his activities and the main source of his income,[3] but he also included wool in his sales of colonial produce. Though the wool sales were a minor feature on which Mort did not concentrate, they were nevertheless a profitable one and when his property manager and later his auctioneer left his firm they both founded concerns in which wool-selling for a time played an important part.[4] Goldsbrough, on the other hand, had been brought up in the wool trade. His apprenticeship in Bradford and his later business life in Shipley had equipped him well and suitably for the wool sorting and packing business he opened in Melbourne in 1848. When he purchased the business of J. & R. Bakewell in 1850 he acquired with it the status of the leading wool broker in Victoria. He reorganized the sales mechanism he had inherited and placed the auctions on a regular periodical basis, but otherwise tended to neglect that phase of his business.

[2] Goddard, *The Life and Times of James Milson*, p. 97.
[3] Cf. Withers, 'The Romance of Wool Selling', 18 Oct. 1913. This concentration is unmistakably reflected in the nature of Mort's advertisements in the *Sydney Morning Herald*.
[4] Richardson, the property manager, became a partner in Richardson & Wrench, the well-known real estate agents of today, which at the time combined real estate and wool sales. O. B. Ebsworth, the auctioneer, started his own wool broking firm in addition to a woollen mill.

His lack of interest may be gauged from the fact that growers were permitted to supply their own auctioneer or to make use of the one who conducted the sales for Goldsbrough on a commission.[5] In fact, like Mort, Goldsbrough was far more interested in pastoral property than in wool. He turned first to selling it and then, in partnership with E. Row and G. Kirk, commenced investing speculatively in Riverina properties.[6]

For both Goldsbrough and Mort wool-selling remained an essentially subordinate activity during the early fifties, overshadowed by stock and property dealings, wool packing, sorting and consigning to England on growers' account, and merely implying recognition of a local trade in wool. It was not until the closing years of the fifties that Goldsbrough and Mort changed the emphasis of their businesses and consciously endeavoured to compete, at least to an extent, with the consignment trade. In that process they laid the foundations of an independent local market, the conception of which far transcended the immediate requirements of sellers and buyers.

The motives of these brokers differed somewhat. The basic assumption in any explanation of Goldsbrough's re-orientation must be that the only reasons which could have led him to concentrate on local selling were the prospects of a greater net revenue from each bale handled and/or a greater volume of trade than he could expect as a mere packer and consignment agent. The selling commission of $1\frac{1}{2}$ per cent to which he was entitled by appropriating, in the view of the growers, the role of the English selling broker, may or may not have exceeded the commission of $\frac{3}{4}$-1 per cent received as a consigning agent.[7] As a warehouseman, he gained the new profits derived from the delivery and receiving charges. The crucial fact was that the absolute volume of consignment business available to him was more limited than his potential share of the possible volume of local sales.

The sources that he could tap for either of these trades—consignment or local sales—were circumscribed by the semi-permanent

[5] The announcement of his acquisition of Bakewell's business included the notice that 'Richard Goldsbrough has also made arrangements for Weekly Sales by Auction of Wool, Tallow, Sheepskins etc. *Vendors selecting their own auctioneers*' (*Argus*, 9 Dec. 1850). My italics. The same arrangement was still in operation in 1855.

[6] H. M. Franklyn, *A Glance at Australia in 1880*, p. 197; also an unsigned article in the *Melbourne Truth*, 2 May 1914.

[7] Goldsbrough's selling commission was based, of course, on realizations in Melbourne; the consigning agent's on realizations in London. The former would exceed the latter as long as London prices were less than 50 per cent higher than those ruling in Melbourne.

obligations of many growers to financial institutions, merchant financiers and consigning agents. From the remainder Goldsbrough could expand his consignment business by improving the quality of his packing and classing services, by making more attractive advances on shipments and by more vigorous advertising and canvassing. The efficacy of these tactics was limited. The really valuable weapon was the power to offer medium and long-term accommodation which would induce growers to change their allegiance from other agents. This he did not have. Merchants accumulated considerable profits from the lucrative import trade, particularly in the early fifties, which they frequently invested in pastoral activity —directly by occupation or indirectly in mortgages—and they afforded, moreover, a convenient channel through which absentee investments might be made. With this Goldsbrough could not compete. His object in coming to Victoria was to restore a somewhat tattered fortune,[8] and his capital resources in the fifties were relatively small.

Goldsbrough's business did prosper and expand. But the purchase of the Bakewells' concern seems to have been financed, partly at least, from the profits of his packing and sorting establishment; and the further expansion into the Row and Kirk partnership had a similar foundation. There can be no doubt that all were profitable ventures—that the combination of sheep-raising, stock and station selling, wool sorting, packing, consigning and broking meant a degree of vertical integration that was of particular value during the gold-rush period—and that his English training and contacts helped make this success possible. Each of these expansions, and the admission of Hugh Parker into the broking partnership in 1857, represented an expansion of Goldsbrough's capital resources and borrowing power. However, increasing personal affluence and expanded capital were insufficient to form a basis for successful competition with an agency like Dalgety & Blackwood.

In that situation, the only method by which Goldsbrough or any similarly placed shipper could expand significantly was by encouraging a local market where that specific disadvantage weighed less.[9] Irrespective of any special concessions which Goldsbrough may

---

[8] Joyce, *Homestead History*, p. 112. Goldsbrough had been caught in George Hudson's railway speculations in Yorkshire.

[9] Other small consigning firms such as Henry Clowes (Joyce, p. 177) were in the same position, but although the dissatisfaction with the merchant consigning agents was growing during the fifties (ibid., pp. 177, 181-2), these small concerns had little chance of success against the more firmly established merchants. While many of them dropped out of existence Goldsbrough went ahead to

have made, a local market could attract untied and sometimes even
tied growers, and he would share with the other brokers their
custom.

These considerations do not apply with quite the same force to
T. S. Mort, whose resources were far more substantial at that time.
His interests, however, were far more widely spread than Goldsbrough's and his ventures in railway promotion, gold-mining, engin-
eering, and the search for efficient refrigeration dispersed capital
which, if concentrated in the wool business, could have secured him
a pre-eminent position in the consignment trade. Mort deliberately
built up his business as a produce salesman and endeavoured to
popularize colonial auctions, but he never felt that the local sale
of wool could displace consignments and even as late as 1870 was
exploring every avenue to increase his consignment trade.[10] Nevertheless Mort, like Goldsbrough, appreciated the potential long-term
importance of the institution he was founding; for both were men of
vision and imagination; both also were attracted to the development
of local selling as a source of immediate profit which did not make
great calls on capital. Mort, perhaps, rose further above the immediate pecuniary question (as he did in many other ventures)[11] and was
able to view the development of the market as an end in itself.
With Goldsbrough, on the other hand, the vision grew out of an
innovatory solution to the problem of business survival and expansion. To attribute varying motives to them does not, however,
diminish the fundamental importance that attaches to the policies
they followed and the effects of their efforts in the establishment of
the colonial auction centres.

In the forties Lyons and Stubbs in Sydney and Hind and the
Bakewells in Melbourne instituted orderly local sales. In the fifties
Goldsbrough and Mort regularized the auction techniques that had
been developed. During the fifties and sixties local selling institutions
continued to develop and grow, partly in response to the deliberate
efforts of those two and partly because of the growth of the trade
as such. Other broking firms, seizing upon the crumbs dropped by

---

become an Australian institution primarily, it is argued here, because of this
diversion of his business into the local sale of the produce.

[10] When this book was already in the publisher's hands I was introduced,
through the kindness of Miss Eirene Mort, to the collection of T. S. Mort's letters
now held by Mr J. L. Mort. This collection, among others, may make possible
the detailed analyses of T. S. Mort's activities as a wool broker and consigning
agent which I hope to incorporate in my projected history of Goldsbrough, Mort
& Co. Ltd.

[11] Cf. the account of his life and activities in J. Jervis, 'Thomas Sutcliffe Mort',
Royal Australian Historical Society Journal and Proceedings, vol. xxiv (1938).

the consigning agents and the two main local sellers, added a competitive drive to the determination of the local practices.[12] The dates
of their establishment reflect the growth and extension of the local
auction system. In the fifties and early sixties the main Melbourne
and Geelong houses were formed; in the late sixties and seventies,
those of Sydney.[13] The effective beginnings of the Adelaide market,
despite the small offerings of auctioneering concerns like Parr &
Luxmoore and E. R. Priestly & Co. from the sixties, were dated
only from 1878 when Elder, Smith & Co. assumed broking functions,[14] and similarly the activities of brokers like Fenwick & Co. in
Brisbane were considered, even as late as 1888, to be of insufficient
size to warrant notice. Attempts were made to establish auction
sales elsewhere—unsuccessfully in Newcastle in the eighties,[15]
successfully in Hobart and Albury near the end of the century.

These brokers in their day-to-day business, in consultation with
one another and with the buyers, evolved an efficient system of
selling. The magnitude of their task is revealed by the fact that the
elementary convenience of printed rather than manuscript catalogues
of the sales was not provided in Sydney until the sixties.[16] Ware-

[12] In Sydney, for example, Durham & Irwin (Irwin & Turner from 1865) became
selling brokers in December 1859; O. B. Ebsworth and Richardson & Wrench
in November 1860; W. Dean in November 1861; J. Brewster (Brewster & Trebeck
from 1868) in October 1862; and James Graham in February 1865. Their lack
of success is indicated by the variety of other occupations which they also needed
to follow.
[13] Harrison & Jones commenced selling in October 1866; James Devlin in
November 1867 (these concerns were amalgamated as Harrison, Jones & Devlin
in 1871); Maiden, Hill & Clark and John Bridges, commenced in the mid-
seventies. These were the main sellers in Sydney, apart from Mort, before the
national concerns such as the Australasian Mortgage & Agency Co. Ltd
opened branches there in the eighties.
[14] This is the opinion expressed by R. B. Skamp (*The Wool Trade . . . in Australia and Tasmania*, p. 13) at the end of the eighties. Green, Parr & Luxmoore
(later Parr & Luxmoore), general auctioneers, held occasional sales of wool from
at least 1860; E. R. Priestly & Co. commenced selling in the seventies. The scale
of these activities was very small—the annual average reported sales by auction
between 1863-4 and 1868-9 did not exceed 820 bales. Even by the end of the
century Adelaide sales were still comparatively small and accounted for less than
10 per cent of the total sales in the four main centres—annual average of
Adelaide sales 1895-6 to 1899-1900, 65,426 bales, of total four centres, 735,136
bales (Bureau of Agricultural Economics, *Statistical Handbook of the Sheep
and Wool Industry*, Table 35).
In 1882 Elder's Wool and Produce Co. Ltd was formed to take over the auction
portion of the wool and produce business of the parent company; see [Price and
Hammond], *Elder, Smith & Co. Ltd.*, p. 37.
[15] Cf. Withers, 'The Romance of Wool Selling', 14 Nov. 1913; Standing Committee on Public Works, 'Report on the Proposed Railway from Narrabri to
Walgett with a branch line to Collarendabri, with Minutes of Evidence', *N.S.W.
V. & P.*, 1900 vol. 5, question 2445.
[16] Cf. Austin, 'Recollections of the Australian Wool Trade', July 1906.

house accommodation was the first problem to demand their attention. Wool-selling required premises in which the produce could be
displayed to the buyers with advantage. Led by Goldsbrough and
Mort they constructed warehouses expressly for the purpose, improving them as business demanded successive extensions of space.
Storage floors were well ventilated, display space was made available on the top floors, where an abundance of windows allowed the
natural light, and careful stowage the space, that buyers needed for
a thorough examination of the wool, and modern equipment
ensured speedy and economical handling.[17] At the same time, as the
volume of the offerings increased it became obvious that the English
practice of making every bale available for that examination before
the sale was both wasteful and unnecessary. A system was worked
out, becoming more complex as the trade widened, which involved
showing only a portion of each lot[18]—an immense saving in time
and labour and one that enabled buyers to value more wool in a
given time. The conditions on which the sales were made were
crystallized, over a period of twenty years or so, by a similar interplay of the interests of brokers and buyers. Conditions imposed by
the brokers and accepted, by default, by the buyers were later
challenged when their application revealed conflict. In 1860, for
example, the implications of sale on the basis of an examination
of a proportion of the lot became apparent and were resolved by
the brokers' formal assumption of the responsibility of guaranteeing
that the shown bales were fair samples;[19] and in the same year the
Melbourne Chamber of Commerce adjudicated a dispute between
the brokers and buyers respecting the allowance to be made for the
weight of the wool-pack (the 'tare') when accounts were being
rendered.[20] Rostering the days on which the brokers sold was a
necessary and convenient move, but one whose main significance
lay in the welding of a number of sellers into one organized market.
It is most readily seen, and achieved its highest expression, in
the use by the brokers of a central saleroom. The use of a central
saleroom was itself a feature of the trade that owed its origin to
the woolbuyers. In 1863 the Sydney buyers insisted that all sales
should be held on the one day in the one place. Lyons Building

---

[17] 'The most imposing structures of the metropolis of the Southern Hemisphere are the banks and wool warehouses' (Franklyn, *A Glance at Australia in
1880*, p. 223).   [18] See p. 129, n. 66.
[19] *Argus*, 5, 17 and 28 July 1860. The dispute arose out of the appeal case
Clough & others v. *Campbell*, reported in the first of those issues, and then proceeded by negotiations between the brokers and buyers.
[20] *Argus*, 11 July 1860.

in George Street served as temporary accommodation until in 1864 the sales were moved to the Sydney Exchange,[21] where they remained until the eighties. Centralization then broke down and was not restored until 1892. Similarly, in Melbourne the demands of the buyers in the nineties led to the use of the Wool Exchange as a centralized selling point.[22]

In these ways the selling institutions developed from the rudimentary auctions at which wool was offered along with a miscellany of other pastoral produce[23] under primitive conditions and on a variety of terms, to the highly formalized, efficient and centralized series of auctions of the seventies and eighties.

2 THE GROWERS AND THE COLONIAL SALES

The evolution of efficient selling institutions was clearly a necessary condition for the growth of the volume of transactions. It is equally clear that this evolution could not have happened without a concurrent expansion in the number of sellers. The hard core of sellers around whom the brokers built their early organization were the small growers. It was to them that the basic attractions of local sales—quick realization and speedy finalization of accounts—appealed most in financial terms, and it was on their clips, small, often mixed, generally of indifferent quality and poorly classed, that the heavy fixed marketing costs in England weighed most heavily. In Victoria in particular, in the sixties and seventies, this class of producers expanded rapidly, partly under the stimulus the selection laws afforded small-scale pastoral production, but mainly as a product of the expansion of agriculture and the growing metropolitan demand for meat. From this change in the structure of pastoral production the Melbourne market drew most of its support during the twenty years before 1875. Even in 1886 it was estimated that most of Melbourne's meat and half the wool sold there was

---

[21] See the 'Wool Circulars', *Sydney Morning Herald*, 21 Nov., 12 and 21 Dec. 1863, and 26 Nov. 1864.

[22] See p. 110, n. 13.

[23] In the forties wool and other pastoral produce were offered by some auctioneers at the same sale as imported goods. Even in the eighties many of the brokers followed the practice of allotting to each day of the week the sale of a different kind. Fenwick & Co. of Brisbane, e.g., advertised (E. Greville, ed., *Official Directory . . . 1884*, end page) the following order of sales: 'Monday—Land, Tuesday—Country Sales, Wednesday—Hides, Tallow, Sheepskins etc., Thursday—Fat Stock Market, Friday—Wool and Leather, Saturday—Horses, Milch Cattle'. The sales of the more important brokers, while including livestock, pastoral properties, etc., revolved primarily around the wool auction.

produced by small flock-owners.[24] Over 3,600 growers patronized the Melbourne and Geelong sales in 1883.[25] The wool they sold amounted to less than one-fifth of the total output of New South Wales and Victoria; yet those growers were equal to just over one-half the number of pastoralists in those two colonies in the censal year 1881.[26] Similar changes in New South Wales in the eighties and nineties, and to a smaller degree in South Australia in the seventies and eighties, were broadly associated with the expansion of local auctions there.

In terms of the suggested motivation for Goldsbrough's deliberate decision to develop the local auction system, there were two basic problems facing him. One was to augment that hard core of small growers by wooing others to whom the sales did not appeal so immediately and so strongly. The second was to attract to Melbourne the representatives of overseas dealers and consumers without whose presence the possibility of local expansion was limited. To an important extent those two phases were interacting and inter-dependent. The station clips, large, well classed and of fairly even quality, attracted far greater buyer attention and claimed higher prices than an equal quantity of farmers' wool. They were the bait needed to lure the foreign buyers. Those same station clips, however, were attracted to the local market only by the higher prices that consumers' and dealers' representatives could afford to pay.

We will defer until the next section consideration of the shift in buying policy. Here our interest is directed to other methods by which brokers attempted to increase the sales by attracting the large clips.

In the first place, they had at their disposal a number of conventional techniques. One of the more obvious of these was personal contact and canvassing. As an investor in Riverina properties Goldsbrough, for example, not only acquired an adequate knowledge of station valuation and an ability to assess the potentialities of grazing lands, but also formed connections which served as a foundation for the large business he later did in Riverina wools. Hastings Cunningham utilized the friendships of his wool-producing days as a basis for his business, while the promoters of the Australasian Agency and Banking Corporation, a consigning agency formed in 1877, pledged themselves to forward through the concern wool

24 Bonwick, *Romance of the Wool Trade*, p. 270, quoting from the Official Handbook of the Exhibition held in Melbourne in 1886.
25 The estimate is that of the *Australasian Trade Review*, 19 Dec. 1883.
26 In N.S.W. in 1881 the number of squatters was 3,179; in Victoria, including dairy-farmers, there were 3,466.

worth £200,000 from their own stations.[27] Brokers like Goldsbrough also maintained a small but efficient staff of canvassers and travellers[28] whose personal interest in clients' problems contrasted vividly with the distance of the English brokers and the less personal attention of some of the consigning houses.[29] So close were the links established in this fashion, in fact, that when a director of Goldsbrough, Mort & Co., who had undertaken much of the outside work, left the firm and became colonial consultant to one of its competitors he took considerable business with him.[30]

The necessity to adopt policies and techniques that would yield the maximum short-run profits consistent with the long-term policy of expanding the market as a whole is most evident in the regulation of brokers' charges. Their revenue was derived from three sources. The selling commission was a percentage charge made to the growers on the realized value of their wool and had its origin, as far as the brokers were concerned, in the general usages of the wool and auctioneering trades. The receiving charge, also levied on the growers, was a flat cash rate per pound of wool entering the brokers' stores, and, covering the costs of warehousing and handling, it underlines the Australian brokers' novel assumption of that function. (While the selling charge varied with the ability of the wool industry to pay, the receiving charges provided an offsetting gamble and an element of stability in brokers' revenue when wool prices were low.) The only charge made to the buyers was one for delivery, again a flat rate per pound irrespective of the value of wool.

Between the sixties and the eighties these charges displayed a remarkable stability, derived both from the trade's adherence to price leaders' rates and a general appreciation of the value of stability as such. They could not afford to discourage potential sellers and buyers by fluctuating rates. The major variation they did introduce in the conditions of sale emphasized the value and soundness of a principle of conservatism and stability. In 1872 the leading

[27] *A.I.B.R.*, vol. 1, p. 160.
[28] In the half-year ended 31 Mar. 1884, R. Goldsbrough & Co. devoted £1,491 out of total expenses of £28,540 to travellers' allowances (R. Goldsbrough & Co., 'Balance Books', Analysis of Profit and Loss).
[29] Not all of the English brokers and the consigning agents were open to such a charge, but the brokers' disabilities, in particular, were heavy. It was written of old clients of a local broker that they 'prefer to see and correspond with particular partners in the management of their business'—J. S. Horsfall, *To the Shareholders of Goldsbrough, Mort & Co. Ltd.: A Reply to Andrew Rowan*, pp. 10-11.
[30] *A.I.B.R.*, vol. 16, p. 327.

Melbourne brokers,[31] in an attempt to turn the growers' agitation to their advantage, abolished a traditional allowance which the buyers had enjoyed—the draft of one pound in every hundred-weight bought.[32] Within a month they were forced to concede a compensating variation and allow them the actual weight of each wool-pack instead of the traditional tare of ten pounds per bale.[33] In the following season the buyers successfully struck against the disallowance of the one pound draft,[34] objecting to being made, in effect, a lever for the abolition of the practice in London.[35]

Apart from their stability, a feature which they shared with London, the Melbourne charges tended to attract growers by the considerable saving in marketing costs which they represented. Not only were the growers relieved of the transport costs to England (which the buyers in the colonies, of course, allowed for in their bidding) but the selling commission of 1½% and the receiving charge of ⅛d. per pound compared favourably with the English selling brokers' commission of 1% (reduced to ½% in 1871), the importing agents' commission of between 1 and 2%, the consolidated warehouse charges of 4s. to 6s. per bale and the loss of many weeks' interest on the value of the clip. The difference in selling costs, excluding all those associated with transport, could amount, in fact, to as much as 0.355d. per pound on wool realizing 12d. per pound in London.[36]

Successful to an extent though they may have been, these tactics and charges were nevertheless capable of influencing only a small

[31] This discussion applies mainly to Melbourne which was by far the most important colonial wool market, but the pattern is the same in other centres. In Adelaide, in 1879, Elder, Smith & Co. announced that 'in order to promote business' they would no longer make a charge to growers for receiving the wool. Four years later, under pressure from the buyers, they reimposed it, at the same time abolishing the charge to buyers for delivery. (Elder, Smith & Co., 'Circular Wool Letters', 20 Aug. 1879 and 30 Aug. 1883, held in the Australian National University.)

[32] The *Argus* contained the following public notice on 29 Aug. 1872: 'We the undersigned woolbrokers of the city of Melbourne in compliance with a written request made by leading wool growers have, after consultation with the shippers, decided to OMIT from our catalogues the DRAFT of 1 lb. per cwt. If special instructions are given to sell with draft they will be attended to.'
The signatories are R. Goldsbrough & Co., Hastings Cunningham & Co., and the London & Australian Agency Corporation Ltd.

[33] Public notice in the *Argus*, 25 Sept. 1872.   [34] *Argus*, 4 Nov. 1873.

[35] See Jules Renard's letter in the *Argus*, 12 Nov. 1873.

[36] See ch. 8, for a discussion of marketing costs. The example in the text assumes that wool fetching 12d. in London will realize only 8d. in the colonies, which is rather extreme. But even if the calculation were based on wool that realized 12d. in both London and Melbourne, the difference still amounts to up to 0.295d. per pound.

minority of the growers. Any large expansion of the market depended, paradoxically, on the brokers' ability to provide long-term finance—the very thing which their inability to do, it is suggested, motivated their concentration on local sales in the first place.

In considering the development of the local markets the role of long-term finance must be considered on two levels. At the level of the individual brokers it appeared partly as a competitive weapon that could be used to retain or extend a broker's clientele. Thereby the number of growers patronizing the local sales rather than the London market might or might not be increased. At the level of the trade as a whole, the development of the local market was incapable of full realization until both long-term and short-term credit could be offered on a large scale without direct reference, either by the local trade or the growers themselves, to sources outside Australia which would draw the produce to England. This was achieved in two ways. The local brokers expanded their financial resources, which enabled them to replace the financiers of some of those growers who formerly consigned to London; and the more important of the English importing houses transferred the centre of their financial operations from Britain to the colonies. The two levels were related through the particular forms of financial support that the brokers adopted for their individual operations. Individually following certain policies determined by the conditions of their own businesses, they developed collectively a set of institutions which forced the English houses to join them.

The conditional nature of long-term finance has already been discussed,[37] but it is necessary to emphasize the restrictions on those conditions. Growers were tied to their financiers; but they were tied to a particular method or place of marketing only if the financier restricted his services in that way. In the case of colonial brokers this meant that they were unable to depend on finance as a method of compelling growers to patronize their sales, as they were unable to dispense immediately with their function as consigning agents. All that could be essayed was an unofficial pressure to induce debtors to try the sales in Melbourne or Sydney first, with an undertaking to provide consignment facilities if the reserve price was not met. (This option had an impressive influence on many medium-sized non-obligated growers who occasionally experimented with different marketing methods.)[38] This pressure may, indeed, have been quite

[37] See pp. 118-22.
[38] Cf. Royal Commission on Railway Construction, 'Report and Minutes of Evidence', *S.A.P.P.*, 1875, vol. 2, paper 22, question 758.

extensive. It certainly impressed contemporary observers in that way, for one of the reasons to which Melbourne's supremacy as a port of shipment and as a colonial market was most frequently attributed was its financial position and the fact that it 'controlled' so many pastoral stations.[39] Moreover, even if the pressure was slight and not always successful, the amount of wool made available under finance agreements was large, and the scope for the pressure correspondingly high. Against station mortgages,[40] stock mortgages, a few freehold mortgages, promissory notes and wool liens (all of which were, if necessary, renewed from year to year to form long-term instruments) Goldsbrough was explicitly offered, in 1866, some 7,000 bales as part security and possibly half that number again which were not formally recorded.[41]

Nevertheless, the restrictions that have been noted meant that their interest in finance as a competitive weapon was limited firstly to protecting and retaining those clients who would otherwise have been forced to seek their accommodation, and take their trade, elsewhere; and secondly, to ensuring that they were able, if approached by a grower who had previously consigned, to take over the financing that had formerly been provided for him somewhere along the consignment chain. These were limited interests, and in fact most brokers' attention was focused on the interest revenue rather than the wool business that borrowing carried with it. Interest was a fickle, but frequently a very profitable, source of revenue. Even in 1870 and 1871, when R. Goldsbrough & Co. were paying out vast sums in interest on 'dead' capital, their net interest receipts amounted to 20 per cent of the gross revenue, and in 1869 it had been 30 per cent.[42] Realistically enough, it was only in depressed periods that the wool business gained under mortgages assumed any major importance in the brokers' eyes.[43]

[39] Cf. Select Committee on the Riverina Districts, 'Report and Minutes of Evidence', *Proc. Vic. Leg. Ass.* 1862-3, vol. 2, paper D42, especially questions 181, 760-1, 961; Select Committee on the River Murray Traffic, 'Report and Minutes of Evidence', *S.A.P.P.* 1870-1, vol. 3, paper 86, questions 26, 272, 398, 1246, 1285; Royal Commission on Railway Construction, 'Report and Minutes of Evidence', *S.A.P.P.* 1875, vol. 2, paper 22, questions 656, 1193, 1217. Royal Commission on the Utilisation of the River Murray Waters; 'Progress Report and Minutes of Evidence', *S.A.P.P.* 1890, vol. 3, paper 34, question 364.

[40] Station mortgages, so-called, were really stock mortgages together with an undertaking to transfer the pastoral lease and the tenant's right to improvements.

[41] R. Goldsbrough & Co., 'Unbound Correspondence' with the Bank of New South Wales.

[42] Ibid. The information has been pieced together from various letters.

[43] In 1892, for example, the Melbourne chairman of directors of Goldsbrough, Mort & Co. Ltd said of a grower who was in grave financial difficulties and unable to meet the company's claims on him that his efforts to secure an English

The process whereby Richard Goldsbrough attained the position of being able to accommodate all the growers requiring his services as a local broker and even to embark on an ambitious campaign of expansion as a pastoral financier was compounded of accident and design. When, in the late fifties, he commenced financing his clients,[44] he was restricted by his dependence on bank credit as the source of his lending power. Unable to compete with other financial institutions by lowering his interest charges, he was forced to liberalize his valuations in order to attract the selling or consigning patronage of unattached growers. This tactic, superimposed on the boom values of the early sixties, was charged with danger. In fact, the restriction of financial competition to this one channel made it reckless and aggravated the effect on broking and other financing firms of the fall in wool prices and the value of pastoral property at the end of the sixties. In the specific case of Goldsbrough, despite the continued prosperity of the wool business, in 1869 and 1870 he was heavily burdened by the payment of interest on 'dead' capital to his bank—capital made available by it and invested in securities which were neither in a position to pay interest nor realizable except at considerable loss.[45]

---

capitalist partner was a satisfactory step 'providing we do not lose the account altogether . . . for he has over 4,000 bales of wool this season'—Goldsbrough, Mort & Co. Ltd, 'Unbound Correspondence': A. W. Robertson to A. Scott, (London Chairman of Directors) 18 Dec. 1892. Even the superficial correlation that exists between the expansion of that company's advances and wool business after 1887 is misleading because, while the advances were made on stations connected with the Melbourne business, most of the apparently new wool business was that gained by the amalgamation with Mort & Co. of Sydney.

[44] This choice of dates is based primarily on a consideration of the facts that Goldsbrough withdrew from pastoral speculation and began concentrating on wool in 1857 (Goldsbrough, Mort & Co. Ltd, *Wool and the Nation*, p. 68), that Richard Goldsbrough & Co., Richard Goldsbrough & Hugh Parker (his partner) do not appear as the owners of any stations in Victoria in 1860 but between them formally owned 27 in 1869 (see 'Return on Pastoral Occupation', *Proc. Vic. Leg. Ass.*, 1869, vol. 2, paper C19) and that the first foreclosure seems to have been made in 1865 (Goldsbrough, Mort & Co. Ltd, 'Unbound Correspondence', J. Walker, Inspector, Bank of New South Wales, to J. Badcock, Melbourne branch manager, Bank of New South Wales, 10 June 1870). These are all consistent with, and point to, some time in the second half of the fifties. (The absence of the Company and the partners from the 1860 run lists may simply mean that mortgages were not registered and therefore formal transfer of ownership was not notified to the Lands Department. This was not an unusual practice even as late as the eighties, and indicates the lender's confidence in the borrower's position. Obviously the probability of registering at least some of the mortgages increased steeply as the number increased.)

[45] Cf. Goldsbrough, Mort & Co. Ltd, *Wool and the Nation*, p. 68. This period of the company's history is well documented in the unbound correspondence between it and the Bank of New South Wales which has been retained by Goldsbrough, Mort & Co. Ltd.

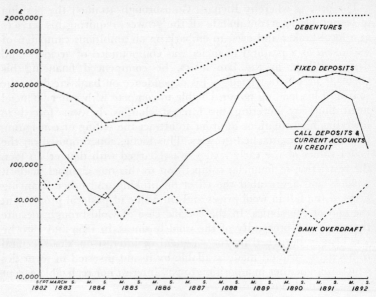

FIG. 5.   Main liabilities, Goldsbrough, Mort & Co. Ltd (semi-logarithmic scale)

(See Appendix, Table XVIII)

The lesson of this crisis was unmistakable. Independence from bank credit would, firstly, permit him to attract trade and fight competition by lowering interest rates and therefore to avoid rashly liberal lending and, secondly, it would reduce the severity of the drain in interest payments during depressed periods. This lesson, it is suggested, lay behind Goldsbrough's break, in 1876, with the bank that had financed him during those years and the transfer of his business to another (of which he later became a director); behind the admission of two new partners in the same year;[46] behind the local promotion and formation of the Australasian Agency and Banking Corporation Ltd in 1876-7 by, among others, J. S. Horsfall, one of Goldsbrough's partners;[47] and behind the subsequent purchase of his business by that concern.[48] Taken in conjunction, these events provided independence from a bank that was associated with unpleasant memories, and expanded capital of his own with which to work, and, finally, the incorporation of his own banking institution, for the Australasian Agency and Banking Corporation had

[46] Ibid., p. 69.   [47] A.I.B.R., vol. 1, p. 164.   [48] Ibid., vol. 5, p. 290 for details.

power to accept deposits, make advances and float debentures through its London office.[49] Gradually the bank overdraft which covered the old company's advances was reduced and deposits and debenture capital became the main source of finance. This process is clearly evidenced in Figure 5. The fact that the firm, because of land legislation, pastoral depression, drought, and perhaps problems of internal management, did not expand advances at all rapidly until 1885-6 in no way reduces the significance of these developments before 1881. It is from that amalgamation that an official chronicler justly dates the company's entry into the field of 'large scale pastoral finance'.[50] The essential point of the story, and the reason for recounting it, is the way in which the firm gained access to an apparently inexhaustible overseas source of funds without in any way compromising the disposal of the wool in which they were invested. Growers could raise capital in England, but it was generally on condition that the clip be sold there. Specialist consignment and importing agencies could dispose of shares and debentures in Britain too, but their internal policies forced the growers who borrowed from them to consign. Goldsbrough showed that broking firms could tap the same capital market and make the funds available to the growers without that restriction.

A parallel course was followed by most of the other major colonial brokers. In 1868 the Melbourne partnership of Cunningham and Macredie was strengthened by the admission of new partners.[51] The new concern, Hastings Cunningham & Co. Ltd, sought limited liability with a nominal capital of £750,000 a decade later,[52] and in 1880 it was given access to British capital by its amalgamation with the newly-formed Australasian Mortgage and Agency Co. Ltd, the head office of which was in Edinburgh.[53] The London & Australian Agency Corporation Ltd, with head office in London, absorbed J. H. Clough & Co. in 1866.[54] Similarly, the incorporation of the various Dalgety partnerships into one company with limited liability, first projected in 1878,[55] was effected in 1884,[56] and its first irredeem-

---

[49] Ibid., vol. 1, p. 160; vol. 2, p. 4. This fact accounts for the mechanism of the amalgamation: the Australasian Agency & Banking Corporation Ltd bought Richard Goldsbrough & Co., though the latter name was retained. By drawing attention to this sequence of events we are not, of course, imputing improper motives to any of the participants.

[50] Goldsbrough, Mort & Co. Ltd, *Wool and the Nation*, p. 70.

[51] H. M. Franklyn, *A Glance at Australia in 1880*, p. 208.

[52] *A.I.B.R.*, vol. 2, p. 196.   [53] Ibid., vol. 4, p. 270.

[54] Clough later severed his connection with this firm (November 1870) and commenced on his own once again, only to be absorbed, in 1880, by the New Zealand Loan & Mercantile Agency Co. Ltd (*A.I.B.R.*, vol. 4, p. 338).

[55] Ibid., vol. 2, p. 196.   [56] Dalgety & Co. Ltd, *A Souvenir*

able debentures issued in 1887.[57] The Union Mortgage and Agency
Co. Ltd, formed colonially in 1884 with a nominal capital of £1¾
million to take over the business of William Sloane & Co.,[58] transferred its domicile to London in 1887.[59] Although both this company
and others like the Australian Mercantile Land and Finance Co.
Ltd (which claimed to have been the first wool finance company to
issue interminable debentures[60]) were not colonial brokers at the
time, their actions reflect the same trend. Some measure of the
extent to which colonial brokers developed, during the eighties,
internal resources from which they could finance both the production and marketing of wool may be gauged from the fact that in
1887 four of them raised a total of £1.3 million in new capital,
mainly in England, while the Union Mortgage and Agency Co.
Ltd, which assumed local broking functions in the following year,
alone raised a further million.[61]

Chronologically this move to secure British share capital and
deposits was initiated in the sixties by some agencies like the Australian Mercantile Land and Finance Co. It was continued by
colonial broking concerns in the seventies and eighties, and then
the participation of colonial firms was strengthened and hastened
as consigning agencies in England sought incorporation, raised
capital in England which was wholly invested in the colonies, and
transferred the emphasis and centre of their businesses with it.

The new and vigorous financial competition between the banks
in the colonies and the various types of pastoral finance and agency
houses after the mid-seventies, and particularly during the eighties,
increased the latitude of choice available to the growers. It became
easier for them to transfer their accounts from one financier to
another. This did not mean, however, that it was any easier for
them to sell their clips in the colonies, for the banks—the interloping
competitors—remained firmly wedded to the London salerooms.
Their large-scale entry into the market provided, in fact, a force
which ran against the prevailing tendency of the English pastoral
financiers to shift their selling activities to the colonies.

The development of the financial resources of the colonial brokers
in these ways, together with the strengthening of the financial
structure of the colonial selling trade as a whole by the migration
to Australia of English-controlled agencies, created conditions in

to Commemorate the Jubilee Year, p. 29.   [57] *A.I.B.R.*, vol. 11, p. 266.
[58] Ibid., vol. 8, p. 549. It later absorbed the wool business of Jas. Turner & Co.,
one of the last large private companies in the trade in Melbourne (ibid., vol. 10,
p. 440).   [59] Ibid., vol. 11, p. 68.   [60] Ibid., vol. 7, p. 254.   [61] Ibid., vol. 12, p. 5.

which it was possible for a substantial proportion of growers to sell in the colonies if they desired to do so. In addition, the growing financial powers of the brokers did actually induce some growers to cease consigning. Loan policy, rate policy and the development of reliable selling institutions augmented with some success the core of small growers on whom the sales had depended in the sixties, and even in 1870 clips of substantial size were being offered in Melbourne. But despite the attractions these policies may have had, and despite the advantage the brokers had in the fact that the transport networks tended to bring the wool through the marketing centres, these factors were in themselves insufficient. The basic criterion by which the large growers were influenced remained the relative returns which were yielded in the two markets.

Changes in relative returns, it will be argued, were primarily a matter of a changing differential between colonial and London prices. This was complicated, however, to the extent that growers varied their selling policies in accordance with their expectations about price changes in the immediate future. The growth of the colonial auctions took place within the context of a falling trend in wool prices. If that fall was expected to show itself throughout each year, it would be to the growers' advantage to sell locally rather than in London where the realization would take place three months later. We have already argued that in general terms the Australian grower did not operate with this degree of flexibility and rationality.[62] Nevertheless, the correspondence of marked falls in prices[63] with pronounced increases in local sales both in individual seasons— 1869-70, 1871-2 and 1879-80—and over longer periods—the early eighties and early nineties—together with the disproportionate fall in sales (compared with the reduction of output) when prices recovered after 1894-5, seem to indicate that some flexibility existed, that it increased as the price differential between the two markets narrowed and that, from a long-term point of view, shifts to the colonial market induced by price trends and afterwards maintained by rigidities, habit or inertia, played a definite part in this relocation.

3 OVERSEAS BUYERS AND THE COLONIAL SALES

The nature of the buyers' interests was an important determinant of the levels at which prices were established in Melbourne and Sydney. Buying for speculative resale at the London auctions neces-

[62] See pp. 88-9.
[63] See pp. 192 ff., Appendix Table XXVII, and Fig. 6 (p. 193), for the price movements.

sarily limited the prices purchasers were able to offer to a figure well below the London equivalent.[64] Those prices reached levels that attracted large growers only when consumers and dealers, whose offers did not need to include provision for a speculative profit on prices below the London equivalent, entered the market. The attraction of this group of buyers was not a thing to which the colonial brokers' policies contributed greatly. The stability of the charges was an advantage, and under pressure they showed themselves unwilling to alienate the buyers' goodwill.[65] The scale of their charges was high, however, averaging 3s. per bale compared with the London rate of 1s. 2d. to 2s.[66] Moreover, the expense of establishing colonial buying branches was high and, in general terms, recoverable only by doing commission buying for other firms. Yet dealers, and then consumers, from the five main consuming nations did in fact transfer at least part of their buying to the colonies in the seventies and eighties.

In a sense this movement was merely part of a wider shift which was then taking place in raw material marketing. It represented no more—and no less—than a movement of the market back closer to the sources of production, whither it was driven by improvements in transport and communications, by the growth and increasing specialization of consuming industries and, above all, by the growing diversity of consumers. The centralization of the market in one consuming area became inappropriate for a truly world-wide consumption. The same phenomenon may be remarked in the cotton, wheat and, later, rubber trades. The tendency was also most marked in the international trade in wool from other producing countries. By 1893 most Argentine wool was sold to Continental buyers in Buenos Aires,[67] and though considerable quantities of Cape wool were still consigned to London in the twentieth century, European, particularly German, buying in South Africa had become common in the eighties.[68]

Associated with this tendency were two other movements which

[64] The *A.I.B.R.* (vol. 1, p. 500) estimated that to pay shipping charges, freight, marine insurance, interest on the investment, cost of realization and a living profit, speculators needed to keep their colonial bids about 20 per cent below the anticipated London realization.

[65] Cf. the case of the alterations in draft and tare in 1872-3 (pp. 157-8).

[66] Colonial rates at ⅛d. per pound on bales of about 290 pounds; London rates calculated on bales of similar weight from wool warehousemen's circulars made available by Brown & Eagle.

[67] Gibson, *The History and Present State of the Sheepbreeding Industry in the Argentine Republic*, pp. 50, 170-8.

[68] The correspondence and activities of Robert Jowitt & Sons, William Rais-

resulted in a closer integration of the international and intra-
national trades in wool and which facilitated the change in the
locations of international wool markets. A specialized class of wool
merchants, for whom there had been little need as long as manufacturers could attend, or be represented at, the central sales,
emerged in France and Belgium and to a smaller extent in
Germany from the sixties onward. It was this class which was to
conduct most of the buying done in Australia on European account.
At the same time national distributive markets developed on the
Continent. There the manufacturers who could not afford to participate in direct importing could obtain foreign wools offered by the
merchants. In addition, domestic wools which had formerly been
disposed of at comparatively scattered fairs began to make their
appearance at these auction centres.

By 1860, Antwerp had already established itself not only as the
major port for the entry of South American wool into Europe, but
also as a major sales centre. Of the 41,000 bales entered in 1860,
25,000 were in transit and 16,000 were offered at the sales. In 1870,
100,000 bales were put on the market and only 11,000 were in
transit.[69] The fall in the business transacted there after 1880 is due
to the gradual rise of other markets which gradually supplanted it
on the Continent. Roubaix-Tourcoing, the centre of the wool textile
industries in Northern France, commenced auction sales of imported
and domestic wools about 1880,[70] and Le Havre, Bordeaux, Hamburg and Bremen became important alternative ports of entry and
sale. Similarly, auction sales of Cape wool had been established in
Berlin by the mid-seventies[71] and, again, other regional centres
competed with it for the growing trade. By the nineties auctions
were also being held in Forst and Leipzig, where imported and
domestic wools were offered side by side.[72] To some extent the
importance of the main national markets was offset after the late
eighties. Increasingly, direct imports by processors and consumers
meant that they were by-passed, that the primary markets in the
producing countries linked producer and consumer directly. The

---

trick & Sons ('Letters to Colonial Purchasers', to Walter Place & Co., Durban,
from 1877 to 1890), and of Jeremiah Ambler & Co. of Bradford ('The Account
Books of Jermiah Ambler & Co.', transactions through John Hall, Port Elizabeth,
from at least 1880; these manuscript records are held by the Brotherton Library,
University of Leeds) and Gustave Ebell & Co.'s account of German interest in
Cape buying (Brodribb, *Results of Inquiries . . ., passim*) are sufficient indication
of this practice.   [69] See Appendix, Table XIX.
[70] F. B. de Beck, *Le Commerce International de la Laine*, p. 58.
[71] Brodribb, *Results of Inquiries . . .*, p. 10.   [72] F. B. de Beck, op. cit., p. 162

fellmongers of Mazamet, for example, did without the intervention of the French wool merchants and conducted their own purchasing first in South America and then, in the nineties, in Australasia. (By developing the extremely suitable natural resources at their command they were able to establish a virtual monopoly both in the purchase of sheep-skins in those countries and in their treatment.[73]) Despite that contrary indication, however, the national distributive markets occupied an essential position in the wool trade in the last quarter of the century. Instead of one central market for colonial wool in London, and another for South American wool in Antwerp, there developed a more complex dual-level system: primary markets in the producing countries which supplied both consumers and dealers, and regional secondary markets which stood between those dealers and other consumers.

All the features of this general movement are also characteristic of the shift in the location of the market for Australian wool: direct purchases by merchants at the colonial auctions, the development of local selling points in Europe, and the growth of consumer purchases in the colonies. Within the framework of the general explanation—the diversity of consumers, the improvements in transport and communications, etc.—special factors are relevant to the specifically Australian case.

In the first place the great expansion of foreign buying in the Australian colonies during the eighties was composed primarily of European purchases. That shift in the location of their purchases accorded well with the prevailing forms of economic nationalism. The fact that France was forced to obtain her supplies of colonial wool from London, and to a slighter extent that her South American wool came from Antwerp, offended the *amour-propre* of her increasingly self-conscious industrial leaders. That dissatisfaction had found expression as early as 1860; in the two succeeding decades frequent, and sometimes bitter, complaints were made in France and Belgium about their dependence on London;[74] and when the volume of business at the Australian sales seemed likely to equal that in London, the news was given joyous reception by the French press.[75] Even modern commentaries on French trading relationships in the nineteenth century credit the shift almost entirely to the desire to break London's monopoly.[76]

[73] Cf. R. Delaby, *Le Marché International de la Laine*, pp. 166-71.
[74] Cf. Renard Bros. & Co., *Antwerp versus London as a Market for Australian Wool*, p. 4; P. Pierrard, *Etude sur l'Industrie Lainière, passim*.
[75] *A.I.B.R.*, vol. 15, p. 577 quoting the *Bulletin du Musée Commercial*.
[76] Cf. Delaby, op. cit., p. 163; F. Maurette, *Les Grands Marchés des Matières*

The attitude, common probably to all developing industrial economies, reflected the altered composition of the European wool textile industries. Continental demand for colonial wool rose with the growth of French, German and Belgian consumption.[77] By the end of the seventies they represented, collectively, a market force at the London sales greater than that of the United Kingdom.[78] It was this that produced and excused Continental bitterness about the dependent status of their woolbuyers, and even British critics were compelled to recognize that their own role constituted little more than that of 'mere brokers and bankers between [the colonists] and foreigners'.[79]

Economic nationalism, however, was in itself not a sufficient motive to have sent French and Belgian buyers to Australia, for in the sixties and seventies manufacturers could obtain their supplies quite successfully, even though distastefully, in London.[80] Yet the economic reality which lay behind this attitude and from which Continental direct buying derived its impetus did in fact lie in the competitive position of the Continental buyers *vis-à-vis* their English rivals. But the emphasis which has been attached to the attitude and the competition is quite misplaced in relation to an explanation of the development of the colonial sales.

The sequence of events was that the first movement to direct colonial buying was made by English dealers and consumers.[81] It was only when those activities began to threaten to undermine Continental manufacturing that any extensive transfer of French and Belgian buying took place. The competitive reality was there, but it operated during the late seventies and eighties, and the importance of the response to it lay in the consummation by Continental buyers of a trend started by the British.

The reasons underlying the British move may be found in the competitive position of the wool textile producers. On the one

---

Premières (Paris, 1933, revised ed.), pp. 70, 86; A. Picard, *Le Bilan d'un Siècle*, p. 354. [77] Cf. Appendix, Table X and pp. 26-33, *passim*.
[78] Cf. Appendix, Table IX.
[79] T. Illingworth, *Our Textile Industries*, p. 32. We cannot, however, agree with Illingworth's estimate (p. 31) that France alone consumed a third of Australian production.
[80] In fact, many trade observers felt that they ruled the market. Cf. Wrigley and Bousfield, *Report on the Woollen Cloth Manufacture of France*, pp. 17, 44; Tariff Commission, 'Evidence on the Woollen Industries', para. 1321.
[81] Some Continental buyers, of course, anticipated the general movement of both British and Continental purchases. Henri Wattine, Renard Bros., and Masurel Fils et Cie were among Continental buying firms operating in the sixties, and direct exports to the Continent had been made in 1859 (Sydney) and 1861 (Melbourne).

hand, in the seventies, the woollen and worsted branches were both faced by the falling prices and narrowing profit margins produced by the 'general depression'. Despite that, production and consumption were maintained—though with irregularities and though sometimes production was only for stock.[82] This led to intensified competition between individual concerns in the raw wool market, since the acquisition of materials that exactly suited their needs—that is, from which the waste was least in their own particular processes— became more than usually essential. For that wool they were prepared, within the broad and depressed limits set by the industry as a whole, to bid with spirit. The same considerations also applied, of course, to Continental manufacturers. On the other hand, both the worsted and woollen industries in England were subject to additional competitive pressures of a different sort.

As we have already seen,[83] the change in consumer fashion away from mixed lustre goods, on which English worsted production had tended to concentrate, to the soft all-wool worsteds in which the French manufacturers excelled, forced the English industry to turn to colonial wool and to adapt its machinery. The adjustment was by no means wholly successful. The industry steadily lost ground and by the mid-eighties had surrendered a large part of the export market in Europe, and French manufacturers were invading the home market.[84] At the same time the superiority of the organization of the English export trade, on which a substantial part of its success had rested, was being challenged, as French manufacturers developed foreign trading channels. The commercial treaties negotiated in the sixties had brought prosperity to both the woollen and worsted industries. Now the reimposition of protective tariffs at the end of the seventies and the beginning of the eighties steadily reduced their markets. Woollen exports suffered most, and worsted exports were maintained primarily by expanded trade in yarn and later in tops and noils.[85]

The growing competition in foreign markets, and the change in fashion, led to increased competition between the woollen and worsted industries in the home market. Although it was to become far more pronounced in the last two decades of the century, this was already apparent in the seventies. Unable completely to meet the challenge of the French manufacturers in the all-wool worsteds, the English worsted manufacturers developed other new fabrics,

[82] Cf. Dobson and Ives, *A Century of Achievement*, p. 40.   [83] See p. 24.
[84] Cf. Sigsworth, 'A History of Messrs. John Foster & Son Ltd.', pp. 129-35, 145.
[85] See Appendix, Table VII, for the role of yarn exports.

also utilizing colonial wools, which tended to displace woollen fabrics—worsted coatings for men's wear, suitings and trouserings. Moreover, though the growing difficulty of distinguishing between woollen and worsted fabrics and processes did not become significant in England until the late eighties, in the seventies the two branches were competing more and more frequently for the same types of wool. Not only was the worsted industry using more of the short merino previously used, in England, primarily by the woollen, but the growing manufacture of tweeds in Scotland and Yorkshire involved the use, by woollen manufacturers, of long wools formerly used solely in the worsted processes.[86]

In other words, the picture of the English industries that emerges during the seventies and early eighties is one of depression, intensified manufacturing competition between the woollen and worsted industries at home and between both of them and foreign industries, and extended competition between the two branches for similar types of wool. These conditions placed an enhanced emphasis on the importance of wool buying. When, therefore, English manufacturers were approached by Australian buying brokers with proposals to purchase on their behalf, they readily succumbed, particularly when those purchases could be linked with return consignments of cloth and the opening of new and direct export channels.[87] For dealers, too, the prospect of being able to buy wool at rates which had afforded profits to speculators whose purchases they themselves had formerly, in effect, bought in the London market, was an attractive one. They operated, initially, through colonial buying brokers, and established their own buying branches only later as circumstances constrained them and the size of their colonial operations allowed them.[88]

Though the movement to colonial buying was initiated by the English trade, the expansion of the colonial markets in the late eighties and nineties was essentially based on the activities of Continental buyers. After 1881 French imports of wool from London declined appreciably, though her consumption continued to rise sharply;[89] by 1900 she imported more than twice as much direct from Australia as from England (and, incidentally, nearly twice as much South American as Australian).[90] In the 1890–1 selling

[86] Baines, *Yorkshire, Past and Present*, p. 663.
[87] Cf. the reciprocal arrangements between J. Raistrick and W. H. Chard ('Raistrick Records', 'Letters to Colonial Purchasers', *passim*.)
[88] Cf. Barnard, 'Wool Buying in the Nineteenth Century: a case history'.
[89] Cf. Tables XI and XIII.
[90] In the three-year period 1898-1900 France imported an annual average of

season 56 per cent of the sales at the colonial auctions were made to Continental interests.[91]

European manufacturers and dealers, it is suggested, moved the scene of their buying to the colonies in order to salve their national feelings and to retain their competitive position with English manufacturers. This second motive is of some importance, since French writers have often argued that the escape from the 'yoke of London' was partly motivated by some specific disadvantages implied in the indirect import, or from some specific advantage which British manufacturers derived from having the market in their own country.[92] This is illusory. Transport costs from London to the French manufacturing centres were no more, and in some cases less, than those to Yorkshire.[93] They might have felt the inconvenience of arranging their transactions through buying brokers, but the English freedom from those intermediaries was only one of degree,[94] and both were equally subject to it when buying in the colonies.

What colonial buying did achieve was to restore French and English competition to their previous relative positions, for bypassing London the English had gained a distinct advantage.

The specific attraction in the colonies for all buyers was the possibility of obtaining wool from what was still, in the seventies and early eighties, a speculative market where, by definition, the prices tended to be below those ruling in London. In formal terms, the buyers' top price was that which they would have to pay in London, less the transport, insurance and exchange costs and the

52.8 m. lb. from the United Kingdom, 86.6 m. lb. from Australia and 228.3 m. lb. from Argentine and Paraguay (Picard, *Le Bilan d'un Siècle*, p. 360).

91 Goldsbrough, Mort & Co. Ltd, *Australian Wool: Its Position and Prospects in 1895*, p. 13. The complete breakdown by destination of the 1890-1 local sales shows the Continent accounting for 56%, England and Scotland 28%, the United States and Canada 6%, and other destinations (including local speculators and manufacturers), 10%.

92 E.g., Picard, op. cit., p. 346; Pierrard, *Etude sur l'Industrie Lainière, passim*.

93 H. Illingworth and J. V. Goodwin, *Special Report prepared for the Tariff Committee of the Bradford Chamber of Commerce* (Bradford, 1876), found that while wool could be transported from London to Bradford in 3-5 days at a cost of 40s. per ton, it took 8-10 days at a cost of 30s. 8d. per ton to carry it to Fourmies and cost only 25s. 10d. per ton to Roubaix. (This report was drawn to my attention by Dr E. M. Sigsworth of the University of Leeds, who kindly lent me a manuscript copy of it together with the authors' summary of the responses to questionnaires circulated to French Chambers of Commerce.) Wrigley and Bousfield, (*Report on the Woollen Cloth Manufacture of France*, p. 16) placed 1878 carriage costs to Bradford and Galashiels at 37s. 6d. and 42s. 6d. a ton respectively, and to Elbeuf and Sedan 35s. The same general claim was still being made in 1904 (Tariff Commission, op. cit., para. 1321).

94 In 1870 approximately two-thirds of the wool sold in London was purchased through buying brokers (*The Sales of Australian Wools in London*, p. 23).

difference in buying costs in Australia and London. The lowest
price acceptable to colonial sellers was the London price less
freight, etc., and the difference in selling costs. As the difference in
selling costs (0.295d. to 0.355d. per lb. at a price of 12d.) exceeded
the difference in buying costs (0.045d. to 0.080d. per lb.),[95] there was
a band of prices at which both sellers and buyers found it more
profitable to operate in the colonies than in London. (This resulted,
of course, from the elimination of the consigning and importing
agents in the colonial market.) Moreover, as this was a market in
which, before the large-scale operation of the dealers and consumers
had attracted many large station clips to the colonial auctions, the
main sellers were weak—willing to accept lower returns to secure
immediate settlement—the gap between colonial and London prices
was wider than the formal calculation suggests. This was why
speculators had been able to buy there for resale in London. In
these circumstances consuming or dealing buyers in the seventies
and early eighties were able to economize in their raw materials by
buying in the colonies.

In addition, Continental and to a slighter degree English buyers
were able to effect savings in transport. When purchasing in London,
Continental buyers had, in effect, to pay for the freight from Australia to London as well as that from London to their mills. Direct
transport from Australia to Continental ports reduced the combined rate, though this entered their calculations only after 1880,
for prior to that date imports were still shipped via London.[96]
Similarly, English manufacturers buying in the colonies tended to
divert their shipments to ports closer to their area.[97] Freight rates
could also be reduced by chartering ships instead of spreading the
load over a number of vessels at the ruling rate.[98] By 1894, when
the scale of prices was no longer that appropriate to a speculative
market, it was estimated that the economies of the market made it
possible to bring wool direct to the Continent from Sydney at a
landed price of at least ⅜d. per lb.—or nearly 5 per cent—cheaper
than from London.[99]

In the early seventies, buyers on American account played, with
the English, an important role in supporting the developing colonial

[95] See pp. 158, 166.
[96] See the Australasian Mortgage and Agency Co.'s market report in the
Australasian Trade Review, 15 March 1882, and R. Goldsbrough & Co.'s in the
Journal of Commerce, 14 Feb. 1883.
[97] J. H. Clapham, *The Woollen and Worsted Industries*, p. 101.
[98] Cf. J. Leach, *Australia v. London as the World's Wool Depot*, p. 11.
[99] J. Leach, op. cit., p. 49.

sales. Tentative inquiries from American consumers in 1870 and
1871 and the swelling volume of business in the following years[1]
arose fundamentally from the increasing protection which was given
to the American wool-growing industry after 1867. Though Sir
Henry Parkes added to the numerous representations for a reduction of the duties,[2] and though aggregate American demand for
Australian wool would have increased had they been removed, their
existence offered a stimulus specifically to the local auctions. In the
first place the construction of the tariff made it imperative that
merino wools in particular should be imported in the greasy state,[3]
and the colonial sales offered a higher proportion of greasy wool
than London whence most American imports had come. (The same
motive may be attributed to some French buyers, for Continental
preference for greasy and English preference for washed and scoured
wool was very marked.)[4] Secondly, taking into consideration transport costs even to Boston, colonial prices were far below those in
London. In 1883 it was calculated, for example, that wool bought
at 20 cents per pound in Sydney cost only 0.65 cents more to land
in Boston, transport and duty paid, than wool bought at the same
price in London.[5] The twenty cents would buy in Sydney wool far
superior in quality to that which they would buy in London.
Unstable as the changes in the tariff and the variable interest of a
few importers rendered them, direct exports to America clearly
stimulated the Melbourne sales considerably in the early seventies.
In the 1871–2 season they amounted to over 20 per cent of the total
sales in Melbourne and Geelong, and to 17 per cent in both 1872–3
and 1874–5.[6]

The activities of buyers from these three centres led to cumu-
lative, competitive imitation. Manufacturers, particularly in Eng-

[1] Cf. R. Goldsbrough & Co.'s market report in the *Journal of Commerce*, 20
July 1871; *Argus*, 12 Feb. 1872. See also Appendix, Table XX.
[2] *Australasian Trade Review*, 17 Jan. 1872.
[3] The duty on washed wool of the Australian varieties was twice, and that on
scoured wool three times, that on greasy wool, and the extra freight payable on
greasy wool (including the carriage of the dirt, etc.) did not offset that advantage.
Cf. the National Association of the Wool Manufacturers of the United States,
The Woolen Tariff Defended and Explained (Cambridge, Mass., 1886), p. 16.
[4] Pierrard, *The Standard Wool-Bale*, p. 24. It is significant that the only
European countries in which, before the middle of the century, sheep were not
washed prior to shearing were France and Spain. French manufacturers carried
this preference into foreign wools while English manufacturers, accustomed
to washed wools, accepted the new style less readily (de Beck, *Le Commerce
International de la Laine*, p. 23).
[5] Cf. The hypothetical cost calculations given in the National Association of
Wool Manufacturers of the United States, op. cit., Appendix C, p. 53.
[6] See Appendix, Table XX.

10 Discharging at the South-West India Docks, London, in the seventies

land, produced what were virtually speciality cloths and their individual needs were confined to a relatively narrow range of wools the supply of which was more or less limited. When one or two went to the colonies direct, the others were forced to follow suit or risk having their supplies cut off before they even reached London.[7] As the market grew, moreover, other factors began to enter their calculations: the savings in transport time which they could effect, and their ability to have new-season wool in the mill six weeks after it reached the colonial port instead of many months later—and therefore in much better condition; and the greater ease with which they could value greasy wool which had not been pressed down in bales for many months.[8] These advantages and the ways in which consumers could reap them became known through the ordinary trade channels and through consular reports which conscientiously reported market developments and trade practices.[9]

The assumption by the buyers of the market risks inherent in transporting the wool to Europe or America can, in retrospect, be seen only as an indication of the competitive pressures to which they were subjected and of the wide disparity between London and colonial prices which initially existed. The competitive pressures became more apparent in the great growth of the colonial sales in the eighties, for this was a period when colonial prices were nearing relative parity with London and when their trend was downward.[10] The growers' willingness to surrender those risks was a function of the impact of the colonial brokers' persistent repetition of the speculative dangers of consignment, of their gradually increasing vague dissatisfaction with the London sales organization and, in the eighties, of the trends in prices.

The considerations presented above, however, throw light only on *why* they were willing to transfer their buying operations. The ability to execute those desires on a wide scale was, as we have already implied, dependent on the buyers' ability to overcome certain obstacles which had barred the expansion of the colonial markets in the fifties and sixties. The obstacles were two: transport

---

[7] Cf. J. Leach, op. cit., p. 23.   [8] Ibid., p. 53.

[9] E.g. F. Gagliardi, *L'Australia*; M. E. Pollett, *Australasie*; *La Nouvelle-Galles du Sud* (Brussels, 1898); *Australasie, 1900* (Brussels 1900); United States Bureau of Statistics (Special Consular Reports), *Australasian Sheep and Wool*.

[10] One would expect that in a period of falling prices manufacturers would prefer to purchase in London for two reasons. There they could purchase small quantities at fairly frequent intervals throughout the whole year; and they could also leave their purchasing later than they could in Australia. Some, like Raistrick ('Letters to Colonial Purchasers', 11 Feb. 1887) did in fact largely withdraw from the colonial markets, but the aggregate movement was otherwise.

and communications, and finance. The opening of the Suez Canal and the construction of the Alpine tunnels, together with the opening of direct shipping lines to the Continent in the eighties, helped surmount the first. More important, perhaps, was the completion of the cable link between Australia and Europe in 1872. This enabled consumers and dealers to communicate price limits and buying orders to their representatives which accurately reflected current conditions in Europe, whereas previously their orders may have been months out of date when they were executed.

The changing structure of the European textile industries which tended to concentrate demand into fewer and more highly capitalized firms,[11] played a large part in easing the financial difficulties of overseas buying. Raw wool merchants, worsted merchant-combers and spinners, relatively large woollen manufacturers and, in France, large vertically integrated worsted mills were more readily able to finance imports out of their own resources. More generally, the scale of their operations meant that they were able to secure credit more easily. It also meant that they were not embarrassed, as small firms were, by a desire to work the wool up before payment was due, and they were therefore able to operate within even the most restrictive credit conditions and conventions. In both the woollen and worsted industry there were, however, firms that could not claim these advantages of scale, and their recourse to banks and acceptance houses caused more complications. It was in order to meet their demands that the inconveniences attaching to this form of financing—the buyer's desire to process the material before the bill was due and the financier's desire to retain title to it until after payment was made—were resolved by the device of supplementary documents, letters of trust, which were exchanged for the bills of lading.

The Continental buyers laboured under an additional handicap which, in fact, played a large part in retaining for so long a monopoly of the sales for London. That handicap was the financial supremacy of the City of London. Not only was it pre-eminent as the money market of the world but it was the key to credits in the colonies, for virtually all their imports came from Britain. Credits had to be opened in Australia before wool could be bought there. But even banks and acceptance houses which were fairly specialized in the wool trade were uneasy about granting credit to foreign buyers, especially if the produce was shipped direct to the Conti-

[11] See pp. 33-9.

nent.[12] One approach to the problem lay in increasing European exports to Australia. It was suggested in the sixties that the lead in direct French buying would be taken by manufacturing textile exporters.[13] This idea was to some extent embodied in the activities of firms like Renard Bros. and the Belgian Export Co., which, from the sixties and eighties respectively, indented Belgian goods and exported wool from the colonies, and of Newell & Co., a merchant firm which acted as buying brokers mainly on American account. For French buyers a specialized channel for securing credits in Australia was provided by the establishment of colonial branches of the Comptoir d'Escompte de Paris in the eighties.[14] In general, however, Continental buyers were forced to arrange their finances through London.

Because of its doubts, London's requirements as to the size and standing of applicants for accommodation were more stringent for Continental than for English buyers. This helped to develop, and was overcome by, a distinctive feature in the structure of the Continental wool importing trade. Though spinners and combers from France, Belgium and Germany were represented at the colonial sales, they played a less important part than their English counterparts. A very large part of the Continental buying in the colonies seems to have been done by groups of three or four large dealers from each main country.[15] They represented the specialized class of dealer-processors that developed when European countries first sought their wool in the producing countries, and they largely resold their purchases on the national secondary markets like Berlin and Roubaix-Tourcoing. They were specialized in foreign buying, and their operations were so extensive, their internal resources so large, and their standing so high that they could obtain credits through London both for themselves and for clients for whom they bought on commission.

4 CONCLUSION

The gradual transfer of buying which developed in this way had

[12] Cf. C. Mackenzie, *Realms of Silver: One hundred years of banking in the East* (London, 1954), pp. 120-4, 149 for an analogous account of the policy of the Chartered Bank of India, Australia and China in respect of bills drawn on European consignees.   [13] Pierrard, *Etude sur l'Industrie Lainière*, pp. 31-2.

[14] It was reported that this extension of the bank's activities was underwritten by a group of French merchants who guaranteed the operations of the first few years (*A.I.B.R.*, vol. 5, p. 71).

[15] There is little direct evidence available on this question. Ours is a qualitative judgment based on conversations with members of the trade, examination of marked sales catalogues and, where available, the detailed lists of wool exports.

far-reaching effects on the prices realized at the colonial sales. While
buyers had been attracted in the first place by the wide differential
between colonial and London prices, as more and more of them
changed their buying policy and came to the colonies that differential was steadily narrowed. The American buyers, in particular,
exerted a market influence out of all proportion to the size of their
purchases. Their preference for light conditioned greasy combing
wools and the way in which, in order to secure suitable parcels from
a fairly restricted supply, they bid prices very nearly the full equivalent of those in London soon became a source of constant delight to
the colonial selling brokers.[16] The French and Belgian buyers, also,
soon turned their attention to better quality wools for which, as
specialist manufacturers, they were willing to pay relatively high
prices.

Although the part played by local colonial manufacturers, producing behind mildly protective tariffs, in bidding up the value of
small lots of possibly inferior wool may not be ignored,[17] the peculiar
service rendered by the French and American buyers was the
attraction to the sales of the large, well-bred station clips. The types
of wool which they sought were those which, in colonial auction
rooms, had often realized insufficient to cover the less flexible costs
of station production and which had not, therefore, been offered
there in significant quantities. It was the demand which these
groups exercised, translated into relatively high prices, which
turned the balance for the large graziers. Their decision, in turn,
together with the financial development of the colonial selling
brokers which made it possible for them to secure their accommodation from colonial concerns, forced the large consigning houses
like Dalgetys to become colonial brokers themselves in the eighties
and so complete the transition from a market centred on London
to one located in the colonies.

16 Cf. the Australasian & Mortgage Agency Co.'s market report, *Australasian
Trade Review*, 16 Jan. 1884.
17 Cf. Royal Commission on the Tariff 'Report and Minutes of Evidence',
Proc. Vic. Leg. Ass., 1883, vol. 4, paper 50, questions 2918-20, 5647-9. In 1884-5
the Victorian textile industry consumed 1,501,000 lb. of raw wool and in the
following year, 1,797,947 lb. (*Victorian Year Book*, 1886).

PART III

THE PRODUCT OF THE
OPERATION OF THE MARKET

8

MARKETING COSTS AND WOOL PRICES

ONE of the major gaps in the source materials of the economic history of the nineteenth century is a body of adequate statistics. The wool trade is better served than others, for it and the wool textile industries were so important to the producing and consuming countries that a comparatively full collection of statistics was built up. Nevertheless, the difficulties are very great. The time units to which figures refer changed basically from time to time and differed between countries; they included different material and were based on different definitions of basic activities and commodities; and they vary from informal guesses and estimates to calculations from official records and censal investigations.[1] To deplore these deficiencies and to lament the inability of the statistical material to meet our requirements is merely to reflect on the comparative youth of organized statistical effort. It is also a confession of our dependence on imperfect data.

In no field is this inadequacy so pronounced as in price statistics. Yet price is the variable in which we are interested, for it was a characteristic of the market that growers did not carry stocks and that, with the unimportant exception of dealers' speculative stocks, the supply of wool equalled the auction offerings and the quantity sold equalled the quantity supplied. The corollary to this was that the effects of movements in supply and demand were absorbed in the prices established.[2] Moreover, from the realizations based on those prices were deducted the charges which the growers had to meet in order to sell their produce.[3] Some of these costs were

[1] Even official records may err. Paul Pierrard, a French woolbuying broker in London and a Fellow of the Royal Statistical Society, in 1887 expressed the view that 'Notwithstanding appearances, *all previous wool statistics are simply delusive and incorrect*' (original italics) (*The Standard Wool-Bale* . . ., p. 8). Cf. also note to Table VI, Appendix.

[2] This is admirably analyzed by G. Blau, 'Wool in the World Economy', *Journal of the Royal Statistical Society*, vol. 109, p. 179.

[3] For most of the growers—for all in fact who did not sell their clips by direct private treaty with the buyers—this statement is quite literally true. The agent who arranged the sale—the English importing agent or the colonial selling broker—paid most of these costs (frequently including freight and insurance) on the grower's behalf and deducted them from the gross proceeds payable on the account sale.

established as the prices of services performed wholly within the market; others were determined independently of the wool market and its structural appendages. All of them played an essential part in the determination of actual realizations.

Here our intention is to bring together what data there are on marketing costs and prices in an endeavour to establish some basic statistical series, and briefly to describe the behaviour of these variables over time.

I   THE COSTS OF MARKETING

The marketing process was a long and fairly complicated one, involving the physical transport of the goods over long distances and the intervention of many skilled market functionaries to bridge economic separation of consumers from producers. To realize his wool it was necessary for the grower to pay for transport, insurance and storage; to pay commissions to the agents who performed middlemen functions; to pay for the weighing, sampling and lotting that preceded the sale; and to pay the costs of holding and publicizing the sale itself.

(a) *Inland Carriage*

The first expense that arose was in the transport of the wool from the sheep station to the coast[4]—either to a port for consignment overseas or to a colonial selling centre. During the sixty years after 1840 the nature and conditions of this inland transport, and with them the costs, changed tremendously.

A most noticeable feature in that period was the gradually increasing efficiency of road transport. In 1840 the grower had to rely almost entirely on bullock-drawn carts which followed ill-defined tracks and rude roads.[5] One aspect of the response to the vast increase in colonial populations which occurred in the fifties was the startling improvement in the number and quality of roads—secondary as well as major—and the establishment of large-scale specialist carrying concerns. Between 1857 and 1864 alone the time and the cost of road haulage, at least on the main highways, was reduced

---

[4] Expenses for packing, sorting and scouring wool are not included here. Though the line of separation may be uncertain at times (for these services were sometimes performed by specialists in the towns), they were essentially costs of producing a given physical commodity rather than costs of marketing it.

[5] Though small, the proportion of wool taken direct to the nearest minor port and then shipped coastwise to the larger ones was larger in the forties than in the last half of the century. In the forties this was the only alternative to road-haulage.

by up to a half.[6] During the following decades the work of improving the roads to serve an expanding and spreading population was
carried on by colonial governments and local authorities,[7] while
larger and more efficient carts were introduced by the carrying firms.
The most significant development, of course, lay in the introduction and growth of river and railway transport. The utilization of
the Murray, Murrumbidgee, Lachlan and Darling Rivers system
terminating in South Australia largely replaced the necessity of
road carriage to Sydney or Melbourne from extensive areas in the
Riverina, northern Victoria and the south-east extremities of South
Australia. Similarly the spread of railway systems after the fifties
directly displaced road carriage in their immediate vicinity. Over
those journeys the costs were substantially reduced. Direct comparisons are difficult to make because of the variable nature of the road
carriage rates and because back-loadings of wool were generally
carried at rates lower than those quoted for the outward trips to
which published tariffs applied; the quotations for wool carriage
which have survived, moreover, are scattered both as to time and
place and are only rarely those which are directly competitive with
railway or river freights. In general terms, however, the saving is
quite apparent. In 1864 road transport from Goulburn to Sydney
took between five and ten days and cost something less than between
£3 and £4 10s. per ton (the outward rate for general merchandise);[8]
in 1869, the first year of the service, railway carriage of wool took
only fourteen hours and cost only £1 7s. 6d. per ton.[9] Similarly, in
1862 the river and road carriage from Hay in New South Wales to
Melbourne was said to vary between £15 and £20 per ton;[10] by 1880
the combined river and rail transport cost was between £4 15s. and
£5 15s. per ton including insurance. While the road carriage from
Hay to Deniliquin—a distance of about ninety miles—was £2 10s.

[6] The journey from Sydney to Albury was reduced from between 40 and 90
days at a cost of £25 to £30 per ton to 21 to 40 days at £7 to £9 per ton; to Orange,
from 18 to 36 days at £18 to £23 was the rule in 1857, while in 1864 it took only
12 to 15 days at £6 10s. to £8 10s. per ton. See the table presented in the 'Report
of the Commissioner on the State of the Roads', *Journal of the Legislative Council of N.S.W.*, 1865-6, vol. 13, p. 237.
[7] In the twenty years 1860-79 an annual average of 13 per cent of the colonial
public authorities' gross outlay on capital goods was associated with roads. See
N. G. Butlin and H. de Meel, *Public Capital Formation in Australia: Estimates
1860-1900*, Australian National University Social Science Monograph No. 2
(Canberra, 1954), pp. 100-3.
[8] 'Report of the Commissioner on the State of the Roads'.
[9] 'Report on the Construction and Progress of the Railways of New South
Wales, from 1866 to 1871 inclusive', *N.S.W. V. & P.*, 1872-3, vol. 2, Appendix 29.
[10] Select Committee on the Riverina Districts, 'Report and Minutes of Evidence', *Proc. Vic. Leg. Ass.*, 1862-3, vol. 2, paper D42, question 203.

per ton, the rail freight from Deniliquin to Melbourne—about 200 miles—was only £2 15s.[11]

In addition to the immediate saving in freight, however, the time saved by these more efficient means of transport was of considerable importance. More rapid carriage meant not only the ability to get the wool to an earlier sales series but also a saving in interest. This is most obvious over long distances. River carriage from properties on the Upper Darling, for example, was about 50s. per ton at the end of the century. It was nevertheless cheaper to pay about 95s. per ton on the railway from Bourke because to the river rate had to be added insurance of about 15s. per cent and because the river trip took about six weeks longer (in a good season when the river was open). On wool worth 15d. per lb. the six weeks' delay, at an interest rate of 6 per cent per annum, meant the actual or imputed addition of about another £1 per ton to the grower's costs.[12] Even on short journeys of 200 miles the difference could amount to 3s. to 4s. per ton.

These comparisons refer to those instances where the rail or river carriage was directly substituted for road haulage. It is important to realize, however, that the pastoral areas directly served by the railway networks, even at the end of the century, were relatively limited. Consequently, while the cost of all wool carriage was reduced to the extent that railway or river transport could be used, the cost of road carriage to the railhead or river port remained a major item in marketing costs, varying widely with distance, location and the state of the weather.[13]

After the arrival of the wool in the main ports two separate cost structures must be distinguished: the one appropriate to wool dispatched for sale in London, and the one appropriate to wool sold in the colonies. Most of these cost items can be identified and, unlike inland transport,[14] measured with considerable accuracy.

---

[11] C. Lyne, *The Industries of New South Wales*, pp. 250, 253.

[12] Royal Commission . . . into the Condition of the Crown Tenants in the Western Division of New South Wales, 'Report and Minutes of Evidence', *N.S.W. V. & P.*, 1901, vol. 4, question 12919.

[13] In the early seventies, for example, the normal rate from Tenterfield to Grafton (about 80 miles) was 2s. per ton-mile but in 1872 adverse weather conditions forced it up to over 3s. ('Collaroy Papers', vol. 5: 'Letters and Papers of R. J. Traill', unknown correspondent to Traill dated 31 Dec. 1872). Similarly at the turn of the century carriage for a distance of about 25 miles from Narrabri rose from a normal 9d. per ton-mile to 1s. and 1s. 2d. in unfavourable weather (Standing Committee on Public Works, 'Report on the Proposed Railway from Narrabri to Walgett . . . with Minutes of Evidence', *N.S.W. V. & P.*, 1900, vol. 5, question 460).

[14] Any measure of the cost to the industry of inland carriage would be at best

(b) *Selling in London*

The main cost incurred in consigning to the London market was ocean freight. This fell throughout the last sixty years of the nine-teenth century as the increasing volume of imports, particularly during the fifties, increased the tonnage of shipping available to the trade, as the larger and speedier steamships were added to the run, and as a result of the opening of the Suez Canal route.

The vastly increased colonial population associated with the discovery of gold led, during and after the fifties, to greatly expanded imports of goods of all descriptions from England. The shipping required to transport these imports increased more rapidly than the wool for export.[15] The bulky wool-bales, instead of provid-ing the main cargo for the round trip, were treated almost as back-loading during the early part of the fifties and, even after the immediate boom in importing eased, the increased facilities per-mitted a permanent reduction in rates.[16] After 1851 the freight rates on washed wool, which had been $1\frac{1}{4}$d. to $1\frac{1}{2}$d. in the forties, rarely exceeded 1d. per lb.[17]

Steamships were first used on the monthly mail runs from Eng-land in 1865. It was not until 1877 that the first steamers not under mail contract arrived. Until that time, therefore, the major part of the clip was lifted by sailing vessel. The popularity of the steamers spread rapidly, however, and seven years later they carried nearly half the exports.[18] Yet the rates were consistently higher than by sailing ship. The reason for the preference for steam transport was, of course, the time saved, which was a major consideration. Speedier

---

a guess. It would be possible to construct tables showing the average costs per lb. of wool by dividing Australia into a large number of fairly small geographical regions, calculating the current transport charges in each year to the main ports from each of them, then weighting those costs according to the regional wool production and finally taking an average. Such an effort would be entirely unwarranted in a study of this nature.

[15] The tonnage cleared out of Port Phillip rose from an annual average of 75,030 in the three years 1848-50 to 634,041 in 1858-1860.

[16] See Appendix, Tables XXI and XXII.

[17] Naturally there could be quite violent short-term fluctuations as the quantity of shipping in the port varied from month to month. Monthly quotations from Melbourne in 1885, for greasy wool by sailer, show the following normal pattern of movement between January and December (in pence per lb.): $\frac{3}{8}$, $\frac{1}{2}$, $\frac{1}{2}$, $\frac{1}{2}$, $\frac{3}{8}$, $\frac{3}{8}$, $\frac{3}{8}$, $\frac{3}{8}$, $\frac{3}{8}$, $\frac{1}{2}$, $\frac{1}{2}$, $\frac{1}{2}$.

[18] In the period 1 July 1884 to 24 Jan. 1885 the percentage of wool exports shipped from the different colonies in steam vessels was:

N.S.W.	Victoria	S.A.	Tas.	W.A.	Q'ld.	Australia
54	43	43	nil	12	97	46

(Calculated from figures presented in R. Goldsbrough & Co.'s monthly wool report, *Argus*, 28 Jan. 1885.)

ocean carriage, the shorter Suez route which steamers could use, and improved internal transport enabled an increasing proportion of the clip to reach the January and even, by the late eighties, the November series of sales in London. This meant a corresponding reduction in the length of time for which export credit was required and consequently in the interest paid.

Insurance had to be provided to cover marine risks in transit to England and fire risk while in the London warehouses. Information regarding these rates is not readily available. Such evidence as there is, however, points to a consistent lowering of the premium on marine insurance throughout the century. Isolated quotations from the period 1843 to 1874 show a fall of over 40 per cent.[19] The improved efficiency and safety of ocean transport and the competition between English and colonial insurance companies, particularly after the late seventies, probably meant a similar gradual reduction in the rest of the period. Fire insurance was a very minor item. Neil Black, in 1848 was paying about 5s. per £100; in 1874 the rate was 1s. 4d. per £100.[20]

The strictly marketing functions of the main agents employed to arrange the sale of the wool in London—the consigning and importing agents—were charged to the growers in the form of the gross commission payable to the consignees. We have already noted the general characteristics of the pricing policy of this group.[21] The average gross commission fell from 2½ per cent of the gross realization in the thirty years preceding the early seventies to 1½ per cent to 2 per cent. Similarly, the commission payable to the English selling broker stood steady at 1 per cent from the twenties to the seventies, when it fell to ½ per cent. Generally this charge was additional to the gross importer's commission. Some consignees sometimes also charged the grower for effecting marine and fire insurance and for paying freight charges for them. Where this happened the charges were small and probably quite variable.[22] If

---

[19] From various account sales for years between 1843 and 1855 in the 'Black Papers', from the *Journal of Commerce*, 28 April 1864 and 12 Jan. 1871, and from Renard Bros. & Co., *Antwerp versus London as a Market for Australian Wool*, p. 14, the following table of premiums per £100 for marine insurance on wool to London may be constructed:

Sept. 1843	60s.		April 1864	35s.
Feb. 1848	50s.		Jan. 1871	35s. plus war
May 1851	40s.			loading
Aug. 1855	60s.		1874	35s.

[20] 'Black Papers': Gladstone & Sargeantson to Black, account sales dated 25 Aug. 1848; Renard Bros. & Co., *Antwerp versus London as a Market for Australian Wool*, p. 14.   [21] See pp. 105-8.

[22] The only specific figure I have seen attached to this service is the ½ per cent

the colonial consigning agents paid these items for the grower, the scale of their charges for the services were governed by the regulations of the Chambers of Commerce. In 1856 the Melbourne Chamber sanctioned charges of $2\frac{1}{2}\%$ on freight paid at the port of departure; $\frac{1}{2}\%$ on the value assured was allowed in Melbourne and $\frac{1}{4}\%$ in Adelaide for effecting marine insurance.[23]

The London selling brokers' charge was 1% between the twenties and the time it was reduced to $\frac{1}{2}\%$ early in the seventies. To this the brokers also added further charges of 4d. per bale to cover sales expenses—the costs of printing the catalogues, advertising the sales, etc. This charge did not vary throughout the century.

Warehousing and the associated services formed a substantial item in the sellers' costs. On 94 bales of wool sent to the sales in 1843 and grossing £1,253, Neil Black paid just over £16 for services itemized on his account sales as dock and town dues, customs entry, cartage and porterage, lotting and showing, taring and making up, re-weighing and warehouse rent.[24] By the sixties these charges had been brought together into one 'consolidated warehouse charge'[25] and formed a considerably heavier burden than they had in the forties. Instead of the 3s. 5d. Black had paid, 4s. 2d. to 5s. 6d. per bale was charged, and instead of forming about 6 per cent of selling costs it formed nearer 12 per cent.[26] Sensitive to changes in wage rates and other operating costs, the warehousemen changed their quotations with a frequency that was not common in most other branches of the trade. The rates charged by Brown & Eagle, which are the same as those of the other warehousemen,[27] illustrate these fluctuations and indicate the slight downward trend

---

of the sum insured mentioned by Sir Daniel Cooper in his letter in *The Times* (16 March 1871). See p. 92.

[23] For the Melbourne scale see, e.g. the *Journal of Commerce of Victoria*, 9 Jan. 1858; for Adelaide, the *South Australian Advertiser*, 1 Dec. 1860.

[24] 'Black Papers': Account sales from Gladstone & Sargeantson, 29 Sept. 1843.

[25] The London & St. Katherine Docks Co.'s scale of charges published on 15 Feb. 1870 include in the consolidated charge the following services—landing, wharfage, carriage to warehouse, housing, 12 weeks' rent, mending, weighing, sampling, supplying documents, taring, piling, transfer of bales to showroom, marking, showing, filling in loose wool, re-weighing, remending, housing bales for delivery, and delivery by land!

[26] The second set of figures are taken from the accounts of the Australian Agricultural Co. relating to its clip of 1868. See Appendix, Table XXIV.

[27] Though nominally the rates differed, the different warehousemen offered discounts to their customers which brought them all to the same level. In 1877, for example, the London & St. Katherine Docks quoted rates of 3s. 8d., 5s., 6s. 3d., 8s. for the four sizes of bales mentioned in Table XXIII, Appendix; but they were subject to a discount of 20 per cent and a further allowance of 15 per cent of the net sum.

that occurred between the end of the sixties and the end of the eighties.[28] Any bales warehoused for more than the twelve weeks allowed for in the consolidated rate were charged rent at the rate of ¾d., 1d., 1½d., and 2d. for each excess week according to their size. This did not change between 1867 and 1889.

In addition to all these selling expenses—defined more narrowly than 'marketing expenses'—the growers' costs should include actual or imputed interest charges. Actual interest payments were made when growers took export advances from their consigning agents or when the agents or consignees made disbursements (freight or insurance) for them before they were in funds from the realization. The rates were governed in the first instance by current short-term bank interest rates in the colonies and the discount on commercial paper drawn on England (the method used by some agents to recover their cash outlay), and in the second instance solely by the short-term interest rates in the colonies or England. It is most probable that a fairly stable margin separated the two sets of rates. The colonial agents could also make a charge for making the advance at all. In 1860 the Adelaide Chamber of Commerce set at 2½ per cent the commission which its members might take for endorsing a bill or for making an advance on produce which was to be shipped. It made the further stipulation that 'when an account is unliquidated at the end of the year the balance is to be charged as a fresh advance, subject to a commission of 5 per cent'.[29]

Where a grower did not take an advance on his realization, the expenses of freight, insurance, etc. were still subject to actual or imputed interest costs. Contemporary commercial statements assumed, in fact, that an allowance would be made for it.[30] Once the colonial auction system had acquired some stature and became a real alternative to the London sales, then it was also reasonable to impute the interest costs for the greater length of time taken for proceeds to be received from a London than from a colonial realization.

Including the financial charges, these costs took a substantial share of the growers' gross income. With set costs like freight and warehousing bulking as large as they did, it is hardly surprising

[28] See Appendix, Table XXIII.
[29] *South Australian Advertiser*, 1 Dec. 1860. This was an obviously fertile field for unscrupulous lenders and it led to many claims of exploitation; see p. 118, n. 43.
[30] E.g., Gustave Ebell's comparison of *pro forma* account sales from the Berlin and London auctions in Brodribb, *Results of Inquiries . . .*, pp. 29-30; also S. S. Smith, *Important Suggestions for a Better Development of Colonial Wool and Leather, etc.*, p. 40.

that, when wool incomes fell so precipitately at the end of the sixties, there should have been an outcry against the 'twenty per cent said to be paid in the shape of discount, commission and agents' charges'.[31]

(c) *Selling in the Colonies*

The two major costs borne by growers who disposed of their clips in the local markets in Sydney, Melbourne or Adelaide were the selling broker's commission and the charge for receiving, weighing, warehousing and showing, known simply as the receiving charge.

These costs varied between the different markets. The Melbourne selling commission seems to have been stable at $1\frac{1}{2}$ per cent. This at least is the rate mentioned in the four specific quotations which have been found.[32] The Sydney quotation in 1864, the earliest reference that has been located, was $2\frac{1}{2}$ per cent, and it was reduced to 2 per cent in 1906.[33] In 1858 the Adelaide Chamber of Commerce set the commission on the sale of produce at auction or through a broker at $2\frac{1}{2}$ to 5 per cent 'depending on circumstances'.[34] By 1879 Elder, Smith & Co. had adopted a sliding scale of charges, debiting $2\frac{1}{2}$ per cent commission on sales of less than £200, and 1 per cent on sales of greater value. Four years later this scale was unchanged.[35] In Melbourne the receiving charge remained stable at $\frac{1}{8}$d. per lb. from 1856 to 1889,[36] and there is no indication that it was changed in the remainder of the century. In Adelaide the grower was relieved of this $\frac{1}{8}$d. per lb. charge in 1879, but only for four seasons.[37] No data have been located concerning the rates in Sydney.

In addition to these charges provision had to be made against fire risks in the warehouse—probably at a nominal rate like 2s. 6d. per £100. Growers who shipped their clips to Melbourne from other colonies could also be charged for lighterage and cartage from the

[31] *Argus*, 6 Feb. 1869, leader.
[32] The sources are: R. Goldsbrough & Co., 'Unbound Correspondence', Goldsbrough to T. J. Gibson, 12 Jan. 1863, duplicate invoices to R. Hogarth (31 Oct. 1881) and M. D. Synnot Bros. (24 Oct. 1881); Royal Commission on the Tariff, 'Report and Minutes of Evidence', *Proc. Vic. Leg. Ass.*, 1883, vol. 4, question 23879; manuscript manifesto prefacing the Victorian Wool Buyers' Association Minutes. It has not been possible to calculate a rate from the commission revenue noted in R. Goldsbrough & Co. Ltd, 'Balance Books', Analysis of Profit and Loss, because the value of the wool sold is unknown.
[33] E. Greville (ed.), *The Official Directory and Almanac of Australia, 1884*, p. 563; also advertisement, Harrison, Jones & Devlin Ltd, in *Australian Country Life*, vol. 1, no. 1 (April 1906). [34] *South Australian Advertiser*, 1 Dec. 1860.
[35] Elder, Smith & Co., *Circular Wool Letters*, 20 Aug. 1879 and 30 Aug. 1883.
[36] This was the rate in 1863, 1881, 1883, and 1889 (see p. 115, n. 32).
[37] See p. 158, n. 31.

wharves.[38] Inland insurance should also be added to the costs of all growers, whether selling in the colonies or in London. The scant indications that exist point to a premium of about £1 per cent for wool sent from inland New South Wales and equivalent regions.[39]

(d) *Marketing Costs and Net Realizations*

In the present state of our statistical knowledge it is not possible to construct tables showing the gross income from wool received by Australian pastoralists, the parts of that income paid to Australian and overseas concerns as marketing costs, or the resultant net incomes which the pastoralists received on the farm or free at the main ports of export or sale. We have neither adequate price and quantity information for accurate gross incomes nor complete figures for the marketing costs.

We can gain some idea of the general relation of marketing costs to gross proceeds, however, by comparing the expenses and receipts relating to the clips of the Australian Agricultural Co. which have been preserved in detail.[40]

It must be noticed, however, that this company did not pay an importer's commission, for the consignee's functions were exercised by its own head office in London. This was a situation which often arose in the case of corporate producers with a London office. Moreover, shipping on their own account, many of these concerns, including the Australian Agricultural Co., escaped the necessity of paying a commission to a consigning agent. Consequently, to the total costs actually paid by the Australian Agricultural Co. must be added the normal gross commission paid to the consignee.

The comparison clearly underlines the scissored effects of price movements and those marketing costs fixed in cash terms. When realizations fell heavily in 1868, 1878 and 1880, the proportion of

---

[38] R. Goldsbrough & Co. Ltd ('Balance Books', Analysis of Profit and Loss) entered as net receipts sums for lighterage, cartage and insurance, all of them very small. These entries seem to be profits made by the firm as a result either of charging growers a higher rate for lighterage than it cost the firm, or by the use of the firm's equipment in carting wool from the wharves (cartage from the railway station was included in the receiving charge) and as commissions or charges on effecting inland and fire insurance.

[39] Royal Commission . . . into the Condition of the Crown Tenants in the Western Division of New South Wales, 'Report and Minutes of Evidence', *N.S.W. V. & P.*, 1901, vol. 4, question 12919 indicates that insurance on wool carried down the Darling system was about £1 per ton in 1900. This was slightly less than £1 per cent. Accounts held by Goldsbrough, Mort & Co. Ltd show that inland insurance covering the journey from Netley station in the extreme south-west of N.S.W. to Melbourne was £1 per cent in 1897.

[40] See Appendix, Table XXIV for costs of selling scoured wool in London, 1865 to 1884, and Table XXV for corresponding costs for greasy wool.

11 The wool floor, London Docks, 1850

costs to proceeds rose sharply. Over short periods when prices were falling, particularly in the nineties, there was a tendency for the same thing to occur.

Over the period as a whole, however, the ratio between costs and gross prices remained remarkably stable. In fifteen of the eighteen years for which data are available the ratio of costs (excluding importer's commission) to the price of scoured wool lay between 6 and 8 per cent; in fifteen of the twenty-four years covered in the data on greasy wool it lay between 8.5 and 10 per cent. Freights, in particular, showed a decided tendency to fall and, as they formed the major single item, this had an important influence in allowing those costs fixed in terms of weight or volume—freights, warehousing and sales expenses—to move in the same general direction as wool prices. Insurance rates do not seem to have changed appreciably, and broker's commission rates changed only in 1870 when they were reduced, for the Australian Agricultural Co. at least,[41] from 1 to $\frac{1}{2}$ per cent. Yet, because these two charges were based on the value (actual or anticipated) of the wool, their relation to proceeds remained the same.

On realization the weight of the marketing costs fell much more heavily on greasy than on scoured wool. The difference is due, of course, to the disproportionately small reduction in freight charges for greasy wool compared with the large difference in price. This discrepancy did not mean, however, that scoured wool was necessarily the most economical to produce. What it could mean is that if there were other grounds for preferring to produce greasy wool rather than scoured wool, as there were, this comparison in costs established a definite inducement to sell it in the colonies so long as the price differential between the alternative markets was not too great, for that course alone avoided ocean transport.

The saving in marketing costs, narrowly defined as the cost of transport, insurance, storage and selling charges, was insufficient, by itself, to induce growers to sell in the colonies rather than in London. Inland transport and insurance costs being the same whether the wool was sold or consigned in the main ports, the focal point of the comparison is the cost of sale at the local auction. Hypothetical costs in Melbourne, based on a receiving rate of $\frac{1}{8}$d. per lb. and a selling commission of $1\frac{1}{2}$ per cent, can be constructed.[42] The saving they indicate suggests that a seller could afford to accept in Melbourne a price between 3 and 9 per cent lower than the

[41] The date at which the trade generally adopted the reduced rate is open to some doubt. See p. 111, n. 21.   [42] See Appendix, Table XXVI.

London quotation and be no worse off than if he had consigned to England. In other words the price spread between the two markets could not exceed, say, 10 per cent, if this saving was the only one the grower made. One estimate at the end of the eighties put the spread necessary to provide a profit for a speculative buyer in the colonies at about 25 per cent. This underlines the dependence of the colonial auctions on the operations of manufacturing consumers and distributive middlemen who alone could afford to pay within the 10 per cent which this comparison suggests was necessary. By the nineties at the latest the differential *had* narrowed to this extent.

In fact, this comparison, and the Australian Agricultural Co.'s cost returns, exclude all financial costs. To the tables relating to London sales need to be added interest charges at rates varying from 6 to 10 per cent per annum, for a period of at least three months, on advances made to cover the time between the wool's departure from an Australian port and the receipt of the proceeds, together with the various commission charges made by agents in granting and renewing the advances, endorsing bills of exchange, etc. This would make a considerable difference to the comparison, for sales in the colonies would require shorter periods of financing and fewer renewals. The price differential that growers would be willing to accept could therefore be extended to closer to 20 per cent. This is in fact about the magnitude of the spread which existed in the late seventies and early eighties.

2　THE PRICES OF AUSTRALIAN WOOLS

There are no satisfactory series of the prices of Australian wools in the nineteenth century. No single series could, of course, serve all the purposes for which we require this information. As we have already indicated,[43] the term 'Australian wool' is misleading, for Australian output comprised a number of broad types of wool each one of which was subject to its own special conditions of supply and demand and for each of which an appropriate price series could be constructed. Series should be collated for Victorian combing wool, for New South Welsh clothing wool, for New South Welsh combing wool, etc., for the crossbred wools from the different colonies and for each of these types in the different states in which they were marketed—greasy, scoured and washed, etc. Those series would form the basic information. To obtain an indicator of the

[43] See pp. 3-8.

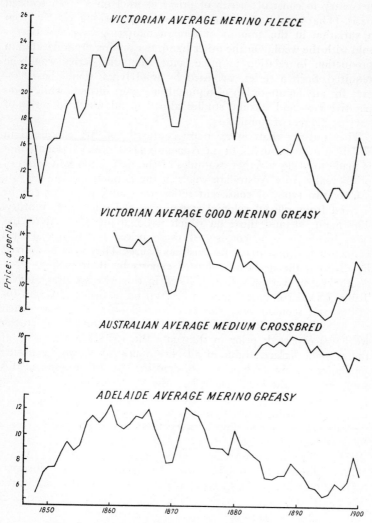

FIG. 6. London prices of some Australian wools
(See Appendix, Table XXVII)

interplay of the supply and demand for each variety it would be necessary to construct series of prices of wool on a clean scoured basis. (That would eliminate price variations arising simply from a variation in the amount of foreign matter—grease and burr—sold with the wool.) On the other hand, to examine gross Australian production in relation to price some composite series would be required. Such a series, weighted by wool types, would be necessary for any computation of national or export income, while comparative cost and income studies also demand weighted series of varying degrees of complexity.

The statistics that do exist are confused and are contained in widely scattered sources. In the Appendix (Table XXVII) an attempt is made to bring together examples of the most important series of prices realized by Australian wools in the London market.

Only two types of consistent series are contained in, or can be derived from, official colonial statistics of the nineteenth century. The main set, and those on which national income analysis has been forced to rely, consists of those prices at which exporters valued their shipments at the customs houses. They may be derived by dividing the declared value of exports by their volume. New South Welsh average values deduced in this way are presented in Table XXVII columns 4 and 5 (see Appendix). Separate values for greasy and scoured wool can be obtained only from 1873, when the Colonial Statistician first took notice of the state in which the wool was exported; prior to that date the series is simply one of the average declared value of all New South Welsh wool exported by sea irrespective of type. It is evident that 'prices' obtained in this way represent the hopes, or at best the formal expectations, of the growers (modified perhaps by the advice of their financiers) rather than actual realizations. Though in periods of relatively stable prices a certain relationship between them and realized prices may be discerned, the frequency with which discrepancies occur reveals the fallibility of the forecasts. (Their correspondence with market values did improve during and after the eighties, but simply because a larger proportion of exports consisted of wool already sold in the colonial markets, and therefore valued in accordance with previously realized, and paid, prices.)

Some colonial statisticians also published average prices realized in London by wool from their own colonies. These were taken from English trade sources, in the form either of annual average prices or average prices obtained at particular London sales series.[44]

[44] E.g. *W. & P.*, *1900-01*, p. 592, gives part of a series extending from 1880

The value and dependability of the English data which they used varied widely. Some of the series constructed by commercial commentators or more or less informed members of the trade have no value for a study of this nature. *The Economist*,[45] for example, was one of many which presented figures framed in terms of price ranges (with a spread of up to three times the lower value), and while this may be the most honest method of presentation, taking account of quality and other differences, it is the least informative.

The most comprehensive, accurate and useful sets of statistics available to us are those computed from trade records by Helmuth Schwartze & Co. (later Buchanan, Schwartze & Co.), woolbuying and selling brokers of London, and by A. Sauerbeck. They consist of end-of-year and/or annual average London prices of a large number of wool types from various countries. Some of them relating to Sydney, Adelaide and Port Phillip merino are included in Table XXVII (columns 2, 3, 6 and 7).[46]

Only one type of series purports to represent the price of 'Australian greasy merino': [47] this is a trade estimate presumably based on the gross realizations of all greasy colonial wool entered in the books of one of the selling brokers. Average prices of such a nature, realized at the February series of sales in London, are recorded in Table XXVII (column 1).

It is clear that the utility of those series is limited. With the exception just noted, each refers only to a specific type of wool. Those referring to specific varieties from specific colonies are eminently suited for a discussion of those wools. But without supplementary information, which is not obtainable, they offer an imperfect basis for wider discussions or for income calculations. Even the more ambitiously phrased 'Australian greasy wool' price series contains defects that make it difficult to use it for many purposes.

---

showing the average prices realized for N.S.W. greasy wool at each of the London sales series.

[45] The 'Commercial History Supplements' to *The Economist* give prices for a number of types of Australian wool in this fashion from at least 1845.

[46] See Appendix. A. Sauerbeck, op. cit., p. 15, gives, in addition to these, annual average and end-of-year prices of two types of Cape wool, average greasy Buenos Aires wool and English Lincoln hoggett and wether wool.

[47] W. H. Chard (*Australasian Wool Markets*, p. 24) presents a chart of annual average prices of 'ordinary 60's topmaking wool, clean scoured basis'. There is no indication of how the basic price series was formed nor of how a clean equivalent was obtained. An unweighted average of the indices of Sauerbeck's prices for South Australian greasy merino and Port Phillip fleece merino is offered by the Bureau of Agricultural Economics (*Statistical Handbook of the Sheep and Wool Industry*, Table 51) as an indication of the movements in 'Australian merino' prices from 1846 to 1947.

It is, firstly, based on an unknown method of computation. How wool from different colonies was weighted and how the average value was obtained is not revealed. This second point applies equally, of course, to the series relating to narrower wool types and probably does not matter as far as *movements* in supply and demand are concerned, for the direction and magnitude of the price movements, not the exactly accurate average determination, are the important things here. The fact that quotations can be obtained quarterly, or even more frequently on occasion, makes this series very useful for that purpose. The uncertainty makes the series suspect, however, when used in income analysis. It is, in any case, an incomplete guide, for it refers only to greasy wool and entirely excludes washed and scoured wool which, until the seventies, formed the greater proportion of exports. Moreover, all these series suffer from one fundamental defect which unsuits them for income calculations or analysis. They refer only to wool sold in London (even the average export valuations are predominantly phrased on that assumption), and they take no account of wool offered and sold in the colonies.

Colonial price statistics themselves are wholly unsatisfactory and inadequate before the end of the century.[48] Series of price ranges of varying lengths may be culled from various official sources[49] or constructed from selling brokers' published reports of sales.[50] The major series of seasonal average prices collected for specific wool types is that made by the Victorian Statistician for the Melbourne market.[51] Even though these prices are based on the calculations of the leading Melbourne wool selling brokers, their accuracy is open to some doubt. Preliminary investigation indicates that they unduly inflate the actual prices realized. In general terms this belief seems to be justified by a comparison of relevant prices realized in London

[48] At the turn of the century Dalgety & Co. Ltd commenced publishing annual series of adequate accuracy.

[49] E.g. *W. & P., 1894*, p. 341, gives in the form of ranges the prices obtained in Sydney by four qualities of each of eight wool types; the first season so treated is 1893-4. Other short series of colonial quotations are occasionally given—e.g. Adelaide prices of greasy and scoured merino, 1861-7, in Appendix M of the 'Report and Minutes of Evidence' of the Commission appointed to enquire into the State of Runs suffering from Drought, *S.A.P.P.*, 1867, vol. 2, paper 14.

[50] Colonial newspapers and commercial journals often carried current market quotations supplied to them by the brokers. They took the form of price ranges and often differed from broker to broker. On 17 Jan. 1883, for example, both R. Goldsbrough & Co. and the Australasian Mortgage & Agency Co. published reports in the *Journal of Commerce* and the *Australian Trade Review*, respectively. Their quotations for average good greasy merino wool were 10½-12d. and 9-10½d. respectively, and for fine crossbred wool 11-12½d. and 10½-12d.

[51] See Appendix, Table XXVIII.

and Melbourne. If we regard the wool sold in Melbourne during, for example, 1884–5 as belonging to the same clip as wool sold in London in 1885 (an assumption only very slightly falsified by the ability to ship new season's wool by steamer to arrive in London before the end of the year), then the comparison shown in Fig. 7 is startling: only once in the ten years between 1885 and 1894 was the Melbourne price for 'fleece and washed wool' below that quoted in London (1888 and 1893); in seven of those years, including the first five years of the nineties, Melbourne greasy wool prices exceeded, or equalled, London prices.

The growth of direct purchases in Australia by English, Continental and American dealers and consumers meant, of course, that colonial prices tended to be the f.o.b. equivalent of London prices. It was possible, under those circumstances, for colonial prices to exceed this equivalent in the short run; it was possible for them to exceed London equivalents by so much that they topped the actual quotations there; it was even possible for them to have done this for a season or more as a result of the impact of market rigidities and special local conditions of supply and demand. It is quite inconceivable that it should have continued for nearly a decade.

It might be suspected that the differences arise from imprecise definitions. This is unlikely. The London greasy prices might be expected to be higher than Melbourne ones because they refer to 'average good merino' while the Victorian figures allegedly include all greasy merino irrespective of quality; but the London quotations are in fact generally lower. London 'average fleece' prices might be expected to be lower than the 'fleece and washed' because fleece wool realized lower prices than either washed or scoured, but once again the specification of 'average' probably nullifies this.

This comparison, of course, merely establishes that either Melbourne quotations are inflated or London prices are too low. Reference to marked sales catalogues from the Victorian auctions indicates that whatever was true of the London quotations, the Melbourne ones are certainly too high. A sample of lots sold at the auctions in Melbourne and Geelong reveals an average price of 8.3d., 7.4d., and 8.2d. for greasy merino and of 13.6d., 11.8d., and 13.4d. for scoured merino realized there in 1886–7, 1887–8 and 1888–9 respectively.[52] The published prices stand at 10½d., 9½d., and 10½d. for greasy and 17d., 15½d. and 18d. for washed wool. The reason for the

[52] These samples have been taken on a 1 in 6 basis from marked catalogues of the sales. The average prices are probably accurate to within plus or minus 5 per cent for greasy and 10 per cent for scoured.

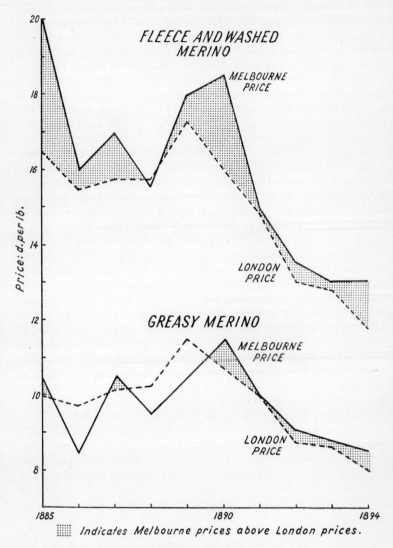

FIG. 7. London and Melbourne prices of Victorian wool

(See Appendix, Table XXIX)

vast discrepancy—up to 25 per cent—lies, it is suggested, in the brokers' omission from all their calculations of all wool not sold in the normal sized bales,[53] and their tendency, perhaps, to demote to lower priced grades (mainly, in the eighties, to low crossbreds) poor quality and damaged merino wool sold at very low prices.[54]

These, then, are the basic price data of the colonial wool trade in the nineteenth century. A selection of the more important of them is shown graphically in Fig. 6. They are subject to two major defects —in their content and accuracy. Some of the series refer to wool types which are readily identified, and some to aggregations of unknown types. Some are undoubtedly accurate both in the year-to-year movements they show and as measures of the prices actually paid at auction for those wools; but a number are, and others may be, grossly inaccurate. Their use, moreover, is limited by the paucity of the information necessary to supplement them. Combined appropriately in a weighted series representing greasy, scoured, fleece and washed wool of various types sold both in the colonies and in England, the more accurate collections could be used for income analysis. Individually, the best of the series reflect movements in the changing relationships between the supply of, and demand for, particular wool types and are essential to any such study. But we do not know enough, particularly about the composition of Australian output and the state in which the wool was marketed before the seventies, to be able to use them in these ways. In other words, they are not only frequently unsatisfactory in themselves but, in the absence of adequate supporting statistical collections, they can meet only the most simple of our requirements.

3 PRICE MOVEMENTS

One of those less sophisticated, but extremely important, things we wish to know about prices is how they moved over fairly long periods of time. The defects of our collection do not prevent us

---

[53] Large numbers of 'bags', 'sacks', 'butts' and 'fadges' were entered in the brokers' catalogues. Almost without exception these lots realized prices lower than other lots. Replying to an attack made on the Victorian Statistician's method of calculating average Melbourne prices (*Australian Trade Review*, 15 March 1882), R. Goldsbrough & Co. detailed the prices at which all their bales of greasy wool at a particular sale had been sold, and argued that the resulting average price was a true indication of prices at that time. They did not include these under-sized packages in their list.

[54] Many bales of 'locks' and of dead and stained wool sold for as little as 1d. per lb. It seems hard to believe that these wools were included, let alone included in their correct category, in calculations which give such high average values.

doing this for changes in the very long run and in the shorter period of about six to ten years, with which this section is concerned. The identification of changes over periods of these lengths is not dependent on the absolute accuracy with which the individual quotations in the series record average prices in given years. It requires rather that wide inaccuracies, like those in the Melbourne series, should be of a broadly consistent nature over time and that irregular inaccuracies should be small percentages of the quoted figures. In the best of the collections we have these conditions are fulfilled. Moreover, the limitations imposed by the relevance of most of the series to a single (though broad) wool type, and by the doubtful nature of the more general, composite, series are less important here. The series show divergent movements over very short periods but in the longer run the correspondence between them is so close that we may speak with confidence of movements in the prices of 'Australian' wool as a whole

(a) *The General Course of Prices in the Long Run*

If we inspect the price series plotted, without any adjustment, in Fig. 6 the broad long-term movements are immediately apparent.

From 1848[55] to 1866 prices generally rose. The movement was a strong and definite one until 1857-8 and then weakened considerably in the first half of the sixties, appearing, in fact, almost as a plateau.[56] The dating of the downturn from this rise varies slightly. Adelaide greasy merino and Victorian fleece and greasy merino, all of which are annual average prices, reach a peak in 1866. New South Wales clothing wool prices, on the other hand, rose only until 1865. The early peak is the product of a different set of supply and particularly of demand conditions.

Equally clear is the general fall in wool prices from at least 1873 to 1894. In contrast to the upward movement in the fifties and early sixties this fall was remarkably steady and persistent. There was no real check to it, nor even any appreciable change in the rate of fall, until an upward movement was initiated in 1895. The magni-

---

[55] Sauerbeck's figures, (Appendix, Table XXVII, columns 2 and 6) show an upturn from 1848. That this was the turning-point of a long movement is confirmed by the sets of price ranges presented by A. Hamilton ('On Wool Supply', *Journal of the Royal Statistical Society*, vol. 35 (1870), Appendix VII). Dating from 1839, and referring to four qualities of wool from each of the five Australian colonies, Hamilton's collection shows an unmistakable fall from that year to 1848.

[56] If the cotton famine associated with the American Civil War is to be connected with any movement in Australian wool prices, it is as a force maintaining this plateau in the face of an impending fall.

tudes of the rise and fall, on the other hand, were surprisingly symmetrical—values in 1848 and 1894 were virtually identical.

It is evident that the division between these two broad movements lay in the second half of the sixties and beginning of the seventies. It is just here, unfortunately, that the picture of the general movement is confused by short-term fluctuations. The short-term trough of 1869-70 and the subsequent abnormal recovery of 1871-2 were partially the product of special forces.

From 1868 to 1872 there was a cyclical upswing in British and European economic activity,[57] and with it an upswing in the demand for manufactured and raw wool until at least the early months of 1870. The continued fall in wool prices during 1869 seems to suggest excess supply. To this was added, from the first third of 1870, growing fears about the stability of European peace. Contrary to expectations the Franco-Prussian War did not mean a net reduction in the demand for wool,[58] but while prices were maintained, or even advanced fractionally, they remained at a very depressed level. The backlog of civilian demand, a possible reduction of output,[59] and the continuation of the cyclical upswing together produced an unprecedented, partly speculative, boom in 1871 and 1872.

If the amplitude of short-term fluctuations is given full consideration, one may view the overall course of the long movements as falling into two cycles. The first would extend from the trough of 1848 to that of 1869-70 with a peak in 1866; the second from 1869-70 to 1894 with a peak in 1872. If one were to discount the full magnitude of these short-term fluctuations, as there is some reason for doing, then the movement of prices appears as a single cycle with troughs in 1848 and 1894 and a plateau of peak prices in the mid-sixties rather than a single peak year. With our present knowledge both patterns are plausible, but any conclusion must rest on a detailed study of Australian, and probably of world, wool production—a task beyond the scope of this study.

A definite upswing in prices commenced in 1895. Although our

---

[57] W. W. Rostow, *British Economy in the Nineteenth Century* (Oxford, 1948), p. 33.
[58] The almost complete withdrawal of French buyers from the London auctions and the reduction in civilian consumption of wool textiles (which affected the English export industries) was 'more than counterbalanced by the exceptional demand for wool suited for blankets, army clothing etc.' (Helmuth Schwartze & Co.'s market report of 23 Feb. 1871, reprinted in the *Journal of Commerce of Victoria*, 13 April 1871).
[59] Cf. Sauerbeck, op. cit., p. 7; also R. Goldsbrough & Co.'s market report, the *Journal of Commerce of Victoria*, 6 April 1871.

series do not show it, this continued until the end of the post-war inflation in 1920.[60]

Within the general pattern of price movements which we have been discussing there were, of course, variations. It was these differences in the rates of change which accounted, at least partly, for the changing composition of Australian flocks.[61] As a result of the changed requirements of the British worsted industry after the end of the sixties[62] and of the differential rates of growth of the European worsted and woollen industries, for example, the prices of Victorian combing wools (despite the expansion of the industry) tended to fall less rapidly than those of clothing merino. For the relatively short period from 1860 to 1877 our series illustrates this divergence (Appendix, Table XXVII, columns 3 and 6). More striking, perhaps, is the contrast between prices for merino and crossbred wools in the twenty years following the late seventies. In Fig. 8 are plotted the index numbers of the prices for Victorian greasy merino and average medium Australian greasy crossbred from 1883 to 1900. The comparison shows clearly that the crossbred wool was not subject to the same general pressures during the period as merino. With this must be associated the relative expansion of crossbred flocks from the seventies.[63] Another major divergence, which our series cannot illustrate, diminished the gap between colonial and London prices, which was an essential condition of the relocation of the market.

(b) Shorter-Term Price Movements

In view of the unsatisfactory nature of our data, short-term movements in the series must be treated with much more caution than the long ones. Minor inaccuracies make the assessment of the magnitude of movement much less certain, while the irregularity with which they may occur means that turning-points may be displaced. Nevertheless, our collections display sufficient correspondence in the main features to warrant some preliminary sketchwork.

Prices fluctuated cyclically around the long-term patterns we have described. Dating them from trough to trough these cycles ran from 1848 to 1854, 1854 to 1858, 1858 to 1862 or 1863 (depending on

[60] The general decline in prices from this peak until 1931 completes a long cycle commencing in 1895. The existence of this 37-year swing lends at least moral support to the interpretation of our nineteenth century data as a single long cycle. On the general nature of the relations between long-term movements in wool supply, consumer income and wool prices, the reader is referred to B. P. Philpott, 'Fluctuations in Wool Prices, 1873-1950', Y.B.E.S.R., vol. 7, no. 1 (March 1955).

[61] See pp. 6-8.

[62] See p. 24.

[63] See p. 6 and Appendix, Table I.

the series taken), 1862 or 1863 to 1869–70, 1869–70 to 1879, 1879 to 1886, and 1886 to 1894. The peaks of these cycles fell in 1853, 1857, 1860, 1866, 1872, 1880 and 1889 respectively. There is also an uncompleted cycle which dates from the trough of 1894 through the peak of 1899.

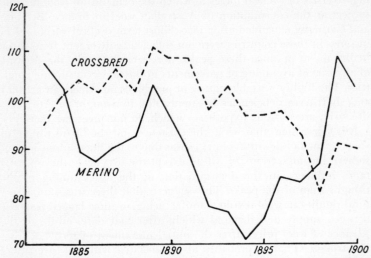

FIG. 8. Prices of Australian merino and crossbred wool, London

One obvious source of these movements lies in the cyclical fluctuations of incomes in the consuming countries. Short-term cyclical troughs in Great Britain, which remained the greatest single consumer of Australian wool throughout the nineteenth century, occurred in 1848, 1855, 1858, 1862, 1868, 1879, 1886 and 1894.[64] Five of the troughs in wool prices coincide with these dates. The other three diverged slightly. That of the early fifties led the trough in British economic activity by a year; that of the early sixties lagged slightly after it; and that of the late sixties occurred well after the British trough. These are not serious differences and, given the existence of pressures specific to the wool trade, are probably to be expected.

With the exception of 1857, 1860 and 1866 the peaks in the series of wool prices showed, however, a persistent tendency to precede those in consumers' incomes. That of 1880 led the British trade cycle peak by three years, and those of 1853, 1872, 1889 and 1899 by a year. This is a far more significant discrepancy. The 1880 peak

64 W. W. Rostow, op. cit., p. 33.

should probably be treated as a purely accidental rise attributable to very short-term forces, and the cyclical peak should probably be moved forward to 1881 or 1882. This adjustment does not, however, overcome the basic problem; the other peaks are not the product of accidental timing. They cannot be explained in terms of the growing diversity of cyclical forces to which the demand for wool became subject as the consumption of Australian wool in France, Belgium and Germany expanded after 1870. Short-term cyclical variations in incomes in those countries were not sufficiently divergent from those in Britain to produce these peaks, nor were the peaks the product of any sort of averaging of movements in the main consuming countries. The highly unstable nature of purchases on American account and short-term deficiencies in supply due to drought in Australia, similarly, are obvious hypotheses which do not meet the facts.

It is clear, then, that while the existence and the broad timing of short termal cycles in wool prices was due to the fluctuations in consumers' incomes, from 1872 (if we except the 1853 peak) they exerted more influence in the determination of the exact timing of the troughs than of the peaks. This suggests that there was some structural rigidity in wool textile manufacturing, or some lagged response between supply and demand which, after that date, inhibited the advance of wool prices after the initial movement of recovery from the trough. That is probably also associated with the overriding influence of the long-term movements, which imparted distinct characteristics to the nature of the short-term cycles.

This influence may be discerned firstly in the changing duration of the short-term cycles. Before 1862 they were fairly short, covering respectively six, four and four years for the three cycles. Subsequently they lengthened to between seven and ten years. This contrast between short cycles before the mid-sixties and longer ones after then is also to be found in the British trade cycle, and is normally connected with rising and falling long-term movements. Similarly, downswing appears only as a very brief interruption to the general upward movement. Between 1872 and 1889, on the other hand, the peaks are weak and the recovery from the troughs uncertain and often feeble. Only in the decade from 1862 to 1872 is the cyclical movement firmly established in all its phases.

The movement of crossbred wool prices provides a striking contrast with these patterns. During the period for which we have statistical data this series was subject to very special demand conditions which paid but scant regard to income fluctuations.

(c) *Conclusion*

Two features emerge very clearly from this description of wool price movements. First, the long-term movements are very strongly imprinted on the series. Up to 1860 the upward movement, and from 1872 the downward movement, are remarkably steady. The only period in which long-term movement could be absent is the sixties. Second, except in the sixties, short-term cyclical fluctuations make very little impression on these long-term changes. Short-term troughs in the period before 1862 were mere checks to the general rise, and short-term recoveries and peaks form almost minor disturbances to the general fall after 1872.

The implications of this are important. These patterns mean that apart altogether from questions of inelasticity deriving from technical considerations, the short-term fluctuations in prices were probably relatively unimportant in the determination of wool producers' output policy. This must be qualified to the extent that given price changes expressed in units of currency were of increasing proportional importance as the general level of prices fell; and to the extent that brief periods of recovery and weak peaks provided a breathing space in between price declines in the period after 1872 and encouraged optimistic expectations about the future course of prices. They also imply that the crisis of the nineties was not so much the product of a short-term cyclical fall in prices as of the conjunction of that and the trough of a long-term movement.

At least until the mid-eighties the absolute profitability of wool production in Australia was sufficiently great, and the optimism of the trade sufficiently well maintained, to induce a continual expansion of output and a high number of new entrants into the industry despite the price movements. Though the attractiveness of the industry as an avenue of investment may have been falling, it retained its superiority over all other colonial activities until the nineties, mainly because of the increasingly capitalized and highly productive nature of wool production. In terms of the content of this study it is important to note that it was also partly maintained until the beginning of the short-term fall in prices in the nineties, because marketing costs fell as much as, or possibly more than, prices. As we saw above, the costs of selling wool in London bore a remarkably steady proportion to realizations in the whole period from the late sixties to the nineties (Tables XXIV and XXV), while the move towards selling wool in the colonies rather than in London, particularly in the nineties, may have been partly motivated by a desire to reduce marketing costs further in an effort to offset the effect of the falling prices.

It is important, finally, to draw attention once again to the deviant behaviour of crossbred wool prices. In both its (apparent) long-term movements and its shorter-term fluctuations this series emphasizes that, while valuable and valid generalizations can be made about the course of 'wool prices', this is essentially a process of lumping together a number of distinct commodities.

A SELECT BIBLIOGRAPHY OF AUSTRALIAN WOOL MARKETING

This is a list of records and publications that are directly relevant to the marketing of Australian wool. It does not include works (to some of which the text and footnote acknowledgments clearly indicate the author's great indebtedness) which deal with wool textile manufacturing or with wool marketing in other countries.

I. MANUSCRIPT SOURCES

The place where each item is held is indicated in brackets at the end of the entry. The dates mentioned refer to the period covered by the material consulted, not necessarily that covered by the entire collection.

Ambler, J. & Co. 'The Account Books of Jeremiah Ambler & Co. 1861-84' (Brotherton Library, Leeds)

Australian Agricultural Co. 'Records', particularly
'Despatches to and from London 1863-1900', and
'Warrah Papers 1865-1900'
(The Australian National University, Canberra)

Australian Pastoral Co. 'Manager's Annual Reports, 1899-1909' (the Managing Agents, Gibbs, Bright & Co. Ltd, Melbourne)

Bank of Australasia
'Letters to London, 1835-51'
'Letters from London, 1835-51'
'Inspector's Circular Book'
'Inspector's Letter Book 1835-6'
(microfilm copies made available by the Australia and New Zealand Bank Ltd)

Black, N. 'The Black Papers 1840-1900' (Public Library of Victoria)

Browne, Eagle & Co. 'Lists of Importers, 1859-1900', miscellaneous Schedules of Rates (Browne, Eagle & Co., London)

Goldsbrough, R. & Co. (from 1888 Goldsbrough, Mort & Co. Ltd).
'Balance Books, 1882-88'
'Balance Books, 1889-94'
'Unbound Correspondence' (miscellaneous dates)
'Minutes, London Board of Directors, 1886-95'
'Minutes, Sydney Board of Directors, 1891-93'
(Goldsbrough, Mort & Co. Ltd, Melbourne)

Hughes, Willans, Irwell & Co. 'Miscellaneous Records' (Hughes, Willans, Irwell & Co., London)

Jowitt, R. & Sons. 'Jowitt Records', particularly
'General Ledgers 1862-97'

'Colonial and Banks Ledgers 1877-1900'
'Interest Accounts 1876-94'
'Purchase Book 1870-1'
'Analysis of Sales and Purchases 1842-58 and 1860-1909'
'Private Copying Book 1863-77'
'Private Business Letters 1877-1909'
(Brotherton Library, Leeds)
Raistrick, W. & Sons. 'Raistrick Records', particularly
'Letters to Colonial Purchasers 1875-90'
(Brotherton Library, Leeds)
Reddihough, J. & Co. 'The Letter Book of John Reddihough
1889-1900' (Brotherton Library, Leeds)
South Australian Woolbuyers' Association. 'Minutes, 1892-1921'
(Victorian & South Australian Woolbuyers' Association,
Melbourne)
Traill, R. J. 'Collaroy Papers'. Vol. 1: 'Tenterfield Station Letter
Book 1852-4'. Vol. 5: 'Letters and Papers of R. J. Traill, 1858-73'
(Mitchell Library, Sydney)
Victorian Woolbuyers' Association. 'Minutes, 1891-1914' (Victorian
& South Australian Woolbuyers' Association, Melbourne)

II. OFFICIAL PUBLICATIONS

AUSTRALIA

Department of Commerce and Agriculture, Bureau of Agricultural
Economics. *Statistical Handbook of the Sheep and Wool Industry.*
Canberra 1949.

NEW SOUTH WALES

Coghlan, T. A. *A Statistical Account of the Seven Colonies of
Australasia.* Sydney, periodically, 1893-1901.
—.*A Statistical Survey of New South Wales, 1893-4.* Sydney 1895.
—.*The Wealth and Progress of New South Wales.*
Sydney, annually, 1887-1905.
Government Statistician. *New South Wales Statistical Register.*
Sydney, annually, 1860-.
'Report of the Commissioner on the State of the Roads.'
Journal of the Legislative Council of New South Wales, 1865-6,
vol. 13.
'Report on the Construction and Progress of the Railways of New
South Wales, from 1866 to 1871 inclusive.' *Votes and Proceedings
of the Legislative Assembly of New South Wales,* 1872-3, vol. 2.
Royal Commission appointed to enquire into the Condition of Crown
Tenants in the Western Division of New South Wales. 'Report
and Minutes of Evidence.' *Votes and Proceedings of the Legisla-
tive Assembly of New South Wales,* 1901, vol. 4.

Select Committee on the Debenture Bill. 'Report and Minutes of Evidence.' *Votes and Proceedings of the Legislative Council of New South Wales,* 1841.

Select Committee on Liens and Mortgages. 'Report and Minutes of Evidence.' *Votes and Proceedings of the Legislative Council of New South Wales,* 1845.

Select Committee on Monetary Confusion. 'Reports and Minutes of Evidence.' *Votes and Proceedings of the Legislative Council of New South Wales,* 1843.

Standing Committee on Public Works. 'Report on the Proposed Railway from Narrabri to Walgett with a branch line to Collarendabri, with Minutes of Evidence.' *Votes and Proceedings of the Legislative Assembly of New South Wales,* 1900, vol. 5.

—.'Report on the Proposed Railway from Temora to Hillston, with Minutes of Evidence.' *Votes and Proceedings of the Legislative Assembly of New South Wales,* 1891-2, vol. 5.

—.'Report on the Proposed Railways for the Riverina, with Minutes of Evidence.' *Votes and Proceedings of the Legislative Assembly of New South Wales,* 1891-2, vol. 5.

SOUTH AUSTRALIA

Commission appointed to enquire into the State of Runs suffering from Drought. 'Report and Minutes of Evidence.' *South Australian Parliamentary Papers,* 1867, vol. 2.

Government Statistician. *South Australian Statistical Register.* Adelaide, annually, 1860–.

Royal Commission on the Land Laws. 'Report and Minutes of Evidence.' *South Australian Parliamentary Papers,* 1888, vol. 2.

Royal Commission on the Necessity for Improved Facilities for the Trade of the South-East. 'Report and Minutes of Evidence.' *South Australian Parliamentary Papers,* 1906, vol. 2.

Royal Commission on the Queensland Border Railway. 'First Progress Report and Minutes of Evidence.' *South Australian Parliamentary Papers,* 1890, vol. 3.

Royal Commission on Railway Construction. 'Report and Minutes of Evidence.' *South Australian Parliamentary Papers,* 1875, vol. 2.

Select Committee on the River Murray Traffic. 'Report and Minutes of Evidence.' *South Australian Parliamentary Papers,* 1870-1, vol. 3.

VICTORIA

Government Statistician. *Victorian Statistical Register.* Melbourne, annually, 1860- .

'Return on Pastoral Occupation.' *Proceedings of the Legislative Assembly of Victoria,* 1869, vol. 2.

Royal Commission on Agricultural and Pastoral Lands. 'Report and

Minutes of Evidence.' *Proceedings of the Legislative Assembly of Victoria,* 1879-80, vol. 3.
Royal Commission on Crown Lands. 'Minutes of Evidence.' *Proceedings of the Legislative Assembly of Victoria,* 1879-80, vol. 3.
Royal Commission on the Banking Laws. 'Report and Minutes of Evidence.' *Proceedings of the Legislative Assembly of Victoria,* 1887, vol. 3.
Royal Commission on the Tariff. 'Report and Minutes of Evidence.' *Proceedings of the Legislative Assembly of Victoria,* 1883, vol. 4.
Select Committee on the Riverina Districts. 'Report and Minutes of Evidence.' *Proceedings of the Legislative Assembly of Victoria,* 1862-3, vol. 2.

FRANCE

Conseil Supérieur du Commerce et de l'Industrie. *Enquête sur le Régime Douanier.* Paris 1890, 4 vols.
Ministère de l'Industrie et du Commerce. A. Picard, *Le Bilan d'un Siècle.* Paris 1906.

UNITED KINGDOM

Board of Trade. *Statistical Tables and Charts Relating to British and Foreign Trade and Industry 1854-1908.* London 1909, Cd.4954.

UNITED STATES OF AMERICA

Department of State, Bureau of Statistics (Special Consular Reports). *Australasian Sheep and Wool.* Washington 1892.

III. PERIODICAL LITERATURE

(a) CONTEMPORARY NEWSPAPERS AND PERIODICALS (Dates indicate first years of publication.)
Argus, Melbourne, daily, 1846- .
Australasian Insurance and Banking Record and Statistical Register, Melbourne, monthly, 1877- .
Australasian Trade Review and Manufacturers' Journal, Melbourne, monthly, 1870- . (Only 1882- available in Australian libraries.)
Dalgety's Annual Wool Review, Sydney, annually, 1897- .
The Economist, Weekly Commercial Times, Bankers' Gazette and Railway Monitor, London, weekly, 1843- .
Journal of Commerce of Victoria and Melbourne Prices Current, Melbourne, fortnightly, 1853- .
South Australian Advertiser, Adelaide, daily, 1836- .
Sydney Herald (from August 1842, *Sydney Morning Herald*), Sydney, daily, 1831- .
Sydney Wool and Station Journal, Sydney, weekly, 1893- .

(b) ARTICLES

Austin, H. 'Recollections of the Australian Wool Trade, 1858-70.' *Australian Country Life* (Sydney monthly) vol. 1, no. 2—vol. 3, no. 6 (May 1906-September 1907).

Barnard, A. 'Woolbuying in the Nineteenth Century: a case history.' *Yorkshire Bulletin of Economic and Social Research,* vol. VIII, no. 1 (June 1956).

—.'Wool prices and Pastoral Policies, 1867-75.' *Economic Record,* vol. XXXI, no. 61 (Nov. 1955).

Blau, G. 'Wool in the World Economy.' *Journal of the Royal Statistical Society,* vol. 109 (1946).

Butlin, N. G. 'Company Ownership of N.S.W. Pastoral Stations, 1865-1900.' *Historical Studies, Australia and New Zealand,* vol. 4, no. 14 (May 1950).

Hamilton, A. 'On Wool Supply.' *Journal of the Royal Statistical Society,* vol. 35 (1870).

Jervis, J. 'Thomas Sutcliffe Mort.' *Royal Australian Historical Society Journal and Proceedings,* vol. 24 (1938).

Mathers, W. J. O. H. 'New South Wales Wool in Great Britain.' *New South Wales Agricultural Gazette,* (1913).

Peacock, R. W., *et al.* 'Farmers' Sheep.' *New South Wales Farm Bulletin,* vol. 1 (1909).

Roberts, S. H. 'The Australian Wool Trade in the 'Forties.' *Royal Australian Historical Society Journal and Proceedings,* vol. 17 (1931).

Thompson, R. J. 'Wool Prices in Great Britain, 1883-1901.' *Journal of the Royal Statistical Society,* vol. 65 (1902).

Trebeck, P. N. 'Improvements effected by the Australian Climate, Soil and Culture on the Merino Sheep.' *Proceedings of the Linnean Society of New South Wales,* vol. 9 (1884).

W[ithers], R. J. 'The Romance of Wool Selling.' *Daily Telegraph* (Sydney) 20 and 27 September, 10 and 25 October, and 14 November 1913.

IV. BOOKS AND PAMPHLETS

Austin, H. B. *The Merino, Past, Present and Probable.* Sydney 1947.

Bagley, L. W. *Efficient Wool Marketing.* Dunedin (N.Z.) 1933.

Bassett, M. *The Hentys: A Colonial Tapestry.* London 1954.

Beck, F. B. de. *Le Commerce International de la Laine.* Geneva 1926.

Billis, R. V., and Kenyon, A. *Pastures New.* Melbourne 1930.

Bonwick, J. *Romance of the Wool Trade.* London 1887.

Brodribb, W. A. *Recollections of an Australian Squatter.* Sydney, n.d. [1881?].

—.*Results of Inquiries and Correspondence in the year 1874, in regard to the Wool Trade, in London, the Continent of Europe and the Colonies.* Melbourne 1875.

Butlin, S. J. *Foundations of the Australian Monetary System 1788-1851.* Melbourne 1953.

Chard, W. H. *Australasian Wool Markets.* Sydney 1926.

Coghlan, T. A. *Labour and Industry in Australia.* 4 vols. London 1918.

Colonial Wool Merchants' Association. *Report of the Sub-committee appointed to consider the communications received from the Chambers of Commerce, Wool Growers and others in the Australian Colonies relative to the management of the London Wool Sales.* London 1872.

Cox, E. W. *The Evolution of the Australian Merino.* Sydney 1936.

Dalgety & Co. Ltd. *A Souvenir to Commemorate the Jubilee Year.* Melbourne 1934.

Delaby, R. *Le Marché International de la Laine.* Paris 1942.

Fison, E. H. *Flocks & Fleeces.* Melbourne 1894.

Fitzpatrick, B. *The British Empire in Australia: an economic history 1834-1939.* Melbourne 1941.

Franklyn, H. M. *A Glance at Australia in 1880: or, food from the South.* Melbourne 1881.

Gagliardi, F. *L'Australia.* Florence 1897.

Goddard, R. H. *The Life and Times of James Milson.* Melbourne 1955.

Goldsbrough, Mort & Co. Ltd. *Australian Wool: its position and prospects in 1895.* Melbourne 1895.

—.*Australian Wool: its position and prospects in 1896.* Melbourne 1897.

—.*Wool and the Nation.* Melbourne 1946.

—.*Wool. The Revival of 1895.* Melbourne 1896.

Goldsbrough, R. & Co. *A Statistical Summary of Wool Exported from the Australian Colonies and New Zealand to Great Britain and Foreign Ports, 1807-82.* Melbourne 1885.

Gooch, Cousens & Co. *Wool Importers.* London 1899.

Graham, J. R. *A Treatise on the Australian Merino.* Melbourne 1870.

Greville, E. (ed.). *The Official Directory and Almanac of Australia, 1883.* Sydney 1883.

—.*The Official Directory and Almanac of Australia, 1884.* Sydney 1884.

Harven, E. J. A. de. *Le Marché de Laines à Anvers: son passer et son avenir.* Antwerp 1879.

Hawkesworth, A. *Australasian Sheep and Wool.* Sydney, 5th ed., 1920.

—.*Wool Production and its Prospects.* Sydney 1891.

Horsfall, J. S. *To the Shareholders of Goldsbrough, Mort & Co. Ltd: a reply to Andrew Rowan.* Melbourne 1889.

Jackson, H. *Broken Fleece.* Sydney 1910.

The Joint Sub-committees of Enquiry appointed by meetings in New South Wales, Victoria, and South Australia. *Report on the Sales of Australian Wools in London.* London 1870.

Joyce, A. *A Homestead History: being the reminiscences and letters of Alfred Joyce of Plaistow and Norwood, Port Phillip, 1843 to 1864.* (Ed. G. F. James) Melbourne 1949.

Leach, J. *Australia v. London as the World's Wool Depot.* Sydney 1894.

Lyne, C. *The Industries of New South Wales.* Sydney 1882.

Mason, L. 'Breeding of Sheep and Improvement of Wool', in *South Australian Industries and Manfactures, being papers read before the Chamber of Manufactures.* Adelaide 1875.

Maurette, F. *Les Grands Marchés des Matières Premières.* Paris, rev. ed., 1933.

Menzies, W. J. *New Methods of Wool Washing.* Liverpool 1882.

Munz, H. *The Australian Wool Industry.* Sydney 1950.

National Association of Wool Manufacturers of the United States. *The Woolen Tariff Defended and Explained.* Cambridge (Mass.) 1886.

Onslow, S. Macarthur. *Some Early Records of the Macarthurs of Camden.* Sydney 1914.

Pierrard, P. *French Parities and Ready Reckoner for Purchasing Wool in London.* London 1891.

—.*Tableaux Synoptiques du Commerce de Laines, Fils et Tissus en Angleterre pendant l'année 1883.* London 1884.

—.*The Standard Wool-Bale and the Improvements Necessary in the Universal Wool Trade.* London 1887.

Plessis, A. F. de. *The Marketing of Wool.* London 1931.

Pollett, M. E. *Australasie: la Nouvelle-Galles du Sud.* Brussels 1898.

[Price, A. G., and Hammond, J. H.]. *Elder, Smith & Co. Ltd.—The First Hundred Years.* Adelaide, privately published, n.d. [1940].

Renard Bros. & Co. *Antwerp versus London as a Market for Australian Wool.* Melbourne 1875.

Riccioli, C. *I Commerci coll'Australia.* Naples 1886.

Roberts, S. H. *The Squatting Age in Australia, 1835-1847.* Melbourne 1935.

Rowan, A. *Letter from Andrew Rowan to the Shareholders of Goldsbrough, Mort & Co. Ltd.* Melbourne 1889.

Satge, O. de. *Pages from the Journal of a Queensland Squatter.* London 1901.

Sauerbeck, A. *The Production and Consumption of Wool.* London 1878.

Schwartze, H., & Co. *The Production and Consumption of Wool.* London 1887.

Shann, E. *An Economic History of Australia.* Cambridge 1930.

Shaw, T. *The Australian Merino: being a treatise on wool growing in Australia.* Melbourne 1849.

Sinclair, A. *A Clip of Wool, from Shearing Shed to Ship.* Sydney 1899; 2nd ed., 1913.

S[kamp], R. B. *Farmers' Wool.* Melbourne 1894.

Skamp, R. B. *The Wool Trade: Its History and Growth in Australia and Tasmania.* Melbourne, n.d. [c. 1888].

Smith, H. B. *The Sheep and Wool Industry of Australasia.* Sydney 1914.

Smith, S. S. *Important Suggestions for a Better Development of Colonial Wool and Leather etc.* Hobart 1857.

Smith, W. M. *The Marketing of Australian and New Zealand Primary Products.* London 1935.

Society for the Diffusion of Useful Knowledge. *Sheep: their breeds, management and diseases.* London 1837.

Southey, T. *Observations addressed to the Woolgrowers of Australia and Tasmania respecting improvements in the breeding of sheep, preparing and assorting wools etc.* London 1830.

—.*The Rise, Progress and Present State of Colonial Sheep and Wool.* London 1848.

Strachan, H. M. *Some Notes and Recollections.* Melbourne, privately published, 1927.

Trebeck, P. N. *Notes on Wool.* Sydney 1882.

Were, J. B., & Son. *The House of Were, 1839-1954.* Melbourne, privately published, 1954.

Westgarth, W. *The Colony of Victoria: its history, commerce, and gold-mining: its social and political institutions: down to the end of 1863.* London 1864.

Wright, H. W. 'Wool Industry' in F. Hutchinson (ed.) *New South Wales: the mother colony of the Australias.* Sydney 1896.

APPENDIX

TABLE I

Breeds of Sheep in New South Wales, 1886 and 1900

	1886	1900
Merino		
Combing	27,915,847	27,158,422
Clothing	10,151,627	9,540,734
Total	38,067,474	36,699,156
Long-woolled	378,383	1,076,284
Crossbred	723,447	2,245,066
TOTAL	39,169,304	40,020,506

Source: T. A. Coghlan, *The Wealth and Progress of New South Wales 1886-7* (Sydney, 1887), pp. 323-4, and *The Wealth and Progress of New South Wales 1900-01* (Sydney, 1902), p. 583.

TABLE II

The Classing of Selected Portions of the Warrah Station Clip, 1881

Group of Sheep	Average yield per sheep							
	Combing wool		Clothing wool		Pieces*		Total	
	lb.	%	lb.	%	lb.	%	lb.	%
Shorn Greasy								
Breeding ewes	2·74	46·1	0·97	16·3	2·24	37·6	5·95	100
Rams	6·15	63·0	—	—	3·61	37·0	9·76	100
Ewe hoggets	3·87	59·2	0·04	0·6	2·63	40·2	6·54	100
Stud ewes	5·03	61·6	—	—	3·13	38·4	8·16	100
Shorn Washed								
3-year wethers	1·78	52·5	0·23	6·8	1·38	40·7	3·39	100
Wether hoggets	1·32	43·0	0·21	6·8	1·54	50·2	3·07	100
Ewe hoggets	1·23	45·5	0·14	5·2	1·33	49·3	2·70	100
Breeding ewes	0·76	27·5	0·65	23·5	1·35	48·9	2·76	100
Purchased sheep	0·53	20·8	0·76	29·8	1·26	49·4	2·55	100

* 'Pieces' here include 'broken' and 'skirting' wool in addition to the wool more usually defined as 'pieces'.

Source: A. A. Co., 'Warrah Papers': 'Average Composition of Warrah Sheep, 1881' (from the MS. collection of Australian Agricultural Company papers at The Australian National University). Cf. also the composition of the 1888 clip from the Boonoke flock, summarized in United States of America Department of State, Bureau of Statistics (Special Consular Reports), *Australasian Sheep and Wool* (Washington, 1892), p. 27.

TABLE III

Estimated United Kingdom Imports of Crossbred Wool from Australia and New Zealand, 1871-82 (in bales)

Year	Australia	New Zealand
1871		25,000 ⎫
1872		30,610 ⎪
1881		176,000 ⎬
1882		185,000 ⎭
1883	92,000	117,000
1884	84,000	124,000

Sources: Trade estimates presented in the Australasian Mortgage & Agency Co., Ltd's market report in the *Australasian Trade Review and Manufacturers' Journal* (Melbourne, monthly), 15 March 1882; by R. Goldsbrough & Co. in the *Journal of Commerce of Victoria and Melbourne Prices Current* (Melbourne, fortnightly), 14 Feb. 1883, and by the New Zealand Loan & Mercantile Agency Co. Ltd in the *Argus*, 11 March 1885.

TABLE IV

Average Quinquennial Production of Wool in the Australian Colonies, as Exported, 1840-99

('000 lb.)

Period	N.S.W.	Vic.	S.A.	Qld.	W.A.	Tas.	Total
1840-4	7,691	2,727	n.a.	n.a.	—	n.a.	n.a.
1845-9	11,801	9,710	n.a.	n.a.	—	n.a.	n.a.
1850-4	15,184	19,665	n.a.	n.a.	—	n.a.	n.a.
1855-9	16,892	20,977	n.a.	n.a.	n.a.	n.a.	n.a.
1860-4	18,728	27,730	13,956	8,948	772	4,704	74,838
1865-9	33,108	49,099	22,256	29,056	1,471	5,224	140,214
1870-4	62,764	60,263	31,886	35,029	1,986	4,939	196,867
1875-9	129,502	77,155	49,235	33,822	3,155	7,192	300,061
1880-4	186,406	75,477	49,944	40,411	4,281	8,303	364,822
1885-9	243,175	66,162	49,377	57,293	7,152	7,382	430,541
1895-9	302,724	81,060	46,221	106,272	11,052	8,122	555,451
1890-4	348,588	77,285	51,628	100,265	9,337	8,941	596,044

Sources: 1840-4 to 1855-9, *Statistical Registers* of the two colonies. Wool exports are assumed to equal wool production. 1860-4 to 1895-9, Commonwealth of Australia, Department of Commerce, Bureau of Agricultural Economics, *Statistical Handbook of the Sheep and Wool Industry* (Canberra, 1949), Table 26, p. 21.

Although the *Statistical Handbook* heads this table 'Production of Greasy Wool', in fact all the figures are simple additions of the weights recorded at the Customs Houses: greasy, scoured, and washed wool are all included.

For the years before separate statistics of these categories were collected in the sixties and seventies there is no readily apparent way of distinguishing between them, nor does it seem possible to calculate the greasy equivalents of scoured and washed wools if the separation could be effected. One solution was proposed by Dr E. Dunsdorfs in a typescript paper ('Trends in the Australian

Wool-growing Industry, 1850-1950') read before a joint meeting of Sections E and G at the 31st meeting of the Australian and New Zealand Association for the Advancement of Science held at Melbourne in 1955. The number of bales of scoured, washed, and greasy wool exported was estimated by sampling selling brokers' reports of sales, the number of bales converted to pounds (because the bale weights varied widely) by applying to average prices in each year a relationship found to exist between bale weight and realized price per pound, and finally the scoured and washed wool converted to a greasy basis by using the relationship between the average prices of the groups. Despite the ingenuity displayed in this construction it is open to grave misgivings both on methodological and historical grounds, and there seems little reason to accept the resultant figures as more than an elaborate guess.

It might also be argued that the crude methods employed up to the sixties and perhaps later mean that there was little difference between the weight of washed and greasy wool, and that as we can convert to greasy equivalents, after separate statistics are provided, we could construct a table of greasy wool exports which would be substantially accurate, for all periods with the possible exception of the sixties. But until far more is known of the techniques of wool washing and the actual yield of washed and scoured wool before the seventies, this remains mere surmise.

The figures presented in Table IV are undoubtedly unsatisfactory, and it must be borne in mind that some of the increased production it shows is illusory, being simply the extra weight due to the change from scoured to greasy production. It is, nevertheless, the only direct guide to output that we have.

TABLE V

Average Quinquennial Sheep Populations in the Australian Colonies, 1840-99

Period	N.S.W.	Vic.*	S.A.	Qld.	W.A.	Tas.	Total†
	'000	'000	'000	'000	'000	'000	'000
1840-4	n.a.	n.a.	n.a.	n.a.	—	n.a.	n.a.
1845-9	5,661	3,880	733	n.a.	—	1,573	n.a.
1850-4	7,654	6,020	n.a.	n.a.	—	2,103	n.a.
1855-9	7,444	5,071	n.a.	n.a.	n.a.	1,704	n.a.
1860-4	6,788	6,861	3,459	4,687	313	1,714	23,822
1865-9	12,735	9,376	4,319	8,022	542	1,664	36,658
1870-4	18,388	10,777	5,090	7,341	699	1,456	43,751
1875-9	25,538	10,235	6,186	6,506	911	1,807	51,183
1880-4	35,536	10,436	6,591	9,618	1,324	1,811	65,332
1885-9	44,113	10,741	6,490	11,905	1,980	1,557	76,835
1890-4	57,971	12,973	7,097	19,658	2,105	1,638	101,505
1895-9	43,468	12,011	5,713	18,006	2,258	1,586	83,109

* Victorian figures are as at 31 March; all others are as at 31 December in the previous year.

† The total includes Northern Territory flocks from 1880-4.

Source: Bureau of Agricultural Economics, *Statistical Handbook*, Table 1, p. 1., and *Statistical Registers* of the colonies.

TABLE VI

Sources of Imports of Raw Wool into the United Kingdom,
1800-1900
(lb. m.)

Year	A'asia	Germany	Spain	S. Amer.	S. Africa	Total*
1800		0·4	6·0			8·6
1810		0·8	5·9			10·8
1820	0·09	5·2	3·5			9·7
1830	1·9	26·7	1·6			32·3
1840	9·7	21·8	1·2	4·3	0·7	49·4
1850	39·0	9·1	0·4	5·2	5·7	74·3
1860	59·1	9·9	1·0	8·9	16·5	148·3
1870	175·0	4·2		12·6	32·7	263·2
1880	300·6	7·1		10·2	51·3	463·5
1890	418·7	6·7		11·1	87·2	633·0
1900	386·3	5·0		35·5	32·2	558·9

* The total includes wool from other countries less important than those shown in the table; it is thus not the sum of the columns. Alpaca is included with the sheep's wool.

Sources: A. Hamilton, 'On Wool Supply', *Journal of the Royal Statistical Society*, vol. xxxiii (1870), p. 502; *Statistical Abstracts of the United Kingdom*. It is necessary to use these figures with some caution, for the Board of Trade improved its collection methods during the century and changes in the statistics often represent simply a greater accuracy than before. In 1869 Messrs J. L. Bowes of Liverpool observed that in 1868 the Board of Trade figures for Australasian wool imported were 47 per cent below the actual figures; as a result of improved techniques it was considered to be understated by only 15 per cent in 1869 (*Argus*, 27 Oct. 1869). Consequently comparisons over time are not strictly possible. As these collections have an authority that trade circulars could not possess, they will have to suffice for our purposes.

TABLE VII

Exports of Worsted Yarn and Fabrics from the United Kingdom, 1857-95

Year	Yarn	Fabrics
	lb. '000	*yds. '000*
1857	23,930*	129,632
1859	22,122*	150,433
1861	26,492*	122,556
1863	30,002	165,835
1865	30,221	233,087
1867	33,571	200,469
1869	35,572	250,062
1870	34,606	235,936
1875	31,139	251,845
1880	25,612	189,940
1885	40,416	198,764
1890	39,510	172,434
1895	59,848	110,674

* Includes woollen yarn.

Source: F. Hooper, *Statistics Relating to the City of Bradford and the Woollen and Worsted Trades of the United Kingdom* (Bradford, 1899), pp. 16-17.

TABLE VIII

Worsted and Woollen Spinning and Doubling Spindles in the United Kingdom, 1850-1904

Year	Worsted		Woollen	
	Spinning	*Doubling*	*Spinning*	*Doubling*
	m.	*'000*	*m.*	*'000*
1850	0·87	n.a.	1·59	n.a.
1861	1·28	n.a.	1·82	n.a.
1871	1·82	n.a.	2·66	n.a.
1874	2·18	400	3·17	158
1878	2·10	456	3·34	318
1885	2·23	536	3·05	231
1890	2·40	669	3·11	300
1904	2·94	845	2·61	211

Sources: A. Redgrave, *Factory Reports, 1875* (London, 1876); Tariff Commission, 'Evidence on the Woollen Industry', paras. 1521-2.

TABLE IX

Quinquennial Measure of British Consumption and Re-exports of Imported Wools, 1840-1900 *(lb. m.)*

Year	Retained Imports	Re-exports	Year	Retained Imports	Re-exports
1840	49	1	1875	200	172
1845	75	3	1880	239	237
1850	63	14	1885	252	267
1855	73	29	1890	309	341
1860	120	31	1895	397	405
1865	135	82	1900	385	196
1870	174	92			

Source: A. Sauerbeck, *The Production and Consumption of Wool;* Tariff Commission, op. cit., para. 1512. These measures include alpaca, goats' hair, etc. Note that the re-export figures do not agree exactly with those in Table XI.

TABLE X

Estimated Consumption of Raw Wool in the Leading Wool Textile Manufacturing Countries, 1855-99 *(lb. m., quinquennial averages)*

Period	U.K.	France	Germany	U.S.A.
1855-9	215·0	n.a.	n.a.	74·6
1860-4	251·0	239·0	n.a.	135·8
1865-9	292·8	319·1	n.a.	203·1
1870-4	330·8	330·0	(155·7)*	230·5
1875-9	342·2	379·3	174·5	240·5
1880-4	336·0	409·5	219·8	343·1
1885-9	392·0	467·5	284·0	391·6
1890-4	452·0	504·7	348·1	409·4
1895-9	493·8	558·2	394·7	466·5

* Three-year average.

Source: Board of Trade, *Statistical Tables and Charts relating to British and Foreign Trade and Industry, 1854-1908*, London, 1909 (Cd. 4954), Table 75.

TABLE XI

Apparent Destinations of British Re-exports of Foreign and Colonial Wool, 1860-1900

(lb. m.)

Year	France	Belgium	Germany	U.S.A.	Holland	Total
1860	15·7	7·9	1·3	n.a.	—	30·6
1861	22·0	15·2	2·9	10·0	—	54·3
1862	19·3	11·3	2·1	7·7	—	48·1
1863	31·5	8·4	2·2	11·1	—	63·9
1864	38·1	9·1	1·4	4·2	—	55·9
1865	50·1	15·1	5·5	7·3	—	82·4
1866	47·3	8·1	3·6	4·5	—	66·6
1867	51·6	19·1	11·5	3·9	—	90·8
1868	59·6	23·3	11·8	4·2	—	105·0
1869	65·2	24·2	12·2	6·4	—	116·5
1870	50·4	18·6	10·9	4·6	—	92·5
1871	n.a.	n.a.	n.a.	n.a.	n.a.	135·1
1872	n.a.	n.a.	n.a.	n.a.	n.a.	137·5
1873	n.a.	n.a.	n.a.	n.a.	n.a.	123·2
1874	n.a.	n.a.	n.a.	n.a.	n.a.	194·4
1875	n.a.	n.a.	n.a.	n.a.	n.a.	189·1
1876	n.a.	n.a.	n.a.	n.a.	n.a.	n.a.
1877	96·0	40·5	28·2	14·7	—	187·4
1878	106·5	40·2	37·3	9·1	—	199·2
1879	107·1	45·7	50·0	29·2	—	243·3
1880	113·3	43·2	41·9	30·7	—	237·3
1881	131·6	47·8	55·1	21·8	—	265·3
1882	118·8	51·1	61·0	26·6	—	263·4
1883	115·6	49·9	68·2	34·8	—	277·1
1884	100·2	53·4	59·9	29·6	30·6	276·8
1885	78·6	55·9	51·1	51·0	28·0	267·6
1886	83·8	70·6	53·4	65·1	35·5	311·9
1887	76·2	82·5	66·4	58·0	32·2	319·0
1888	85·7	77·4	80·7	61·2	30·1	338·9
1889	88·0	79·6	91·4	67·1	33·0	363·4
1890	90·3	62·7	83·2	67·2	32·1	340·5
1891	104·4	69·1	99·4	80·2	26·5	384·1
1892	82·6	76·4	118·9	90·3	58·2	430·1
1893	75·6	76·0	85·4	52·6	51·3	345·7
1894	86·8	66·1	104·4	53·0	31·6	344·9
1895	96·0	49·5	120·4	125·2	8·2	404·1
1896	96·1	47·6	106·7	67·9	12·5	334·4
1897	73·0	44·4	79·5	155·2	14·6	370·8
1898	96·8	46·4	79·2	42·5	12·5	282·7
1899	93·3	43·3	100·1	42·2	7·9	291·8
1900	52·7	26·8	53·0	47·9	9·8	195·3

Source: The Economist (London), annual 'Trade Supplements'.

TABLE XII

Structure of the English Worsted Spinning Industry, 1850-90:
Percentage of Plant Operated by each Factory Type

Year	Factory Type	Doubling Spindles	Spinning Spindles	Power Looms	Workers %
1850	Spinning only	n.a.	48·3	—	28·4
	Spinning and weaving	n.a.	51·7	60·4	52·2
	Weaving only	n.a.	—	39·6	19·4
1861	Spinning only	n.a.	49·1	—	25·9
	Spinning and weaving	n.a.	50·9	59·5	58·0
	Weaving only	n.a.	—	40·5	16·1
1867	Spinning only	65·6	55·7	—	33·8
	Spinning and weaving	34·4	44·3	63·3	52·4
	Weaving only	—	—	36·7	13·8
1874	Spinning only	58·0	50·7	—	33·7
	Spinning and weaving	42·0	49·3	50·3	45·1
	Weaving only	—	—	49·7	21·2
1878	Spinning only	67·3	54·4	—	30·4
	Spinning and weaving	32·7	45·6	48·2	45·2
	Weaving only	—	—	51·8	24·4
1885	Spinning only	61·9	57·4	—	32·5
	Spinning and weaving	38·1	42·6	48·2	43·5
	Weaving only	—	—	51·8	24·0
1890	Spinning only	65·9	60·2	—	34·5
	Spinning and weaving	34·1	39·8	43·1	41·8
	Weaving only	—	—	56·9	23·7

Source: Sigsworth, 'A History of Messrs John Foster & Son Ltd.', p. 204.

TABLE XIII

Estimated Quinquennial Wool Production and Consumption (lb. m.)
in the Main Consuming Countries, 1875-1900

(Note: Production appears in column A, consumption in column B)

Year	Germany		France		Austria-Hungary		Italy		United States		United Kingdom	
	A	B	A	B	A	B	A	B	A	B	A	B
1875	83	150	n.a.	376	n.a.	n.a.	n.a.	n.a.	197	232	162	340
1880	n.a.	181	n.a.	403	50	38	22	38	232	357	149	355
1885	58	248	104	439	n.a.	n.a.	n.a.	n.a.	308	375	136	346
1890	n.a.	307	130	462	35	57	n.a.	n.a.	276	378	138	407
1895	32	414	91	507	n.a.	n.a.	21	49	310	509	135	480
1900	28	316	86	447	n.a.	n.a.	n.a.	n.a.	289	437	141	474

Source: Production of all countries, and consumption of Austria-Hungary and Italy: Tariff Commission, op. cit., paras. 1509-10, Tables 1 and 2.
Consumption in Germany, France, United States and United Kingdom: *Statistical Tables and Charts Relating to British and Foreign Trade and Industry (1854-1908)* (Cd. 4954, 1909), Table 75.
The Tariff Commission figures include alpaca, vicuna, etc. consumed, which are excluded in the Board of Trade estimates.

TABLE XIV

Quinquennial Production of Raw Wool in the New Countries,
1860-1900 *(lb. m.)*

Year	Australia	S. America	S. Africa	New Zealand
1860	59	43	26	6
1865	109	137	33	19
1870	173	197	43	37
1875	258	220	51	54
1880	354	256	60	67
1885	376	356	50	86
1890	462	260	93	103
1895	617	443	85	116
1900	445	222	31	141

Sources: Australia: Bureau of Agricultural Economics, op. cit., p. 21, Table 26; South America and South Africa, 1860-85: Helmuth Schwartze & Co., op. cit.; 1890-1900, R. J. Thompson, 'Wool Prices in Great Britain, 1883-1901' *Journal of the Royal Statistical Society*, vol. lxv (1902), p. 512; New Zealand: *New Zealand Year Book, 1903*.

TABLE XV

Charges for Wool Buying – R. Jowitt & Sons, 1886

Selected price of wool in saleroom	Number of instances in which agreements specified payments above cost price of:										
	$\frac{1}{4}$d.	$\frac{3}{8}$d.	$\frac{1}{2}$d.	$\frac{5}{8}$d.	$\frac{3}{4}$d.	$\frac{7}{8}$d.	1d.	$1\frac{1}{8}$d.	$1\frac{1}{4}$d.	$1\frac{3}{8}$d.	$1\frac{1}{2}$d.
7d.	1(1)	—	3(2)	1(1)	1(2)	—	—	—	—	—	—
10d.	(1)	1	1(2)	1	3(3)	—	—	—	—	—	—
13d.	—	—	1(1)	—	2(4)	1	2(1)	—	—	—	—
17d.	—	—	(1)	—	3(1)	—	3(3)	—	—	—	(1)
21d.	—	—	(1)	—	1	—	2(3)	1	2(1)	—	(1)
25d.	—	—	(1)	—	1	—	2(2)	—	2(2)	1	(1)
28d.	—	—	(1)	—	1	—	2(2)	—	2(1)	—	1(2)

Note: These rates were set in contracts made with various clients between 1879 and 1885; agreements made between 1879 and 1884 are shown in brackets.
Source: 'Jowitt Records', 'Jobbing [erased] Order Book'.

TABLE XVI

Distribution of Charges made as Importing Agents –
R. Jowitt & Sons*

	Rates of Commission							Total
	$\frac{3}{4}$%	1%	$1\frac{1}{4}$%	$1\frac{1}{2}$%	$1\frac{3}{4}$%	2%	$2\frac{1}{2}$%	
Charged to seller	—	3	1	6	—	9	3	22
Rebated to agent	2	7	2	1	—	—	—	12
Net to Jowitt	2	10	3	6	1	—	—	22

* These charges were made under individual agreements negotiated between 1876 and 1893.
Source: 'Jowitt Records': 'Jobbing [erased] Order Book'.

TABLE XVII

*Estimated Sales at the Wool Auctions in Sydney, Melbourne
and Geelong, 1859-60 to 1899-1900*   (*Number of Bales*)

Selling Season	Sydney	Melb. & G'long	Total
1859-60	5,827	23,521	29,348
1860-1	6,454	27,719	34,173
1861-2	8,512	22,893	31,405
1862-3	9,760	45,178	54,938
1863-4	10,925	38,754	49,679
1864-5	10,983	29,539	40,522
1865-6	12,475	43,349	55,824
1866-7	13,311	47,534	60,845
1867-8	12,001	40,460	52,461
1868-9	14,084	36,850	50,934
1869-70	25,140	62,844	87,984
1870-1	18,153	50,696	68,849
1871-2	21,887	85,599	107,486
1872-3	17,816	69,287	87,103
1873-4	15,850	75,754	91,604
1874-5	18,740	107,885	126,625
1875-6	23,973	94,241	118,214
1876-7	34,292	114,265	148,557
1877-8	32,897	123,533	156,430
1878-9	32,374	111,212	143,586
1879-80	51,905	133,879	185,784
1880-1	48,094	130,187	178,281
1881-2	79,091	169,788	248,879
1882-3	79,413	171,645	251,058
1883-4	115,875	189,227	305,102
1884-5	112,906	197,934	310,840
1885-6	116,576	178,153	294,729
1886-7	128,734	180,045	308,779
1887-8	162,511	188,050	350,561
1888-9	209,252	214,875	424,127
1889-90	234,419	279,360	513,779
1890-1	251,314	247,508	498,822
1891-2	278,304	292,694	570,998
1892-3	362,365	310,828	673,193
1893-4	401,830	305,715	707,545
1894-5	425,135	328,142	753,277
1895-6	415,538	315,543	731,081
1896-7	401,048	310,385	711,433
1897-8	445,808	286,625	732,433
1898-9	447,517	280,397	727,914
1899-1900	399,893	312,465	712,358

Sources: The figures for Sydney, 1859-60 to 1883-4, and Melbourne and
Geelong, 1859-60 to 1882-3, have been calculated directly from the catalogues
of each sale, which were published in the *Sydney Morning Herald* and *Argus*
after the sale, or from the brokers' weekly or monthly reports published in the
same newspapers.

Sydney, 1884-5 to 1893-4: H. W. Wright, 'Wool Industry' (p. 68) in F. Hutchinson (ed.), *New South Wales: the mother colony of the Australias* (Sydney, 1896),
pp. 66-75. Sydney 1894-5 to 1899-1900: *W. & P. 1900-01*, p. 591.

Melbourne and Geelong, 1883-4 to 1890-1: Withers, 'The Romance of Wool

Selling', 15 Oct. 1913. Melbourne and Geelong 1891-2 to 1893-4: T. A. Coghlan, *A Statistical Account of the Seven Colonies of Australasia 1895-6* (Sydney, 1896), p. 149. Melbourne and Geelong, 1894-5 to 1899-1900: Bureau of Agricultural Economics, op. cit., Table 35.

The 'selling season' covers the period October to March for Melbourne and Geelong up to 1882-3, and for Sydney up to 1883-4. Thereafter it is taken to extend only to February. The justification for this lies in the improved transport facilities which, by the eighties meant that except in exceptional circumstances the bulk of the clip had been received in the main ports by the end of that month.

'Sales' as far as possible refer only to wool sold in the auction room and exclude wool bought in at the sale under owners' bid and later disposed of by private treaty.

Figures of the quantities of wool offered at the sales are not presented here because the duplication involved in the re-offer of wools bought in or withdrawn from previous sales inflates them beyond correction and renders them useless either as a measure of the growers' willingness to try the local markets or as an indication of the efficiency of the sales in clearing the supply coming to the markets.

TABLE XVIII

Main Liabilities incurred to Secure Funds, R. Goldsbrough & Co. and Goldsbrough, Mort & Co. Ltd, 1882-92

Balance Date		Call Deposits and Current A/cs in Cr.*	Fixed Deposits	Debentures	Bank Overdraft
		£	£	£	£
Sept.	1882	145,654	520,743	66,700	797,465
Mar.	1883	150,647	448,014	66,700	491,294
Sept.	1883	99,458	391,781	110,700	692,462
Mar.	1884	59,713	318,771	189,400	396,804
Sept.	1884	50,934	233,256	220,800	571,769
Mar.	1885	73,031	245,123	277,500	324,345
Sept.	1885	59,304	242,811	326,000	535,963
Mar.	1886	56,753	273,642	376,900	457,564
Sept.	1886	78,036	269,309	504,800	563,238
Mar.	1887	119,788	349,806	675,900	372,263
Sept.	1887	162,382	439,088	759,100	398,933
Mar.	1888	198,619	556,071	910,200	272,839
Sept.	1888	391,794	612,339	1,020,200	189,420
Mar.	1889	595,300	620,754	1,149,000	276,383
Sept.	1889	351,789	686,403	1,455,800	265,978
Mar.	1890	212,204	478,478	1,790,800	66,122
Sept.	1890	212,285	590,837	1,921,400	409,308
Mar.	1891	348,151	586,662	2,012,720	307,743
Sept.	1891	446,962	630,095	2,027,105	441,397
Mar.	1892	374,511	605,675	2,034,990	486,042
Sept.	1892	139,022	533,573	2,074,855	682,155

* Current A/cs in Cr. were those accounts which Goldsbrough's clients held in the firm's own banking department. Generally the individual accounts were small and were left with the firm to meet payments which it made on behalf of the clients – government rents, taxes, incidental purchases, etc. Because of their nature they would not have been an important credit base. The amount of call deposits, also held in the firm's banking department, cannot be separated from the current accounts.

Source: Goldsbrough, Mort & Co. Ltd, 'Balance Books'. The change in name from R. Goldsbrough & Co. to Goldsbrough, Mort & Co. Ltd, occurred in 1888 when the firm of Mort & Co. Ltd was acquired.

Appendix

TABLE XIX

Antwerp's Trade in South American Wool, 1840-1900

(Number of Bales)

Year	Arrivals	Sales	Wool in Transit
1840	6,300	n.a.	n.a.
1850	21,294	n.a.	n.a.
1860	41,834	16,302	25,532
1870	111,767	100,736	11,031
1880	n.a.	98,922	n.a.
1890	45,348	35,823	9,525
1900	31,428	25,999	5,429

Source: F. B. de Beck, *Le Commerce International de la Laine*, p. 164.

TABLE XX

Direct Wool Exports from Melbourne to the United States, 1866-7 to 1882-3

(in bales)

Year	Exports	Year	Exports
1866-7	1,200	1876-7	7,576
		1877-8	5,071
1871-2	18,659*	1878-9	—
1872-3	11,851†	1879-80	17,551
1873-4	9,745	1880-1	3,372
1874-5	19,042	1881-2	11,070
1875-6	5,032	1882-3	5,794

* Including about 1,800 bales addressed to Montreal.
† Including about 1,900 bales for Montreal.
Source: R. Goldsbrough and Co., 'Annual Review of the Wool Market', *Argus*, 14 Feb. 1883.

TABLE XXI

Freight Rates on Washed Wool from Melbourne to London, at Selected Dates, 1845-55

(pence per lb.)

Date	Rate	Date	Rate
Dec. 1845	$1\frac{1}{2}$	Dec. 1851	1
Dec. 1847	$1\frac{1}{2}$	Nov. 1852	$\frac{3}{4}$
Feb. 1849	$1\frac{1}{4}$	Dec. 1853	$\frac{7}{8}$
Jan. 1850	1	Jan. 1855	1
Feb. 1851	$\frac{3}{4}$		

Source: Newspaper reports of freight rates, published as commercial news.

Table XXII

Quinquennial Wool Freight Rates from Sydney and Melbourne to London, 1845-90
(pence per lb.)*

Date*	Sailing Ship Greasy wool Sydney	Sailing Ship Greasy wool Melbourne	Sailing Ship Washed wool Melbourne	Steamship Greasy wool Melbourne	Steamship Washed wool Melbourne
Dec. 1845	—	—	$1\frac{1}{2}$	—	—
Jan. 1850	—	—	1	—	—
Jan. 1855	—	—	1	—	—
Oct. 1860	$\frac{5}{8}$	$\frac{3}{4}$–1	n.a.	—	—
Dec. 1865	$\frac{1}{2}$	$\frac{1}{4}$	$\frac{1}{4}$	—	—
Nov. 1870	$\frac{3}{8}$	$\frac{1}{2}$	$\frac{5}{8}$	—	—
Nov. 1875	$\frac{3}{8}$	$\frac{1}{2}$	$\frac{5}{8}$	$\frac{3}{4}$	1
Nov. 1880	$11/16$	$\frac{1}{2}$	$\frac{3}{4}$	$1\frac{1}{8}$–$1\frac{1}{4}$	$1\frac{1}{4}$–$1\frac{1}{2}$
Nov. 1885	$\frac{3}{8}$	$\frac{3}{8}$	$\frac{1}{8}$	$\frac{1}{4}$	$\frac{7}{8}$
Nov. 1890	$7/16$	$\frac{1}{2}$	$\frac{7}{8}$	$\frac{1}{4}$	$\frac{7}{8}$

* Sydney rates are annual averages; Melbourne are monthly. The two are therefore not comparable. All these rates were subject to an additional 5 per cent primage.

Sources: Sydney: *W. & P., 1900-01*, p. 99 (yearly averages, 1857-1900). Melbourne: 1845-55, see sources to Table XXI; 1860-90, periodical (generally monthly) reports on freight published in the *Argus* by shipping agents and/or colonial wool brokers.

With the exception of 1860, for which October is the only quotation, the figures that have been selected for 1860-90 are the averages of those months in which the greatest part of the clip was exported.

Table XXIII

Warehouse Rates Charged by Messrs Browne & Eagle, 1868-89

Date	Consolidated rates charged on bales weighing: 1 cwt. and under 1 cwt. 2 qr.	1 cwt. 2 qr. and under 3 cwt. 2 qr.	3 cwt. 2 qr. and under 5 cwt.	5 cwt. and under 7 cwt. 2 qr.
	s. d.	s. d.	s. d.	s. d.
31 Dec. '67	3 0	4 2	5 6	6 9
1 Jan. '68	3 8	5 0	6 6	8 0
15 Feb. '70	3 3	4 6	6 0	7 6
28 Nov. '71	3 8	4 2	5 6	7 0
24 July '72	3 8	5 0	6 6	8 0
29 Sept. '73	2 6	4 0	5 0	6 0
1 Jan. '77	2 6	3 6	4 3	5 6
1 May '82	2 6	3 5	4 3	5 5
1 Oct. '89	3 0	4 0	5 0	6 5

Source: Broadsheets setting out the charges, published by the firm at irregular intervals, copies of which have been retained by it. I am obliged to the present company for the opportunity to examine them.

TABLE XXIV

Marketing Charges on Scoured Wool Paid in England by the Australian Agricultural Company, 1865-84

(pence per lb.)

Year of clip	Gross Price	Costs (see legend below) I	II	III	IV	V	VI	VII	Costs as % of gross price* VIII	IX
1865	23·15	0·59	0·30	0·57	0·15	0·01	0·23	1·85	7·99	10·49
1866				n.a.†						
1867	18·89	0·34	0·03	1·03	0·22	0·01	0·19	1·82	9·70	12·20
1868	13·78	0·46	0·03	0·81	0·20	0·01	0·14	1·65	11·96	14·46
1869				n.a.						
1870	24·60	0·61	0·03	0·78	0·21	0·01	0·12	1·77	7·20	9·70
1871	25·58	0·61	0·03	0·86	0·15	0·01	0·13	1·80	6·99	8·99
1872	24·00	0·57	0·03	0·79	0·18	0·01	0·12	1·70	7·10	9·10
1873	24·31	0·57	0·03	0·79	0·14	0·01	0·12	1·66	6·83	8·33
1874	24·04	0·57	0·02	0·77	0·14	0·01	0·12	1·64	6·81	8·31
1875	20·86	0·55	0·03	0·54	0·15	0·01	0·10	1·38	6·62	8·12
1876	20·58	0·55	0·03	0·57	0·16	0·01	0·12	1·43	6·93	8·43
1877	24·13	0·55	0·03	0·67	0·15	0·01	0·12	1·53	6·35	7·85
1878	16·33	0·50	0·03	0·66	0·14	0·01	0·08	1·43	8·74	10·24
1879	24·72	0·54	0·03	0·67	0·16	0·01	0·12	1·53	6·19	7·69
1880	20·28	0·55	0·03	0·65	0·15	0·01	0·10	1·50	7·38	8·88
1881	24·09	0·50	0·03	0·78	0·16	0·01	0·12	1·60	6·62	8·12
1882	22·88	0·49	0·03	0·63	0·15	0·01	0·11	1·43	6·23	7·73
1883	19·65	0·35	0·03	0·70	0·17	0·01	0·10	1·35	6·89	8·39
1884	18·53	0·29	0·02	0·67	0·16	0·01	0·09	1·25	6·73	8·23

* These percentages have been calculated with data taken to the third decimal place. Sometimes, therefore, the second decimal place will differ from figures calculated on the basis of the figures in the table.

† Available only as general costs for scoured and greasy wool together.

Legend: I Sea insurance   VI Broker's commission

II Fire insurance   VII Total costs

III Freight   VIII Total costs as % of gross price

IV Warehouse charges

V Sales expenses

IX As VIII, with the addition of importer's commission, taken as 2½% from 1865 to 1870, 2% in 1871 and 1872, and thereafter 1½%.

Source: A. A. Co., particulars of the clip of each year enclosed with communication in 'Despatches from London'.

TABLE XXV

Marketing Charges on Greasy Wool Paid in London by the Australian Agricultural Company, 1876-99

(pence per lb.)

Year of clip	Gross Price	Costs (see legend below)							Costs as % of gross price*	
		I	II	III	IV	V	VI	VII	VIII	IX
1876	11·73	0·33	0·01	0·77	0·11	0·01	0·06	1·29	10·98	12·48
1877	10·04	0·27	0·02	0·51	0·11	0·01	0·05	0·97	9·62	11·12
1878	7·74	0·28	0·02	0·52	0·11	0·01	0·04	0·97	12·51	14·01
1879	11·18	0·30	0·01	0·54	0·11	0·01	0·06	1·02	9·10	10·60
1880	9·05	0·30	0·01	0·52	0·10	0·01	0·05	0·99	10·88	12·38
1881	11·36	0·26	0·01	0·64	0·11	0·01	0·06	1·09	9·58	11·08
1882	10·73	0·27	0·01	0·51	0·11	0·01	0·06	0·97	8·99	10·49
1883	9·30	0·20	0·01	0·51	0·10	0·01	0·05	0·89	9·56	11·06
1884	8·83	0·16	0·01	0·52	0·12	0·01	0·05	0·87	9·82	11·32
1885†	7·23	0·16	0·01	0·35	0·14	0·01	0·04	0·70	9·65	11·15
1886	8·54	0·12	0·01	0·43	0·13	0·01	0·03	0·74	8·70	10·20
1887	8·10	0·12	0·01	0·49	0·12	0·01	0·04	0·79	9·70	11·20
1888	7·93	0·14	0·01	0·39	0·13	0·01	0·04	0·72	9·03	10·53
1889	10·44	0·11	0·01	0·58	0·12	0·01	0·04	0·90	8·58	10·08
1890	9·07	0·08	0·01	0·78	0·14	0·01	0·05	1·07	11·74	13·24
1891	7·53	0·09	0·01	0·62	0·15	0·01	0·04	0·91	12·01	13·51
1892	8·24	0·10	0·01	0·47	0·15	0·01	0·04	0·78	9·47	10·97
1893	7·54	0·07	0·01	0·68	0·15	0·01	0·04	0·95	12·60	14·10
1894	6·58	0·07	0·01	0·54	0·14	0·01	0·03	0·81	12·27	13·77
1895	8·19	0·08	0·01	0·46	0·15	0·01	0·05	0·75	9·15	10·65
1896	7·51	0·06	0·01	0·48	0·14	0·01	0·04	0·74	9·83	11·33
1897	8·46	0·06	0·01	0·47	0·14	0·01	0·04	0·73	8·65	10·15
1898	8·51	0·07	0·01	0·68	0·14	0·01	0·04	0·96	11·29	12·79
1899	12·85	0·10	0·01	0·57	0·15	0·01	0·06	0·90	6·98	8·48

* See note * to Table XXIV.

† In this year part of the clip was lost by shipwreck. It was not subject to many of these costs but the insurance claim is included in the gross proceeds and that quantity of wool included in the net weight of wool sold; therefore some of the figures in the table show averages which are too low.

Legend: I Sea insurance   IV Warehouse charges   VII Total costs   IX As VIII, with the addition of importer's
        II Fire insurance   V Sales expenses   VIII Total costs as % of   commission, taken as
        III Freight   VI Broker's commission   gross price   1½%

TABLE XXVI

Cost of Selling Wool of Different Values in Melbourne

Wool price	*Total*		*Selling commission*		*Receiving charge*	
d. per lb.	*d. per lb.*	*% of price*	*d. per lb.*	*% of price*	*d. per lb.*	*% of price*
6	0·215	3·58	0·090	1·50	0·125	2·08
7	0·230	3·29	0·105	1·50	0·125	1·79
8	0·245	3·06	0·120	1·50	0·125	1·56
9	0·260	2·89	0·135	1·50	0·125	1·39
10	0·275	2·75	0·150	1·50	0·125	1·25
11	0·290	2·65	0·165	1·50	0·125	1·15
12	0·305	2·54	0·180	1·50	0·125	1·04
16	0·365	2·28	0·240	1·50	0·125	0·78
17	0·380	2·24	0·255	1·50	0·125	0·74
18	0·395	2·19	0·270	1·50	0·125	0·69
19	0·410	2·16	0·285	1·50	0·125	0·66
20	0·425	2·13	0·300	1·50	0·125	0·63
21	0·440	2·10	0·315	1·50	0·125	0·60
22	0·455	2·07	0·330	1·50	0·125	0·57

TABLE XXVII

London Prices of Selected Types of Australian Wool, 1846-1900

(pence per lb.)

	Price and Types (see legend below)						
Year	*1*	*2*	*3*	*4 5*	*6*	*7*	*8*
1846	–	–	–	–	18	–	–
1847	–	–	–	–	16	–	–
1848	–	5½	–	–	13	–	–
1849	–	7	–	–	16	–	–
1850	–	7½	–	–	17	–	–
1851	–	7½	–	–	17	–	–
1852	–	9	–	–	19½	–	–
1853	–	9½	–	–	20	–	–
1854	–	8¾	–	–	18	–	–
1855	10¼	9¼	–	14·6	19½	–	–
1856	11½	11	–	16·2	23	–	–
1857	12	11½	–	17·9	23	–	–
1858	9¼	11	–	19·9	22½	–	–
1859	12½	11½	–	20·5	23½	–	–
1860	14	12⅝	24	21·0	24⅛	14⅞	–
1861	13	10¾	20½	23·4	22⅛	13⅜	–
1862	11	10½	21½	20·5	22	13⅜	–
1863	11½	10⅞	21½	19·9	21⅞	13¼	–
1864	11½	11½	21	21·4	23¼	14¼	–
1865	10½	11⅜	22½	18·3	22⅜	13¾	–
1866	12½	12⅛	20½	18·3	23⅝	14⅜	–
1867	13	10½	17	18·9	21½	12½	–
1868	9½	9⅜	16½	17·5	20	11⅝	–
1869	8½	7¾	15½	14·8	17	9⅞	–

Price and Types (see legend below)

Year	*1*	*2*	*3*	*4*	*5*	*6*	*7*	*8*
1870	9½	7⅞	14	13·8		17	10⅛	–
1871	7½	10⅛	23½	17·3		21¼	12⅜	–
1872	12	12⅜	25	15·9		25¾	15½	–
1873	12½	11¾	22	12·0	18·7	25	15¼	–
1874	11¾	11½	20	11·7	19·1	23½	14⅝	–
1875	11¾	10⅝	19	11·5	19·3	22	13½	–
1876	12½	9⅛	19½	10·1	17·8	20¼	12⅛	–
1877	14	9⅛	18	10·3	17·6	20¼	12⅛	–
1878	10½	9⅛	–	9·9	16·1	20	12	–
1879	10	8½	–	10·5	17·3	18¾	11⅝	–
1880	11½	10⅝	–	10·8	24·0	21½	13½	–
1881	12	9¼	–	10·9	16·9	19½	12	–
1882	12	9	–	10·5	17·2	19¾	12½	–
1883	12	8½	–	10·6	18·1	19	12⅛	8·8
1884	11	8⅛	–	10·5	18·3	18¼	11½	9·5
1885	10	6¾	–	8·9	15·2	16½	10	9·7
1886	8½	6¾	–	8·3	14·1	15½	9¾	9·5
1887	11	7	–	8·4	14·7	15¾	10⅛	9·9
1888	10	7	–	8·2	13·9	15¾	10¼	9·5
1889	10½	8¼	–	8·6	14·9	17¼	11½	10·3
1890	11	7½	–	7·0	13·9	16	10¾	10·1
1891	10	6⅞	–	7·4	–	14¾	10	10·1
1892	8½	6	–	7·2	–	13	8¾	9·1
1893	8½	6	–	6·8	–	12¾	8⅝	9·6
1894	7¾	5⅜	–	6·0	–	11¾	8	9·0
1895	9½	5⅝	–	6·6	–	13	8⅜	9·0
1896	9	6⅜	–	7·1	–	13	9⅜	9·1
1897	9	6	–	6·8	–	12¼	9¼	8·7
1898	10	6⅝	–	7·3	–	13¼	9¾	7·5
1899	13½	8½	–	10·3	–	17¼	12¼	8·5
1900	15*	7⅛	–	–	–	15¾	11½	8·4

* September series of sales.

1. Australian greasy merino, Feb. prices
2. Adelaide average greasy, annual average price
3. N.S.W. average clothing fleece, end-of-year price
4. N.S.W. average export valuations, greasy
5. N.S.W. average export valuations, scoured and washed
6. Victorian average merino fleece, annual average price
7. Victorian average good merino greasy, annual average price
8. Australian average medium, cross-bred greasy, annual average price

Sources: Column 1: Compilation of Helmuth Schwartze & Co. (Buchanan, Schwartze & Co.). This has been reproduced in part or in entirety in many places. Our source: anon. article 'Historical Sketch of the Wool Industry', *Clarion* (Sydney, monthly), 25 May 1901, p. 36. Columns 2 and 6 (1846-59), 2, 6 and 7 (1899 and 1900): *Journal of the Royal Statistical Society*, various dates. Columns 2, 3, 6, 7 (1860-77): A. Sauerbeck, *The Production and Consumption of Wool*, p. 15. Columns 2, 3, 6, 7 (1878-98): F. Hooper, *Statistics relating to the City of Bradford and the Woollen and Worsted Trades of the United Kingdom* (Bradford, 1899), p. 28. Columns 4, 5: *Statistical Register of New South Wales*, annually. The method of derivation is described (text, p. 193). Column 8: R. J. Thompson, 'Wool Prices in Great Britain, 1883-1901', *Journal of the Royal Statistical Society*, vol. 65 (1902), p. 508.

Table XXVIII

Seasonal Average Wool Prices at the Melbourne Sales, 1884-5 to 1893-4

(pence per lb.)

Season	*Greasy merino*	*Greasy crossbred*	*Fleece and washed wool*	*Scoured wool*
1884–5	10½	9	20	19
1885–6	8½	8	16	15
1886–7	10½	9	17	18
1887–8	9½	8	15½	16
1888–9	10½	10	18	17½
1889–90	11½	11	18½	19½
1890–1	10	9	15	16½
1891–2	9	8¾	13½	15
1892–3	8¾	8½	13	14½
1893–4	8½	8¾	13	14½

Source: *Victorian Year Book*, 1894.

Table XXIX

Comparison of the Reported Prices of some Victorian Wools in London and Melbourne, 1885-94

(pence per lb.)

*Year**	*Greasy merino*			*Fleece and washed merino*		
	Melb. price†	*Lond'n price‡*	*Melb. price cf. Lond.*	*Melb. price†*	*Lond'n price§*	*Melb. price cf. Lond.*
1885	10½	10	+ ½	20	16½	+3½
1886	8½	9¾	−1¼	16	15½	+ ½
1887	10½	10⅛	+ ⅜	17	15¾	+1¼
1888	9½	10¼	− ¾	15½	15¾	− ¼
1889	10½	11½	−1	18	17¼	+ ¾
1890	11½	10¾	+ ¾	18½	16	+2½
1891	10	10	0	15	14¾	+ ¼
1892	9	8¾	+ ¼	13½	13	+ ½
1893	8¾	8⅝	+ ⅛	13	12¾	+ ¼
1894	8½	8	+ ½	13	11¾	+1¼

* Equivalent to season 1884-5, etc.
† From Table XXVIII.
‡ From Table XXVII, column 7.
§ From Table XXVII, column 6.

INDEX